Leadership Studies

NEW HORIZONS IN LEADERSHIP STUDIES

Series Editor: Joanne B. Ciulla, *Professor and Coston Family Chair in Leadership and Ethics, Jepson School of Leadership Studies, University of Richmond, USA*

This important series is designed to make a significant contribution to the development of leadership studies. This field has expanded dramatically in recent years and the series provides an invaluable forum for the publication of high quality works of scholarship and shows the diversity of leadership issues and practices around the world.

The main emphasis of the series is on the development and application of new and original ideas in leadership studies. It pays particular attention to leadership in business, economics and public policy and incorporates the wide range of disciplines which are now part of the field. Global in its approach, it includes some of the best theoretical and empirical work with contributions to fundamental principles, rigorous evaluations of existing concepts and competing theories, historical surveys and future visions.

Titles in the series include:

The New Russian Business Leaders
Manfred F.R. Kets de Vries, Stanislav Shekshnia, Konstantin Korotov and Elizabeth Florent-Treacy

Lessons on Leadership by Terror
Finding Shaka Zulu in the Attic
Manfred F.R. Kets de Vries

Leadership in Context
Four Faces of Capitalism
Mark N. Wexler

The Quest for Moral Leaders
Essays on Leadership Ethics
Edited by Joanne B. Ciulla, Terry L. Price and Susan E. Murphy

The Quest for a General Theory of Leadership
Edited by George R. Goethals and Georgia L.J. Sorenson

Inventing Leadership
The Challenge of Democracy
J. Thomas Wren

Dissent and the Failure of Leadership
Edited by Stephen P. Banks

Corporate Governance and Ethics
An Aristotelian Perspective
Alejo José G. Sison

Rethinking Leadership
A New Look at Old Leadership Questions
Donna Ladkin

Leadership Studies
The Dialogue of Disciplines
Edited by Michael Harvey and Ronald E. Riggio

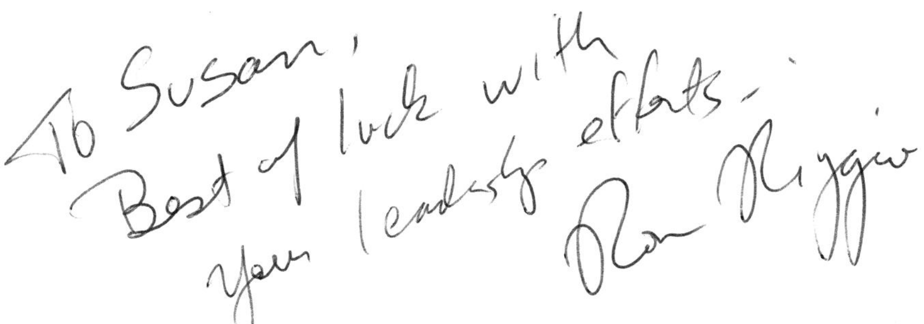

Leadership Studies

The Dialogue of Disciplines

Edited by

Michael Harvey

Washington College, USA

Ronald E. Riggio

Claremont McKenna College, USA

NEW HORIZONS IN LEADERSHIP STUDIES

Edward Elgar

Cheltenham, UK • Northampton, MA, USA

Published by
Edward Elgar Publishing Limited
The Lypiatts
15 Lansdown Road
Cheltenham
Glos GL50 2JA
UK

Edward Elgar Publishing, Inc.
William Pratt House
9 Dewey Court
Northampton
Massachusetts 01060
USA

A catalogue record for this book
is available from the British Library

Library of Congress Control Number: 2011924157

ISBN 978 1 84720 940 5 (cased)

Typeset by Cambrian Typesetters, Camberley, Surrey
Printed and bound by MPG Books Group, UK

Contents

Contributors

Joanne B. Ciulla, Ph.D., Jepson School of Leadership Studies, University of Richmond

Michael A. Genovese, Ph.D., Director, Institute of Leadership Studies, Loyola Marymount University

George R. Goethals, Ph.D., Jepson School of Leadership Studies, University of Richmond

Michael Harvey, Department of Business Management, Washington College

Margo Hittleman, Ph.D., Senior Fellow, Dorothy Cotton Institute, Center for Transformative Action, and Natural Leaders Initiative, Cornell Cooperative Extension

Crystal L. Hoyt, Ph.D., Jepson School of Leadership Studies, University of Richmond

Stefanie K. Johnson, Ph.D., University of Colorado, Denver, School of Business

Anu M. Mitra, Ph.D., Union Institute & University

Susan Elaine Murphy, Ph.D., School of Strategic Leadership Studies, James Madison University

Sonia M. Ospina, Ph.D., Research Center for Leadership in Action, New York University

Norman W. Provizer, Ph.D., Professor of Political Science and Director of Leadership Studies, Metropolitan State College of Denver

Ronald E. Riggio, Claremont McKenna College

Robert J. Sternberg, Ph.D., Provost, Oklahoma State University

Lawrence A. Tritle, Ph.D., History Department, Loyola Marymount University

Stephen P. Turner, Ph.D., Department of Philosophy, University of South Florida

Nicholas O. Warner, Department of Literature, Claremont McKenna College

J. Thomas Wren, Ph.D., Jepson School of Leadership Studies, University of Richmond

PART I

Introduction

1. Introduction: the dialogue of disciplines

Ronald E. Riggio

The discussion and study of leadership is old – stretching back to the earliest of written texts. As Bernard Bass (Bass and Bass, 2008) notes in *The Bass Handbook of Leadership*, "Myths and legends about great leaders were important in the development of civilized societies" (p. 4). Leaders and leadership are important themes in the ancient Greek and Latin classics, in the Old Testament of the Bible, in the Hindu religious texts, and in the Canons of Confucianism. Bass also notes that Egyptian hieroglyphs for *leader*, *leadership* and *follower* were written over 5000 years ago. So leadership is woven into the very fabric of civilization.

Taken further, the roots of leadership are likely "hard-wired" into the DNA of humans, and of all social animals. Dominance hierarchies are critical to the structure of social groups, and the higher that animals go in the evolutionary chain, the more the behavior of dominant "alpha" males or females begins to look like the evolutionary roots of leadership. These social animal packs look to the alpha "leader" for direction, for protection, and the pack leader plays a critical role in keeping the social order. For instance, in wolves, the pack's dominant male plays a critical role in hunting activities and initiating travel, while the dominant female takes the lead in protecting the pack and in nurturing pups (Mech, 2000). Indeed, scholars in animal behavior have recently begun to explore parallels between pack animals' dominance behavior and leadership (for example, Bonanni et al., 2010). We are, after all, merely social animals. Unfortunately, the discipline of animal behavior and its perspective on leadership is not included in this collection, but most other relevant disciplines are.

What is included here is a variety of disciplinary approaches to the study of leadership, ranging from the arts and humanities, to the social sciences, and to more applied perspectives. Our intent was to gather leadership scholar experts from various disciplines and have them provide an overview of how their particular discipline approaches the study of leadership as well as providing some of the key findings, theories, and/or concepts associated with their discipline's study of leadership. In the integrative final chapter, the disciplinary perspectives are interwoven by Michael Harvey and framed around seven questions that groups and leaders must answer. Harvey uses these questions, derived from the disciplinary inquiries of our leadership scholars, to create a model of how and why leaders might (or might not) be effective.

LEADERSHIP IS STUDIED THROUGH DISCIPLINARY LENSES

Traditionally, the topic of leadership has been studied in different ways by different disciplines. In a discipline such as political science, the study of leadership has focused a great deal on "elites" – leaders of kingdoms, nations, or political movements – and how they have shaped political processes and outcomes (Hargrove, 2004). Other disciplines, most notably psychology (and psychiatry), have also focused on the leader, but are more concerned with the inner workings of the leader's personality and how the leader's characteristics and behavior influence followers. Historians take a different approach. They focus more on the historical context and the forces that push and pull the leader into action. Each discipline brings its own perspective and approach to the study of leadership.

This creates something akin to the old (and overused) story of the blind men and the elephant, with each discipline feeling a different piece of the leadership elephant and trying to conceptualize the entire beast. Not only are we each studying different aspects of leadership, but we are using different methodologies. Historical analyses, case studies, qualitative and quantitative analyses, are all methodologies used in leadership studies, with different disciplines leaning more heavily on one methodology rather than others. This means that not only do we have different disciplinary points of view, but in describing leadership (the elephant), we are speaking different languages.

The problem is exacerbated by the tendency for the disciplines that study leadership to be "ivory towers" – with scholars staying within their own discipline, writing for and reading only the disciplinary journals, and believing in the correctness (and superiority?) of their home disciplinary approach. Like the blind men, their perspective and understanding is severely limited.

Many scholars are drawn to study leadership because it is a rich and important topic. Leadership, particularly in Western cultures, is also a "hot" topic, as evidenced by the constant attention given to leaders in government and business, and the many wildly popular books on leaders and leadership. Indeed, those high-profile leadership scholars who have successfully crossed over to the more popular media, are often labeled "leadership gurus". It's hard to imagine top scholars in other disciplines – chemistry, music, engineering – being called "gurus". Despite this attraction, however, it is difficult to study leadership in some disciplines, where leadership is a marginal or peripheral topic. Moreover, in order to carry out the most impactful scholarship in leadership, requires an ability to cross disciplines and integrate information from many different perspectives.

So in some ways, this collection is a primer on leadership studies. It is an introduction to the perspectives, methods and findings of each of the represented disciplines. We hope that through an understanding of how different disciplines approach the study of leadership, and by focusing on the major themes in each discipline, we will be able to establish some common ground for conceptual and research progress in the field of leadership studies.

ABOUT THE BOOK

This collection begins with an introductory section and chapters focused on the interdisciplinary nature of leadership studies and how that has impacted the field in the past, currently and in the future. Riggio addresses the question of whether leadership studies is (or should/could be) a distinct academic discipline. He concludes that it is an "emerging discipline", and he has hopes that the disciplinary divisions that characterize the field can be successfully overcome.

Joanne B. Ciulla, one of the founding faculty of the first school of leadership studies, discusses the history of the Jepson School of Leadership Studies at the University of Richmond, and the experiment of having scholars from different disciplines reside in a single school, with a common focus on leadership. Ciulla suggests that leadership as a topic of study is a natural fit with the liberal arts. She also argues that the study of leadership is best approached from a traditional disciplinary perspective.

The second, and largest, section of the book covers the disciplinary approaches to leadership studies. The chapters are arranged in a somewhat historical order, beginning with the classical origins of thinking about leadership, especially in Greek philosophy, moving through the traditional social sciences, and into newer perspectives in the arts and humanities.

Michael A. Genovese, a political scientist, and Lawrence A. Tritle, a historian, discuss how leadership is portrayed in the classic literature of early Western civilization. Focusing on early political philosophers and historians, from Plato to Plutarch and forward to Machiavelli, they demonstrate that the understanding of political leadership requires knowledge of the history, culture and philosophy in which the leaders of the ancient empires were embedded. They conclude that understanding of the evolution of leadership, and key concepts such as constitutionalism and democracy, need to be approached through an interdisciplinary study of the Classics.

In her chapter, "Handmaiden and queen", philosopher Joanne B. Ciulla presents a primer on how philosophy has contributed to the study and understanding of leadership. She characterizes Anglo-American analytic philosophers as supporting the study of leadership (they are the "handmaiden"), and European continental philosophers as attempting to answer the big questions about leadership (and life; they are the "Queen"). Ciulla also relates her own personal journey as one of the first philosophers to jump fully into leadership studies, wrestling with questions such as the definition of leadership and what constitutes a *good* leader.

Historian J. Thomas Wren discusses history's unique approach to the study of leadership. According to Wren, history looks at particulars, not patterns. The social sciences seek to use patterns to predict future leadership behaviors and outcomes. History looks to the past to understand the present and the future. Wren outlines the methods of historical analysis used to study leadership, and argues that historical analyses have much to contribute to our understanding of leadership, particularly history's emphasis on "context", "characters", and "complexity".

Stephen P. Turner takes a look at sociologist Max Weber, and his seminal contribution to leadership through the theory of charismatic authority. In this chapter we get a glimpse into a sociological interpretation of charisma and charismatic leadership and their implications for leadership today – a century after Weber developed the theory. In the second sociology chapter Sonia M. Ospina and Margo Hittleman suggest that sociology has contributed an understanding of the social structures that make different forms of leadership possible. Moreover, they argue that the trend toward studying leaders and followers, and their interactions, ignores the larger and critically important social context. Ospina and Hittleman argue that leadership research will be richer if it incorporates a "sociological lens".

Psychologists George R. Goethals and Crystal L. Hoyt explore psychology's many contributions to leadership studies. Using classic case studies of leaders, Goethals and Hoyt answer the questions of what makes leadership necessary, possible, and what makes leadership effective. Beginning with evolutionary theory, and incorporating key theories from social psychology, the authors cover a wide landscape of leadership issues in their effort to show how psychology has contributed mightily to our understanding of leaders, leadership processes and leadership outcomes.

In the first of our management chapters, Ronald E. Riggio suggests that the ultimate reason that management scholars and business schools are interested in leadership is to make business managers and leaders more efficient and effective. However, he observes that as management theories became more sophisticated, and research work more intense, the leadership theories became mechanistic and took much of the human element out of leadership. More recent management theories and research have restored that human element, and have begun to incorporate broader disciplinary perspectives into the study of leadership.

The second management chapter, by Susan Elaine Murphy and Stefanie K. Johnson, focuses on the dichotomy that exists in US and Western business schools and management faculty. On the one hand, business schools purport to develop better business leaders. Business school faculty, who are focused on making important research contributions to theory on management and leadership practices and to teach about these theories, assume that knowledge will lead to better practice. On the other hand, effective leadership is as much "art" (meaning leadership skills) as it is science. Murphy and Johnson challenge the traditional business school model and suggest that a revolution needs to take place if business schools are indeed going to produce better leaders. This chapter has important implications for leader education and development for all disciplines.

Norman W. Provizer discusses why political science has not contributed more to the study of leadership, despite its central role in analyzing governing processes. Using an analysis of power as a prime example, Provizer argues that political science has much to offer the study of leadership and he reviews some of his discipline's most important contributions.

Using the concept of stories as an important vehicle for understanding the complexities of leaders and leadership, Robert J. Sternberg gives us insight into the approach some educational scholars have used to frame leadership. With illustrations from recent US Presidential elections, Sternberg discusses the impact that a good, consistent, and moving leader story can have. In the process, he touches on issues of perceived leader authenticity and the role that media portrayals of leaders can have on determining who gets to lead and how that leader's story plays out.

As a professor who studies literature and film, Nicholas O. Warner shows the enormous capacity of literature to aid our understanding of leadership and leadership processes. Picking up on the theme of stories in the previous chapter, Warner shows us how storytelling (through literature, plays, films, music, poetry) can shape our ideas about leaders and leadership and can reflect how a culture thinks (and should think) about leadership.

Anu M. Mitra, in her "Learning how to look" chapter shows us how an appreciation of the arts can help facilitate understanding of leadership. Mitra presents an arts appreciation program that, through systematic observation and reflection, allows leaders (and anyone) to enhance their capacity to understand the complexity of the world around us and to solve problems.

Michael Harvey closes the book by integrating the various disciplinary perspectives and drawing some common threads together. We will, however, allow you to read that later. For now, go forward, and enjoy the multidisciplinary field of Leadership Studies.

REFERENCES

Bass, B.M. and R. Bass (2008), *The Bass Handbook of Leadership*, New York: Free Press.

Bonanni, R., S. Cafazzo, P. Valsecchi and E. Natoli (2010), "Effect of affiliative and agnostic relationships on leadership behaviour in free-ranging dogs", *Animal Behaviour*, **79**(5), 981–91.

Hargrove, E.C. (2004), "History, political science, and the study of leadership", *Polity*, **36**(4), 579–93.

Mech, L.D. (2000), "Leadership in wolf, *Canis lupus*, packs", *Canadian Field-Naturalist,* **114**(2), 259–63.

2. Is leadership studies a discipline?

Ronald E. Riggio

With the understanding and acknowledgement that what I say in this chapter is controversial, I will argue that leadership studies is a distinct discipline, albeit a discipline that is "emerging". I have every expectation that a generation from now leadership studies will be a recognized discipline and universities that do not have departments of leadership studies (or at least programs devoted to leadership) will be in the minority.

I will begin with a discussion of what constitutes an academic discipline and then review the evidence that leadership studies is currently an emerging discipline, on the verge of becoming recognized as a "stand-alone" discipline in the next several decades. I will also address the topic of this book, namely the multidisciplinary nature of leadership studies as it currently exists. Finally, I will make recommendations for faculty involved in academic leadership studies programs (or academics who are in the area of leadership studies) to hasten the process of disciplinary recognition.

First, let me state that there are some of us who firmly believe that leadership studies has already arrived as a distinct discipline, but there are scholars who devote their research partially or entirely to the study of leadership who vehemently disagree that leadership studies is, or will ever become, a discipline. The argument against usually revolves around the notion that leadership is a topic of study and not a "discipline", or the scholar intends to hold firmly to his or her traditional discipline, as in "I am a political scientist who happens to study leadership".

Years ago, Georgia Sorenson and I, as members of the board of the International Leadership Association, were tasked with exploring this very issue of "Leadership studies as a discipline". Georgia and I admitted up front that we were "true believers" in the distinction of leadership studies as a discipline, and James MacGregor Burns also professed his allegiance. However, when I hosted a roundtable discussion on the topic at a meeting of the International Leadership Association, it was very clear that many leadership scholars disagreed. Indeed, these individuals argued that not only is leadership studies not a distinct discipline, but to pursue that path was futile and would be a detriment to the recognition of leadership as a legitimate topic of academic investigation. I respectfully disagree.

WHAT IS AN ACADEMIC DISCIPLINE?

The *Oxford English Dictionary* defines an academic discipline as "a branch of learning or scholarly instruction". The Wikipedia definition suggests that an academic discipline is a branch of knowledge that is taught and researched at the university level. Therefore, the departmental structure of universities plays a large part in acceptance of an area of study as an academic discipline. Indeed, this may be the litmus test of the title question: when (and if) a majority, or a significant percentage, of universities have departments of leadership studies, the discipline most likely will have fully emerged.

The National Academies (nationalacademies.org) serves as the US agency that advises on issues involving science and higher education. In 2001–02, a Panel on Taxonomy and Interdisciplinarity was created to both revise the existing taxonomy of academic disciplines and to explore interdisciplinary issues, including how to identify interdisciplinary fields. The taxonomy distinguishes: (1) life sciences; (2) physical sciences, mathematics and engineering; (3) arts and humanities; and (4) social and behavioral sciences. One difficulty is that leadership studies crosses the humanities and social sciences categories. Needless to say, leadership studies is not in the taxonomy, either as an existing or emerging discipline (emerging disciplines include: film studies; ethnic studies; and gender studies (in the arts and humanities), and organizations, occupations and work; and science and technology studies (in the social sciences)).

In 2005, The National Academies surveyed over 200 universities (primarily research universities) focusing on their doctoral programs in order to develop a Taxonomy of Fields. Traditional fields were common (mathematics, political science, philosophy), as were recognized interdisciplinary fields (American studies, neuroscience, and one identified as language, societies and culture). Additional programs were more rare and recent and are considered as emerging disciplines, which includes the aforementioned film studies and gender studies, but new emerging disciplines include bioinformatics, and nanoscience. Leadership studies was not designated because none of the surveyed universities had doctoral programs in leadership studies. However, the last decade has seen remarkable growth in both graduate and undergraduate degree-granting programs in leadership studies, but the vast majority of these programs are not in top-tier research universities. When graduate programs with leadership in the title show up in research universities, they are typically associated with another discipline. Most common are masters and doctoral programs in educational leadership that are typically found in Schools of Education, and graduate programs in organizational leadership found in business schools.

Only very rare cases currently exist in higher education where leadership studies programs are housed in stand-alone schools. Most notable are the Jepson School of Leadership Studies at the University of Richmond (see Chapter 3, this volume), and more recently the University of St Thomas and its School of Leadership Studies (which offers a BA in *organizational* leadership) and Regent University's School of Global Leadership and Entrepreneurship (which offers graduate degrees). My prediction is that the number of schools of leadership will grow, but that this process will be rather slow, with leadership programs housed in other schools (for example, the University of San Diego's school of education has reformed into the School of Leadership and Education Sciences), but eventually breaking off to form stand-alone units – driven primarily by the programs' growing size.

My prediction that 20–30 years into the future, leadership studies will be a distinct discipline is pure speculation (and as a social scientist, I realize the folly of trying to predict the future). It is based, however, on my reading of the small body of literature on academic disciplines, and examples of areas of study that have emerged as full-blown disciplines. A review of this work will allow us to better understand the process of how an academic discipline emerges.

An interesting and succinct review by Del Favero (n.d.) suggests that there are four methods for classifying disciplines. The first is termed *codification*, and refers to whether a distinct body of knowledge can be circumscribed by those researching the field. When scholars reach a high level of agreement on what that body of knowledge consists of, then disciplinary status is assumed. There has been a great deal of discussion on this topic of whether leadership contains a bounded body of knowledge. To determine if there is some generally agreed-upon body of knowledge in leadership studies, let's look at the popular textbooks.

First it is important to note that there is a wide number and range of textbooks on leadership, and that the authors of these competing textbooks hail from multiple disciplines. For example, the most popular textbooks in leadership include those authored by Peter Northouse (2010), Hughes, Ginnett and Curphy (2009), and Gary Yukl (2009), and a dozen or so others. Northouse's home discipline is Communication. Hughes, Ginnett and Curphy are all psychologists (Richard Hughes is a clinical psychologist, with past associations with the US Air Force and the Center for Creative Leadership). Gary Yukl is also a psychologist, but with a career in a department of management. The vast majority of authors of textbooks used in courses on leadership hail from management/business, but other leadership textbook authors include a scholar with doctoral degrees in science, and a co-author with degrees in clinical leadership and nursing (Porter-O'Grady and Malloch, 2003), and one of the most popular ancillary texts – a book of readings on leadership – is edited by a historian (Wren, 1995).

What is most noteworthy for our discussion, however, is not just the diverse background of leadership textbook authors, but the fact that the content of the major textbooks is surprisingly similar. The theories reviewed, the structure of tables of contents, and the history of theory and research in leadership are often quite similar. Indeed, leadership texts seem to follow the same implicitly agreed-upon core body of knowledge. This argues, consistent with the concept of codification of a discipline, that there is high consensus on the topics studied in leadership, even if a majority of leadership scholars (or even textbook authors) would not accept that leadership studies is a distinct discipline.

A second approach to identifying an academic discipline is the quite popular concept of *paradigm development*, discussed by Thomas S. Kuhn (1962) in his popular and highly-cited work on scientific revolutions. A physicist, Kuhn argues that disciplines possess an ordered body of knowledge, an accepted methodology for conducting research in the discipline, and a general, unifying theoretical perspective – a grand theory, so to speak. While Kuhn's work applies well to the physical sciences, it is less applicable to the social sciences. While the social sciences do tend to have a shared methodology for conducting research, there are no grand, "unifying" theories in most social science disciplines. This is the case in leadership studies as well, despite the very interesting, multi-year attempt by a group of scholars to explore the possibility of a "grand theory of leadership", the story of which is recounted in an edited book (Goethals and Sorenson, 2006).

While there is no general theory of leadership, there are constructs, such as charismatic leadership, systematic classifications of leader behavior, and interactionist models of leadership, that have been widely and thoroughly researched, some for nearly 100 years. In terms of methodology, most leadership scholars adhere to the quantitative and qualitative methodologies shared by several of the social sciences, including sociology, psychology, education, political science, and others. In any case, the Kuhnian notion of an accepted paradigm may apply to the physical sciences, but is not as applicable to the social sciences, including leadership studies.

A third approach is the Biglan model, as researched by psychiatrist, Anthony Biglan (1973a, 1973b). Using a variety of scaling techniques, Biglan asked faculty members from research universities and liberal arts colleges to evaluate various disciplines (of course, leadership studies was not among them, but educational administration, journalism, and home economics were included). He found that scholars clustered the disciplines based on dimensions such as "hard" and "soft" (sciences vs. humanities, respectively), "pure" and "applied" disciplines, with science, mathematics, humanities on the pure end of a continuum, and accounting, engineering, and education on the applied end. Another dimension concerned the methodological approach of "creative" versus "empirical" disciplines, which distinguished the humanities from the social and physical sciences. No doubt, using the Biglan method, leadership studies would cluster with the "soft" social sciences, using primarily (but certainly not exclusively) empirical methods, with some applied emphasis. But here is the problem: philosophers, historians, and others from the humanities who study leadership would probably not agree with that placement, and that is one reason why the debate over whether leadership studies is a defined and unique discipline continues.

Drawn from both the Kuhnian model of paradigm development and Biglan's research methodology, is the notion of *consensus*. Consensus refers to whether those involved in a field agree upon a shared knowledge base, methods of inquiry, but also whether there is similar education and training, a cohesiveness within the community of scholars, and professional structures that draw the scholars together. Disciplines can be characterized as being high or low in consensus, and leadership studies would clearly fall under the "low consensus" category. In my opinion, it is this low level of consensus that has been the stumbling block for leadership studies reaching disciplinary status.

A hallmark of an academic discipline is the establishment of academic journals dedicated to the field. Leadership studies has several. To some extent, academic disciplines are shaped and defined by the work that is published in its journals. *The Leadership Quarterly* (published by Elsevier) was begun in 1990, and was the first scholarly journal completely devoted to publishing research on leadership. Although the majority of studies published in *The Leadership Quarterly* are from scholars trained in management or psychology, the sub-title of the journal, "An International Journal of Political, Social, and Behavioral Science", suggests its interdisciplinary nature. *The Leadership Quarterly* is one of the highest ranked journals in both management and applied psychology.

In 1993 the *Journal of Leadership Studies* was founded, and it is now called the *Journal of Leadership and Organizational Studies* (published by Sage). The "organizational" emphasis suggests that this journal is slanted toward management/organizational behavior, but the vast majority of papers published are in leadership studies. Sage also publishes a distinctly interdisciplinary journal simply titled *Leadership* (founded 2005), and there are a number of other journals focusing primarily on leadership research (for example, John Wiley publishes a new journal that took the old title *Journal of Leadership Studies*; there are also practitioner-oriented journals, such as *Leader-to-Leader*, published by Jossey-Bass). Clearly, leadership studies has several representative journals that help define the field. It is quite unusual that an area of study would have so many dedicated journals without being recognized as a distinct discipline.

In addition to dedicated, disciplinary journals, the Library of Congress implicitly recognizes many academic disciplines by categorizing books by discipline. For example, the older and more traditional disciplines, such as science, world history (American history has a separate designation), education, political science, and music, all have separate designations, represented by letters of the alphabet. Some disciplines are clustered together, such as social sciences and the combined category for "Geography, Anthropology, and Recreation". But where are books on leadership classified? There is indeed a separate subject heading in the Library of Congress for "Leadership", but books on leadership are classified into four subcategories associated with other disciplines: applied psychology (books with the BF code that represents the larger philosophy category), social psychology (HM, the catch-all social sciences disciplinary category), management (HD), and military science (which has its own classification letter of U). There are no leadership classifications in other disciplines; most notably absent are political science and education. Clearly leadership research and writing is done in both of these disciplines, but books emanating from scholars in these disciplines are classified in one of the four leadership categories. The classification of leadership books is sometimes surprising. For example, the Library of Congress classification of James MacGregor Burns' (1978) seminal book, *Leadership*, is classified as HM, which puts it in the same category as books written by sociologists and social psychologists, although Burns is a US Presidential historian and political scientist. I actually corresponded about this issue with Library of Congress librarians. They agreed that there should probably be a single disciplinary classification for the topic of leadership, but noted that making such a change to the system was difficult, costly and rarely done.

Another characteristic of an academic discipline is a professional organization that represents the discipline, has a significant number of scholars as members, and holds annual conferences, or publishes journals, to disseminate research in the discipline. This is an area of difficulty for leadership studies. There currently is no single organization that represents leadership studies, although there have been some very serious attempts. We will discuss the travails of these organizations shortly.

So in terms of everyday operations, what characterizes an academic discipline? Obviously, faculty share a common disciplinary identity and are classified and housed in the same unit (school or department) on campus. Faculty teach a distinct content area; courses are labeled with the disciplinary title ("leadership" or "leadership studies"). There are a number of academic journals dedicated to research in the discipline. There are national and/or international organizations that are devoted to the academic discipline, and those disciplinary organizations play a key role in defining and promoting the discipline. Like labor unions, the strength of a disciplinary organization is partly determined by the percentage of scholars who are members. Attempts are being made to create such a disciplinary organization for leadership studies, but it has been a difficult struggle. In sum, however, leadership studies looks very much as if it is emerging as a unique discipline.

THE INTERDISCIPLINARY NATURE OF LEADERSHIP STUDIES

It is important to note, consistent with the theme of this book, that leadership studies is mostly composed of scholars who are primarily trained in multiple traditional disciplines, and much of the work that is done in studying leadership crosses disciplinary lines. As graduate programs in leadership studies grow, however, we expect a greater percentage of leadership scholars will have degrees specifically in leadership. The fact that leadership studies is emerging from traditional disciplines is an old story. Many of today's recognized disciplines were born from other disciplines. Psychology, for example, began as a branch of philosophy. (In the Library of Congress system, psychology rightly shares a letter, "B", with its parent discipline of philosophy, as does religious studies). William James, one of the fathers of American psychology, was a philosopher and had a medical degree. Early contributors to psychoanalytic psychology (and psychiatry), such as Sigmund Freud and Alfred Adler, were also trained in medicine. The branch of psychology that has transformed into cognitive neuroscience, also has roots in physiology.

Areas that are recognized as *emerging disciplines*, such as gender studies, ethnic studies, and studies of specific countries or regions (for example, American studies; Latin American studies), began with scholars focusing on a common topic area. They are, similar to leadership studies, composed of scholars trained in various disciplines, but graduate degrees are also being granted specifically in the emerging discipline. In short, the path that leadership studies is on has been trod before by both recognized and emerging disciplines.

Public Administration went through the same sort of disciplinary emergence several decades ago. Public Administration is an interdisciplinary "blending" of political science, sociology, philosophy, economics, law and business administration. Some trace the earliest roots of this discipline to the founding of the American Society for Public Administration in 1939, but it took about a generation (30 years or so) for public administration to move from its earliest beginnings to disciplinary status. We might use the mid-1990s as the date of the beginning of leadership studies, so it is still in the "infancy" stage.

LEADERSHIP STUDIES: THE STRUGGLE FOR RECOGNITION

Leadership studies is a lost and orphaned stepchild. It is related to several disciplines – management/organizational behavior, industrial and organizational psychology (I/O psychology), educational administration – but it has no real home. In recent conferences of the Society for Industrial and Organizational Psychology (SIOP), leadership is one of the two biggest research topics (along with testing and selection). At the Academy of Management meetings, presentations on leadership research and practice also constitute one of the largest topic categories. Despite its popularity, leadership has not been accepted as a separate area by the Academy of Management, largely due to bad timing. A decade ago leadership scholars appealed to the Academy for divisional status (which would mean that programming time and resources would be allocated to leadership research, on a par with other divisions, such as the Human Resources Division, Entrepreneurship Division, and Organizations and the Natural Environment Division). Leadership, whose scholars currently are members of the divisions of organizational behavior, organization development and change, business policy and strategy, and others, was denied division status. The group, known as the Network of Leadership Scholars, then applied for "Interest Group" status, but was also denied that designation (which would have given Academy resources/programming time to leadership scholars). So, leadership currently has a "network" status within the Academy of Management, with virtually no resources other than webspace on the Academy of Management website (but try to find it!).

A dozen years ago, the International Leadership Association (ILA) was founded and has held annual conferences since then. The ILA states that it is "the global network for all those who practice, study and teach leadership". Although the ILA strives to be the professional association for leadership scholars, only a small fraction of leadership scholars are members of the ILA. In all fairness, the International Leadership Association is trying to bring together leadership scholars, practicing leaders, leadership consultants, and those who teach leadership, both within the higher education curriculum, but also outside the curriculum and outside higher education. The broad reach of the ILA, and its efforts to serve multiple and differing constituents has hampered it becoming the agreed-upon academic "home" for leadership scholars.

There is also a great deal of academic politics that have prevented leadership studies from achieving disciplinary status. Several established disciplines claim leadership as their own – psychology, management, and, surprisingly, some in political science. There is resistance by many to the establishment of a distinct discipline when their own discipline has scholars researching the topic of leadership.

To some in the Academy, the study of leadership is not seen as rigorous, and the plethora of popular trade books on leadership – books that have little or no grounding in academic research – simply reinforces that notion. Leadership scholar Tom Cronin (1984) did a very good job of outlining the 10 main reasons that colleges and universities have resisted the teaching of leadership (and, we assume, leadership studies as a discipline; Cronin's article was written before the establishment of most programs in leadership studies). In addition to the perception that leadership studies lacks rigor, is *vocational* in nature, involving training of skills rather than academic content, Cronin notes that there is a belief that leadership studies is "unscientific", and too abstract a construct. (Note that the last two decades of serious research on leadership has assuaged some of this concern, but not all of it). Cronin also suggests that the very fact that leadership is so complex and requires investigation from multiple disciplinary perspectives is somewhat intimidating given the increasing specialization of higher education. This leads to the interesting conclusion that leadership, with its inherent complexity and need for an interdisciplinary and multidisciplinary understanding, is the perfect topic of study for liberal arts colleges (Wren et al., 2009).

Hastening Recognition of Leadership Studies as a Discipline

First and foremost, scholars and educators must strive for academic rigor. Graduate programs must place high value on sound, scholarly research. Doctoral students, in particular, should be well schooled in state-of-the-art research methods and data analysis techniques. Because it is a social science, the complexity of leadership studies requires sophisticated, multivariate analyses in order to understand the multiple forces (leader qualities, follower characteristics, situational elements, etc.) that impact the process of leadership.

Those teaching leadership in university classrooms need to maintain high levels of academic rigor as well. Although it is very important to emphasize that the study of leadership is practical in nature (that is, it is OK to focus a portion of a curriculum on the development/acquisition of leadership skills and development of potential), it is important to avoid taking the "easy path" of assigning only/primarily trade book versions of leadership concepts that are really designed for a general, not an academic, audience. It is encouraging to note that the best-selling leadership texts used in the college classroom tend to do a good job of representing the scholarly literature and avoid presenting a too watered-down version of leadership.

The 2001–02 National Academies panel recommended that fields that have granted 500 degrees in a five-year period should be designated as emerging or full disciplines. Graduating students with degrees such as organizational leadership or educational leadership, as opposed to the more general term of leadership studies, likely cause greater confusion and make the field look fragmented, or "tacked on" to existing disciplines (for example, education, business). If undergraduate and graduate degrees are interdisciplinary or multidisciplinary in nature, and if they focus primarily on leadership, then adopting the term "leadership studies" seems appropriate and would probably hasten recognition of the discipline.

Those of us with serious interests in leadership studies need to develop and nurture our emerging discipline. This means joining and participating in the scholarly societies dedicated to the study of leadership (for example, International Leadership Association, the Academy of Management's Network of Leadership Scholars, and others), supporting the journals devoted to leadership studies, and identifying with the discipline (I admit that I find it easier to tell a stranger that "I'm a psychologist" rather than "a leadership scholar", even though I have to deal with the psychology stereotype baggage of assuming that I am a psychotherapist; but I now proudly admit that I study leadership, even though that often confuses the listener).

So, what is the takeaway message of this chapter? I suggest that leadership is an emerging discipline that will continue to grow and develop, and ultimately receive academic recognition. Only time will tell if that is true. In fact, I believe that leadership is such an important topic that leadership studies will become a distinct and recognized discipline (I just received a LDRNET email from a leadership scholar who suggests that if we don't figure out how to apply good leadership practices, we [the human race] may have no future). Hopefully, with its combination of scholarly rigor and practical applications, universities of the future will wonder how they ever got by without a leadership studies department.

REFERENCES

Biglan, A. (1973a), "The characteristics of subject matter in different academic areas", *Journal of Applied Psychology*, **57**(3), 195–203.

Biglan, A. (1973b), "Relationships between subject matter characteristics and the structure and output of academic departments", *Journal of Applied Psychology*, **57**(3), 204–13.

Burns, J.M. (1978), *Leadership*, New York: Harper & Row.

Cronin, T.E. (1984), "Thinking and learning about leadership", *Presidential Studies Quarterly*, **14**, 22–34.

Del Favero, M. (n.d.), "Academic disciplines: disciplines and the structure of higher education, discipline classification systems, discipline differences", accessed at http://education.stateuniversity.com/pages/1723/Academic-Disciplines.html.

Goethals, G.R. and G.L.J. Sorenson (2006), *The Quest for a General Theory of Leadership*, Cheltenham, UK and Northampton, MA, USA: Edward Elgar.
Hughes, R.L., R.C. Ginnett and G.J. Curphy (2009), *Leadership: Enhancing the Lessons of Experience*, 6th edn, Boston, MA: McGraw-Hill Irwin.
Kuhn, T.S. (1962), *The Structure of Scientific Revolutions*, Chicago, IL: University of Chicago Press.
Northouse, P.G. (2010), *Leadership: Theory and Practice*, 5th edn, Thousand Oaks, CA: Sage.
Porter-O'Grady, T. and K. Malloch (2003), *Quantum Leadership: A Textbook of New Leadership*, Sudbury, MA: Jones and Bartlett.
Wren, J.T. (ed.), (1995), *The Leader's Companion*, New York: Free Press.
Wren, J.T., R.E. Riggio and M.A. Genovese (eds) (2009), *Leadership and the Liberal Arts*, New York: Palgrave Macmillan.
Yukl, G. (2009), *Leadership in Organizations*, 7th edn, Upper Saddle River, NJ: Prentice-Hall.

3. The Jepson School: liberal arts as leadership studies

Joanne B. Ciulla

> Thus some appear to seek in knowledge a couch for a searching spirit;
> others, a walk for a wandering mind; others, a tower of state;
> others, a fort, or commanding ground; and others, a shop for profit or sale...
> (Francis Bacon, 1605: 23)

Around twenty years ago, I joined the faculty of the University of Richmond to help design the Jepson School of Leadership Studies. The easiest way to understand Jepson is as a liberal arts school with an explicit focus on the study of leadership. Our students take courses in history, philosophy, psychology, political science, and so on. These courses draw on the methodology and content of a discipline to understand leadership as a phenomenon and a practice. So as a school, we are multidisciplinary and some of our classes are interdisciplinary. By taking a liberal arts approach to leadership studies, the Jepson School is not doing anything new, but rather reapplying the original intent of liberal arts education, which was not to learn a craft or useful skill, but to acquire knowledge that is good in itself and to educate citizens to live and make choices in a free society (Jaeger, 1986). Hence, the Jepson School is as much about the liberal arts as it is about leadership studies. In this chapter, I will briefly discuss the place of leadership studies in the liberal arts and then go on to describe the development of the Jepson School and how, from its inception to today, it grapples with the practical and philosophical challenges of being a liberal arts school of leadership studies.

People often think of a leadership school as some sort of training program. Yet when you think of it, the very idea of leadership *training* is an oxymoron. Training implies development of a skill in conformity to certain practices and procedures. Leadership would seem to be the opposite of this. While leadership requires certain skills, I am not so sure that leadership itself is a skill. If anything, leadership is more about initiative, perspective, imagination, morality, and the ability to think well and understand people and the world around us. Ideally, a liberal arts education provides the foundation for leadership and life in human society.

THE LIBERAL ARTS

In the ancient world, scholars considered the liberal arts to be those needed for free people to seek a good life (Artistotle, 1984). For Aristotle, our real work in life is the work of being human. The ultimate end of life is happiness. Self-sufficiency and freedom from fear, material needs, and commitments allow us the liberty to develop ourselves as human beings. The word "school" comes from the Greek word for leisure "scholé", which meant to stop and have quiet or peace (DeGrazia, 1962). Education and war, not work, provide people with virtues such as temperance and discipline needed for free time, or the time away from working for the necessities of life. The liberal arts also free the mind so that it is not ruled by the passions, ignorance or prejudice. Aristotle believed that education for free time, not work, would teach people how to engage in activities that are good in themselves, because it is these activities that make humans unique from animals. In a similar vein, the Roman Cicero said that education should separate the truths needed for life's necessary cares from knowledge that is pursued for its own sake. It is ironic that most students today pursue a liberal arts education so they can get a job, when ideally it was meant to teach them how to use their freedom or discretionary time.

Aristotle believed that education should cultivate five virtues of thought: *technê* – craft or technical knowledge; *epistêmê* – descriptive knowledge of the world; *sophia* – wisdom or thought about universal ideas; and *nous* – the higher mind, soul or intellect. The fifth is *phronêsis*, or practical wisdom about how to act or bring about change or a particular end. It is also associated with prudence. Education should cultivate all of these virtues, but *phronêsis* is of particular importance for leadership. Aristotle writes:

> Practical wisdom is the only virtue peculiar to the ruler: it would seem that all other excellences must equally belong to ruler and subject. The excellence of the subject is certainly not wisdom, but only true opinion; he may be compared to the maker of a flute, while his master is like the flute player. (Aristotle, 1984: 2027)

Both Plato and Aristotle started schools. They both understood the idea of educating young people to reason and see the world in different ways by exposing them to a variety of subjects. For example, Plato believed that everyone, especially rulers, needed to study geometry (see Ciulla, 2004a; see also Ciulla, 2004b). Aristotle suggests that at a minimum, students should study reading, writing, drawing, physical training and music (Aristotle, 1984: 2121–28). From the Greek and subsequent Roman tradition, medieval scholars such as St Augustine depicted the liberal arts as resting on seven pillars. The imagery of the seven pillars came from Proverbs 9.1 in the Old Testament: "Wisdom has built her house; she has hewn out its seven pillars". The first three, or the *trivium*, are the verbal arts of logic, grammar and rhetoric. The second four, or the *quadrivium*, are mathematics, geometry, music and astronomy. These two divisions later evolved into what we call the arts and sciences.

If you read the mission statements of liberal arts schools, most of them say something about developing future leaders. So you might wonder, if the liberal arts already educate people for leadership, then why do we need a leadership school or leadership programs? I think that there are several things to consider in answering this question. First, a liberal arts education does not magically produce leaders. Before college education was easily accessible to students from a wide variety of social and economic backgrounds and there were as many liberal arts colleges as there are today, most of the people who received a liberal arts education were from well-off families or members of the elite. It is not surprising that places like Oxford, Cambridge, Harvard and Yale produced leaders, because their students were often in line to take over the family business, or well positioned to go into politics, for example. Elite universities produced leaders in a large part because students came from elite families or well connected families. Students who did not come from elite families learned from their classmates and made connections to elite networks while at school. In a sense, many of these students, by virtue of their lot in life, were born to take on leadership roles, whether they were good at them or not. The same was certainly true in Aristotle's time.

As higher education became democratized, universities enrolled students from all sorts of families. While students from wealthy, poor or modest means benefited from the liberal arts, the connection between liberal arts education and leadership may not have been as evident to people who had not grown up in families of influence or who were not surrounded by people from families of influence. As more people became better educated, there were also changes in the way that people ran businesses and government organizations. The command and control, centralized system of scientific management was geared towards an uneducated, industrial work force. By the mid-twentieth century, it began to give way to more decentralized ways of working in organizations, which resulted in more roles for leaders. This is one reason why, in the latter half of the twentieth century, writers such as James MacGregor Burns (1978), John W. Gardner (1989), and Warren Bennis (1989), wrote about the urgent need for more people who had the ability to take on leadership roles. All of these writers indicated that the higher educational system needed to offer something more than the traditional liberal arts.

Another reason for a leadership school or program is because liberal arts schools have changed. Students increasingly go to university to study business or get credentials for a job. One might argue that, in Aristotle's terms, universities are becoming more like centers for the servile arts (workers) than the liberal arts (free citizens). For instance, undergraduate students who major in business often take fewer courses in the liberal arts school than other students. They learn many useful things, but they may not get the full benefit of the liberal arts. They could miss out on what is perhaps the most important insight of the liberal arts tradition – we can only understand what knowledge is useful if it is based on knowledge of the good. The good is not just what is good for the individual, but what is good for the individual in the context of some greater good that usually includes a good for society as well. Aquinas writes:

> In order that man may make good use of the art he has, he needs a good will, which is perfected by moral virtue; and for this reason the Philosopher says that there is a virtue of art; namely, a moral virtue, in so far as the good use of art requires a moral virtue. (Aquinas, 1947: Q.57 article 3, Reply Objection 2)

The courses that teach students about the good tend to be in the humanities. When parents or students regard universities as trade schools that prepare them for the job market, they seek only the instrumental goods of education, sometimes at the expense of learning things that are intrinsically good. By making liberal arts universities more like trade schools (what Aristotle would call teaching the servile arts), we may be educating students to be workers, but not leaders.

When we designed the Jepson School in 1991, distinguished researchers lamented the lack of progress in leadership studies, despite the growing number of studies and articles on the subject. After reading some of the leadership literature, I could see why they were concerned. Most of what was then called leadership studies came from researchers in psychology and management. Hardly any of the literature was from the humanities. The humanities help us understand the context and values that shape the relationship of leaders and followers and the phenomenon of leadership itself. Without the humanities, leadership studies was a little like watching a movie without the sound. The research showed us things, but we could not hear what they meant. It is against this backdrop that my colleagues and I set out to design the Jepson School of Leadership Studies. Our task was to reinvent a liberal arts school around the study of leadership and to expand and enrich the field of leadership studies.

THE JEPSON SCHOOL

Let me start the story of the Jepson School at the beginning. The school was born in May 1987 when Alice and Robert S. Jepson gave the university of Richmond a $20 million challenge gift to develop a school for leadership education. The Jepson gift funded a school – not a center or a program. The

Jepsons also seemed to know that if you want to build an institution, you need bricks. In 1992, they donated an additional $5 million to complete the building that houses the Jepson School. The story behind the founding of the school is important because it explains why the school was able to make an impact on leadership education and leadership studies. As a separate school housed in a building with its name on it, the Jepson School was built to last. It also started with three endowed chairs and funds for a full-time faculty, who would get tenure and promotions based on their teaching and scholarship in leadership studies. These elements provided a stable environment for innovation, curriculum development, and teaching that was conducive to cross-disciplinary cooperation and research.

Before the Jepson School was built and the faculty hired, a university committee had put together the basic plan for it. In the draft proposal, they articulated the mission of the school in the following way: "The primary task of the school is to provide a rigorous and disciplined education with a focus upon ethical and responsible leadership."[1] The committee then went on to describe the purpose of the school:

> The school's degree programs must be focused on producing in students the knowledge, experience, and abilities needed to be effective and constructive leaders in a variety of contexts. A solid foundation in the liberal arts and sciences, coupled with the study and preparation for leadership, holds the potential to prepare men and women who will approach leadership opportunities with a measure of skill, compassion, integrity, ability, and breadth of understanding that is sorely needed in our nation and world.

This statement was later translated into the mission of the school, which was to educate students "*for* leadership and *about* leadership."

In July 1991, I left The Wharton School for what I felt was one of the greatest opportunities in higher education – designing a new kind of institution from the ground up. The University of Richmond had already hired the Dean, Howard Prince, and the Associate Dean, Stephanie Micas. James MacGregor Burns had also signed on as a Senior Fellow. I was the first tenure track faculty hired as an endowed chair in leadership and ethics (my graduate and undergraduate degrees are in philosophy). My three colleagues soon followed – Richard Couto (political science), Karen Klenke (industrial psychology), and William Howe (education). The Dean was a behavioral psychologist and the Associate Dean's background was in women's studies. From July 1991 until the beginning of the spring semester of 1992, the faculty and two Deans developed all aspects of the school from admission procedures, to curriculum, to the introductory course.

This was an exciting but, at times, a very difficult process. It entailed seemingly endless conversations about what the school should look like. The first and most difficult stumbling block was unpacking what "for and about leadership" meant. As academics, the "about leadership" part was easy, but the "for leadership" part was not. Most of us did not think that the school should be doing leadership "training". My colleagues discussed what we wanted our students to be like when they graduated. In addition to leaving with a strong liberal arts education, we wanted them to be the sorts of people who took responsibility for the world around them. Not all of our students would be presidents or CEOs, but at a minimum they would be the good citizens – the kind who, rather than complain about a pothole, would gather their neighbors together to do something about it. We hoped that the difference between our students and students in a regular liberal arts program would be that our students would not only feel responsible for the world around them, but they would have explicitly learned from the liberal arts how leaders influence and work with others. After this discussion, I captured our thoughts in the mission and philosophy statement. We stated the mission of the school this way: "The Jepson School develops people who understand the moral responsibilities of leadership and who are prepared to exercise leadership in service to society."[2]

The "for and about leadership" was also tied to questions about how we selected our students. Were we supposed to be picking students based on leadership potential? (Our students apply to the Jepson School during their sophomore year at the university.) We did not want to be in the business of picking out who would be a leader. This was offensive to some of us on a few levels. First, because it seemed presumptuous and second, because both trait research and history show that there is no written-in-stone criteria for predicting who will be a leader. Even if there were, then such "born leaders" would, in theory, not need to take our program. The task of identifying future leaders is especially difficult, given how much students can change and mature in the last two years of college. Finally, the idea of selecting leaders based on their leadership potential precluded letting students in who were interested in studying leadership. In the end, we accepted students based on their grades and their essays about why they wanted to join the school. We decided that it would be best to have students with a variety of interests, backgrounds, and personalities in our classes. This scatter shot approach has served us well. To this day, I am often surprised by which of our graduates actually end up in significant leadership positions years after they graduate.

In the end, we found some very acceptable solutions to the "for" question. Service learning, action research, speakers, and leaders in residence would provide students with hands-on and practical knowledge *for* leadership. We also pledged to experiment with pedagogy. Small interactive classes and the cohort effect created by having a selection process would allow us to create an active learning community in the school. Students would learn the skills and practical parts of leadership through doing things and interacting with leaders that we brought into the program. Today, one or more of these elements can be found in most leadership programs. The one simple reason why a liberal arts school of leadership studies may produce more leaders than a regular liberal arts program is because when students study a subject, they often want to practice it – art students want to be artists, psychology students want to be psychologists, chemistry students want to be chemists, and so on. In the same vein, when students study leadership, they frequently become interested in taking on leadership roles. Over the years, our students have consistently held key leadership positions on campus – during some years they have held almost all of those positions. In part, this is the result of self-selection, but I do not think it accounts for all of it.

DEVELOPING THE CURRICULUM

When it came to developing the curriculum, there was some tension between the disciplines of the various faculty and Deans, but we were actually able to design the curriculum in one day. We first agreed to have an introductory course called The Foundations of Leadership Studies. Next, we formulated the core courses starting with critical thinking and ethics and leadership. We had an extended debate over history as a core course. I was the only person from the humanities in the group. I really thought a core course in history was essential. Instead, we ended up with what we later learned was a bad compromise – a course called The History and Theories of Leadership.

The discussion about critical thinking exemplified the challenge of a multidisciplinary program. I envisioned a course that focused on epistemology, informal logic, and philosophy of science as a means of developing critical reading, writing, listening, and argumentation skills. The social scientists wanted a research methods course. I thought that the study of knowledge itself would be a better all-purpose tool for our students. I was rightly outvoted on this. We then had to grapple with the question: which discipline's method should we teach? Our students would be taking courses and reading literature from a variety of disciplines. Critical Thinking was supposed to help our students critically read and discuss materials from all of the liberal arts. Again, we made an easy but problematic compromise and decided to have the course address research methods in all disciplines from psychology to literary theory. We ended up with a course called Critical Thinking and Methods of Inquiry. The fourth core course, Leading Groups, was not controversial.

The core curriculum consisted of Critical Thinking, History and Theories of Leadership, Leading Groups, and Ethics and Leadership, which later became Leadership Ethics. Experiential learning formed the last element of the core. Since a founding idea of the school was moral leadership, we wanted to make sure that ethics was not just a course in the curriculum, but a part of other courses and experiences in the school. Hence, we required all of our majors to engage in community service and take a service learning class. The course was mainly a forum for discussing students' on-site experiences. We later increased the number of credits for this class and created a regular academic course to go with service learning called Justice and Civil Society. In addition to this class, majors were required to do an internship. During the first six years of the school, all students were required to do a senior project. We later changed this requirement to a series of senior seminars and, since the ethics course touched on many aspects of the program, it became de facto the capstone course.

After formulating the core courses, we moved on to the electives. These were grounded in two broad variables in leadership studies – the context of leadership and competencies of leadership (or things leaders need to know about). The context courses included community leadership, international leadership, political leadership, leadership in social movements, and leadership in formal organizations. The basic competency electives were also easy to identify: conflict resolution, decision-making, motivation, organizational communication, leading individuals, and leading change, to name a few. Today we have a very wide range of electives that still fall into these general categories such as: Leadership in Historical Contexts; Statesmanship; Leadership and Religious Values; Gender and Leadership; Leaders and Artists; Reason, Rhetoric and Leadership; Psychology of Good and Evil and so on. We have since abandoned the context and competency categories, but I still think they are helpful ways to think about a leadership curriculum. Any leadership program or comprehensive study of leadership needs to take a balanced look at what leaders know and do and the influence of the contexts in which they operate.

Designing the curriculum was a piece of cake compared with our effort to design the first Foundations of Leadership Studies course. Through years of teaching and research, established disciplines like psychology or philosophy have forged a general consensus about what students need to know in an intro course. This was not the case in leadership studies in general and definitely not the case for a liberal arts approach to the topic in 1991. There were some textbooks on leadership, such as Gary Yukl's *Leadership in Organizations* (1989), but they tended to offer a limited view of leadership studies that was mostly based on research in management and psychology. There was also a massive amount of literature in the popular press that was not really appropriate for this program.

Our first Foundations of Leadership Studies course was a disaster for all who taught it and took it. Out of what were sometimes heated debates, we put together 600 pages of readings and a syllabus that really did not hang together.

Around mid-semester, our students called us to a meeting and demanded that something be done with the course because we were driving them crazy. Despite our failure to put together a very coherent course, we were rather pleased with the way that our students intervened and offered constructive criticism. That was exactly the sort of behavior we hoped to see in them. Many of the students from that course stayed on and joined the first class of the Jepson School, which was formally inaugurated in the fall of 1992.

I think the biggest problem we had with that course is that none of us really knew what the foundations of leadership studies were and I am still not sure that our faculty or colleagues in the field would agree on what they are today. As Thomas Kuhn (1970) notes, one indication that a field of study is mature is when there are standard textbooks in it. There are some good leadership textbooks out there today, but I do not think that they represent a consensus of what one should learn in an introduction to leadership studies course (for example, see Northouse, 1997 and later edition, 2009). Three years after the first course, my colleague Tom Wren carved down and organized the 600 pages of reading from the original Foundations of Leadership Studies course into a reader called *The Leader's Companion* (1995). This helped reshape the course into something more manageable and it also offered the first model of a liberal arts leadership studies reader.

THE CHALLENGES OF IMPLEMENTING AN INTERDISCIPLINARY CURRICULUM

It is rare that any program gets the curriculum right from the start, and we were no exception. Because we are a liberal arts school, we have a multidisciplinary faculty teaching a curriculum that consists of a number of interdisciplinary courses. This creates some unique challenges. It is one thing to devise a list of new courses and quite another to actually teach them and find faculty to teach them. For example, I taught Critical Thinking and Methods of Inquiry. As a philosopher, the critical thinking part was easy. There are plenty of good textbooks in this area – logic is still logic, and the same is true for epistemology and philosophy of science. All I did was insert examples and exercises that would apply to leadership. My problem was with research methods. I knew something about research methods in history, literature, philosophy, and the natural sciences but I did not know much about the social sciences. We had similar problems with History and Theories of Leadership. This course required knowledge in both history and the social sciences. Since we did not have enough faculty to team-teach these courses, the content of them was sometimes a bit lopsided. Depending on who taught it, students either got a strong dose of history or a strong dose of the social science theories of leadership. After teaching it for a while, some faculty managed to master both sides of the course.

Interdisciplinary courses raise a number of questions about the level of expertise needed in the various disciplines for a course to meet the same level of academic rigor as single-discipline courses. Professors sometimes make the mistake of trying to put too many things into an interdisciplinary course. This allows them to skate with ease through material from a number of disciplines, but such courses run the risk of fragmentation and failure to treat subjects with sufficient depth. Our Foundations of Leadership Studies course had a related problem. It was supposed to be a survey course, but our faculty did not like teaching things they did not know well or find interesting. They solved the problem of fragmentation and depth by teaching what they knew best. As a result of this, we eventually got rid of the Foundations of Leadership Studies Course by splitting it into two required courses – Leadership and the Social Sciences, and Leadership and the Humanities. This makes practical sense, but it raises the question of how knowledge of the humanities and social sciences complement, reinforce, and enrich our understanding of leadership. The old foundations course also served the function of teaching new faculty about the various areas of leadership research. One concern is that faculty who do not have a good sense of the whole field will be unable to tie what they do in their courses to the rest of the curriculum.

We later divided Critical Thinking and Methods of Inquiry into two courses – Critical Thinking, and Research Methods. Research Methods focuses on method in the social sciences. We still struggle with what to do about these two courses. We recently made them into two half-semester courses taught by different professors. Undergraduates in any program need to have a course that develops critical skills and skills that aid in the organized collection of information. The half semester of each short-changes both courses, but this may be adequate for an undergraduate program. In graduate education, however, an in-depth focus on method is fundamental for future research and a student's development as a teacher and scholar.

The ideal solution for interdisciplinary courses is to have them team-taught. This is a costly solution that few schools and departments can sustain over time. We have team-taught a number of courses at Jepson with faculty from other parts of the university. These courses have covered leadership in art, science, literature and economics. We funded several of these courses with a Keck Foundation Grant that Jepson, Claremont McKenna, and Loyola Marymount received in 2005. Team-teaching is a great way for faculty to learn new subject areas but faculty need to teach a course more than once to develop it and refine their knowledge of a subject. Leadership courses require time to experiment, make mistakes, and refine the material. Some of us at the Jepson School published textbooks after we felt we had got a course right. For example, I published my book *The Ethics of Leadership* (Ciulla, 2003) after getting the kinks out of my leadership ethics course and Gill Hickman published *Leading Organizations* (1998) based on her experience teaching Leadership in Formal Organizations.

HIRING AND DEVELOPING LEADERSHIP STUDIES FACULTY

Hiring faculty for a multidisciplinary and interdisciplinary program is challenging. The Jepson School started out with four faculty members and hired two more the second year – Tom Wren (history) and Gill Hickman (public administration). In the early years, our job advertisements were usually for people in leadership studies. We received hundreds of applications from people with Ph.D.s, many of whom were practitioners such as retired generals, consultants, business people, and a myriad of others who wanted to share their personal knowledge and leadership experiences with our students. We often invite such practitioners into our classes or to give talks, or to serve as our Leader in Residence. At this time, we do not have positions for "professors of practice". We soon discovered that the best way to advertise for a position in our school was to search for people who, first and foremost, had a strong disciplinary background in a liberal arts discipline.

One hallmark of a discipline is an implicit or explicit method of research. At this time, leadership studies is not itself a discipline – it is a field that includes many disciplines. We get a number of job applicants who have Ph.D.s in leadership studies, but we have noticed that their research does not always rest on a solid foundation in one or more of the liberal arts. The danger of interdisciplinary graduate programs is that students can end up without a discipline. We then look at the candidates' research and background to see if they are able to connect what they know and have done to future teaching and research in leadership studies. Job candidates from specific disciplines can also present problems. While Ph.D. work in interdisciplinary programs sometimes lacks depth and rigor, single-discipline candidates are sometimes so narrowly focused that it is difficult to see how they could teach our courses or, for that matter, many courses in their own discipline. At this time, the disciplinary make-up of the Jepson School faculty looks like this: we have two faculty members from philosophy, two from religion, three from political science, three from social psychology, one from history, one from public administration, one from international studies, and we will soon have another faculty member from one of the humanities. Our Dean is an economist.

FINDING BOUNDARIES AND KEEPING FOCUSED

As we have added faculty, we have added many new courses and research on leadership. Perhaps one of the greatest challenges of a leadership studies curriculum is finding a balance between what needs to be taught and what the available faculty can and will teach. You can make just about any subject into a leadership course. The difficulty is drawing the line between what is really about leadership and what is about something that has only a thin connection to leadership. This issue is conceptually difficult and – as one might imagine – politically volatile. Yet, if a liberal arts approach to leadership studies is about anything and everything, then it is no longer a leadership program. It is the worst sort of interdisciplinary program – a collection of courses that lack a coherent connection to each other.

When we designed the curriculum, we were concerned about the danger of fragmentation so we decided that our courses should be carefully sequenced. By having students take courses in a certain order, we hoped to have the core courses build on each other. The course sequence also reinforced the cohort effect, which is very useful in a program where most classes are largely discussion, and group assignments are quite common. In addition to tight sequencing, we began to offer students the option of taking a leadership concentration. Before we started the school, the university had stipulated that all of our students were required to have a minor or second major. They thought that a second major or minor would answer the "Leadership for what?" question. We soon discovered that a number of our students were taking two or sometimes three majors or minors on their own. Usually the major or minor complemented their work in leadership studies. We decided to get rid of the major or minor requirement and introduce leadership studies concentrations. Now, if students are interested in areas such as international leadership, law and leadership, political leadership, religious leadership, and so on, we help them put together a program of courses from Jepson and in other departments in the university. This allows them to follow their interests without having to cobble together several minors or another major. Students who take a concentration have a faculty supervisor and they write a thesis in their senior year.

LIBERAL ARTS POSTGRADUATE PROGRAMS

Ever since the day that The Jepson School opened its doors, we have received requests to give training programs for business, government and community groups. We turned down most of them because we were too busy teaching and doing our own research. During the first year, I was approached by the Virginia Foundation of Police Executives to develop a program for police chiefs and other senior officers from around the state. Since the mission of our school included the idea of service to society, I thought that we should do something for this important group of public servants, but only if that "something" was what we were already doing in our classes. I outlined a proposal that I thought the Virginia Foundation of Police Executives would reject. It was a miniature version of our undergraduate liberal arts program. This meant that participants would take everything from Critical Thinking to Leadership and Literature. The foundation liked the idea and so did the people who eventually attended the program. My colleagues did a wonderful job delivering short versions of their regular courses. The program ran as a Jepson program for over ten years.

The police executive program was a useful learning experience because the original plan for the Jepson School included the development of a master's degree program. We did indeed design one in 2002. I drafted the following description of the program:

> The Jepson School's executive Masters of Leadership Studies (MLS) is a selective and intellectually rigorous liberal arts leadership program for mid-career professionals. The MLS curriculum rests on three assumptions about leadership. The first and central assumption is that leaders must have a broad perspective on the world and the place of organization and work in it. There is no better vehicle for doing this than the liberal arts. Insights from areas such as history, anthropology, international studies, sociology, and literature help participants expand their worldviews and gain new insights into their organizations and themselves. Second, leadership is about anticipating, analyzing and solving problems within complex systems. Courses in this program focus on developing analytical ability and imagination to create viable strategies for creating, implementing and foreseeing change in organizations and society. The MLS program offers intensive work in logic, critical thinking, systems thinking, creativity and change. Third, perhaps the most difficult part of leadership is relationships with people. The people issues permeate all parts of this program, but are specifically addressed in sessions on ethics, groups, and organizations. These sessions are taught using literature from philosophy, religion, and the best social science on individual and group behavior.

We faced a number of practical challenges implementing this program, such as cost – it would be quite expensive because we only wanted about 20 students in the class. The size of the potential pool of applicants in the Richmond metropolitan area was a concern because the university did not have a hotel facility, so most students would have to commute or make their own hotel arrangements. Staffing was problematic since some faculty did not want to teach in the program. In a small program, we also hoped for an interesting group of people with diverse backgrounds and experiences from both the non-profit and for-profit sectors. Despite these challenges, we were able to get a pool of applicants for the first class – and then we had a revelation. We had required all of our applicants to take the GREs (Graduate Record Exam). At the meeting to select our first class, we discovered that many of the applicants' scores were fairly low, except for one applicant who got an 800. Some of the lower scores were interesting people with years of experience who had been out of school for a long time. While we wanted these people in the program, we wondered if some of them could pass our courses. What would we do if they could not? This was designed as an academic master's degree program, analogous to one in a topic like history or psychology, so we did not want to lower our standards. We began to think about what failure of a course would mean to someone whose employer was paying for the program, or for someone who would be attending on a scholarship. Despite the fact that we were very clear about the program as a liberal arts program, I think that there was still the perception that it was a training program. At the selection meeting we made the difficult decision not to go forward with the program. In retrospect, I think it was the right choice. We had not sufficiently worked through the conceptual and practical challenges of such a program. Today the good graduate programs in leadership studies are not liberal arts programs. They tend to focus more on leadership practice and be grounded in the study of business, psychology, strategy, and so on.

This is not to say that liberal arts programs should not be done, but rather that it is often difficult to explain to employers the value added of taking impractical courses such as literature for leadership development. Having taught leadership seminars for a number of business and government groups over the years, I am not alone in noticing the powerful ways in which working adults translate lessons from areas such as philosophy and literature into practical applications regarding leadership and their work. For example, in the 1950s, executives at the Bell Telephone Company were concerned about how to develop leadership talent within the company. Many of the up-and-coming managers were good at their jobs, but did not have a college education. They believed that "A well trained man knows how to answer questions; an educated man knows what questions are worth asking."[3] The company sent promising managers through a ten-month liberal arts program at the University of Pennsylvania. There they took short courses on everything from James Joyce's *Ulysses* to the *Bhagavad Gita*. The company carried out a survey of the participants and found that they read more widely, were more curious about the world, and they tended to see more than one facet to any given argument after going through the program. In short, managers developed two very important leadership qualities. They had widened their perspective on the world and improved their critical thinking skills. The company considered the institute a success, except for one problem. The managers who participated in the program were more intellectually engaged and confident, but they were also less inclined to put the company's bottom line ahead of the interests of other stakeholders such as the community and their families. While the company wanted to develop competent, intellectually engaged leaders, they were not very comfortable with leaders who might put the interests of other stakeholders ahead of the company's bottom line. In short, these managers internalized the most important lessons of the liberal arts – knowledge is only useful if it is for some greater good, and the ultimate end of knowledge is happiness and the good life. Perhaps this is the main reason why leadership studies should be a liberal and not a servile art.

LEADERSHIP STUDIES AS THE LIBERAL ARTS

The liberal arts approach provides a foundation of knowledge needed for life. A liberal arts leadership studies program uses the study of leaders and leadership as a focal point for that foundation. The study of leadership will never be complete without the arts and the sciences. The humanities supply a rich foundation for understanding the context of leadership and they offer a gigantic repository of information about morality and human behavior that spans over time and across cultures. In an ideal field of leadership studies, social scientists would test the results of their research against what we know from subjects such as history, literature, philosophy and religion, and scholars from those fields would test their observations and interpretations against research carried out by social scientists in the laboratory and the field.

As I argued earlier, undergraduate students who choose to study leadership are probably more likely to want to be leaders than liberal arts students in general. Jepson School graduates rarely aspire to get graduate degrees in leadership studies. They move on to jobs in business, public service or non-profits, or they study law, medicine, public administration, education, religion, or some other academic discipline. In short, a liberal arts leadership studies degree is not something one takes to prepare for graduate work in leadership studies or to be a leader. It serves as an intellectual and moral foundation for doing whatever it is that students choose to do or study in life. Nonetheless, by adding a leadership focus to the liberal arts, we hope that our students will be more inclined to take on the moral responsibilities of leadership and citizenship and know more about what it takes to do it well.

NOTES

1. Draft 4: "Proposal for the Jepson School of Leadership Studies", University of Richmond Faculty Committee, 1989.
2. Draft of the Jepson School Philosophy Statement from 3 September 1991.
3. The description of this program is from Davis (2010).

REFERENCES

Aquinas, Thomas (1947), *Summa Theologica, Part I–II,* translated by Fathers of the English Dominican Province, New York: Benziger Brothers.

Aristotle (1984), *Politics*, translated by B. Jowett, Jonathan Barnes (ed.), *The Complete Works of Aristotle,* Princeton, NJ: Princeton University Press.

Bacon, Francis ([1605] 1900), *Advancement of Learning and Novum Organum*, New York: The Colonial Press.

Bennis, Warren (1989), *On Becoming a Leader*, Reading, MA: Addison-Wesley Publishing.

Burns, James MacGregor (1978), *Leadership*, New York: HarperCollins.

Ciulla, Joanne B. (2003), *The Ethics of Leadership*, Belmont, CA: Wadsworth/Thompson.

Ciulla, Joanne B. (2004a), "Aristotle", in *Encyclopedia of Leadership Studies*, vol. 1, Thousand Oaks, CA: Sage Publications, pp. 43–6.

Ciulla, Joanne B. (2004b), "Plato", *Encyclopedia of Leadership Studies*, vol. 3, Thousand Oaks, CA: Sage Publications, pp. 1202–06.

Davis, Wes (2010), "The 'Learning Knights' of Bell Telephone", *The New York Times*, 16 June, A25.

DeGrazia, Sebastian (1962), *Of Work, Time and Leisure*, New York: Twentieth Century Fund.

Gardner, John W. (1989), *On Leadership*, New York: The Free Press.

Hickman, Gill R. (1998), *Leading Organizations: Perspectives for a New Era*, Thousand Oaks, CA: Sage Publications.

Jaeger, Werner (1986), *Paideia: The Ideals of Greek Culture, Vol. I*, translated by Gilbert Highet, Oxford: Oxford University Press.

Kuhn, Thomas (1970), *The Structure of Scientific Revolutions*, Chicago: University of Chicago Press.

Northouse, Peter N. (1997 [2009]), *Leadership: Theory and Practice*, Thousand Oaks, CA: Sage Publications.

Wren, Thomas (1995), *A Leader's Companion*, New York: The Free Press.

Yukl, Gary (1989), *Leadership in Organizations*, Upper Saddle River, NJ: Prentice Hall.

PART II

The disciplines

4. Leadership and the Classics

Michael A. Genovese and Lawrence A. Tritle

The study of leadership is as old as the study of politics and history. It crosses and covers most academic disciplines. That our academic disciplines have become so balkanized into narrowly self-defined fields makes both the integration of knowledge and the study of leadership difficult. Seemingly only a true renaissance person could master the breadth and scope of so inclusive a field, which explains the present joint effort of this essay: the task of understanding leadership involves a multidisciplinary endeavor in which concepts and historical and political figures are examined from several or more perspectives at once. We hope to contribute but one element to this grand puzzle by examining what the study of the Classics might contribute to the understanding of leadership broadly defined.

We approach our topic from the academic disciplines of political science and history/Classics. We have team-taught a course on *Leadership and Ethics: Ancient and Modern*, as part of a grant from the Keck Foundation and have approached the subject of leadership from the perspective briefly noted above. By "Classics" we mean the study of the cultures and politics of ancient Greece and Rome (a Eurocentric view, perhaps, but one that taps into the core of what has become known as Western civilization). By "leadership" we mean the art and science of directing and mobilizing group efforts to achieve mutually desired goals. Thus, our question is: *what can the study of the Classics contribute to our understanding of leadership?*[1]

THE IMPORTANCE OF THE CLASSICS FOR THE STUDY OF LEADERSHIP

Why bother with the work of old, dead, white guys? Partly because it is the foundation of Western civilization; partly because most of the important questions and problems with which we deal today were asked (and perhaps, answered) by the ancients; partly because the frameworks of our cultures and politics were grounded in that era. In short, the Classics serve as the foundation for who we are, what we think, what we believe to be important, and what continues to vex us. How could we *not* study the Classics?

We study the Classics, not to the exclusion of other voices, other cultures, other races, other religions, other genders, excluded and marginalized voices, but in addition to studying all these many contributions.[2] As leadership studies must be – by definition – inclusive and encompassing, it must embrace a wide range of approaches, perspectives, voices and interests. And so we study the Classics not to exclude, but to engage; not to assert superiority, but to illuminate how we got here and why that matters; not to narrow but to expand understanding.

The Classics serve as the foundation of the study of leadership. This has been the case not only since antiquity itself with the study and writing of lives of great men, but also since colonial America. In the eighteenth century young Americans, as well as their counterparts in Britain and elsewhere in Europe, read Plutarch's *Lives of Noble Greeks and Romans*, a work that began to appear in various European languages with Thomas North's 1579 translation. Plutarch provided readers with both good and bad examples of political leaders, ranging from Pericles of Athens (good) to Mark Antony of Rome (bad).[3] To the modern era, such basic, even simplistic categories, lacking in subtlety and context, may seem naive, yet grounded in Plutarch's analysis are the foundations of leadership studies. Didactic and moral treatments made role-modeling easy for astute observers, which explains the popularity of Plutarch in the education of young Americans and Europeans.[4] For in the lives of such figures as Pericles and Antony, one can find the key questions, central conflicts and paradigmatic responses to the dilemmas faced by those who dare to lead.

WHAT MATTERS?

Essentially there are two strands we wish to pursue in employing the Classics in the study of leadership: questions of political philosophy and matters of history. The first set of questions that emerges from the study of great political thinkers and political philosophy will be essentially normative, that is, what ought to be and why? The second set of concerns is primarily descriptive, and concerns who actually rules, how, and on what basis. What ought to be and what is are often at odds.

While today, the "scientific" study of leadership allows us to develop theories, test them, and arrive at plausible conclusions of what factors shape and move political and social reality, the ancients had to rely on logic, persuasion, and an emerging empiricism still in its nascent stages. History and the lives of the great and powerful served as their laboratory. And yet, in this era the perennial and perplexing questions of leadership were confronted, and their work serves as the basis of all that follows.

CLASSICAL POLITICAL PHILOSOPHY CONFRONTS HISTORY

Normative political theory from the classical period asks several key questions that continue to haunt us into the modern era: *Who should rule? On what basis? How should society be organized? Are leaders born or made? How should "the people" be defined and what role should they play in politics? Who should get what, and on what basis?*[5]

Who Should Rule?

Among the first to ask this question in the classical era was the Greek historian Herodotus, writing in the last quarter of the fifth century BC. Herodotus not only posed the question in terms of authority, but staged the debate in the court of the Persian king, Darius.[6] Here Herodotus explored the tripartite classification of regimes, essentially three different models of leadership: rule by the one (monarchy), rule by the few (oligarchy), and rule by the many (democracy), that had first been posed by the poet and statesman Solon in the early sixth century BC.[7] The Herodotean model, however, which philosophers, historians and orators would address throughout antiquity, was itself a product of the Athenian democracy of the later fifth century BC, an era dominated by one of the great leaders of all time, Pericles.

The heir of two great Athenian families, Pericles emerged as one of several demagogues or popular leaders (demagogue acquires its negative connotation after Pericles) in the mid-fifth century BC. He sponsored several measures that dramatically influenced Athenian democracy and society: pay for jury service which enabled poorer Athenians to participate in the democracy; the establishment of Athenian legal identity whereby Athenian citizenship would be restricted to those with Athenian fathers and mothers. He resisted Spartan overtures in the disputes that resulted in the great and catastrophic Peloponnesian War (431-404 BC), and while his firmness may be admirable, it also contributed to the single greatest disaster that befell the Greeks.[8]

In his life of Pericles, Plutarch continues the view of Periclean greatness that began with Pericles' own contemporary, the historian Thucydides. Thucydides saw Pericles as a talented statesman and orator, who led the democracy with a vision of Athenian greatness, best seen in the speech Thucydides ascribes to Pericles, the famous Funeral Oration, also known as the "School of Athens" speech.[9] In speaking over the Athenian dead of the Peloponnesian War's first year, Pericles outlined the ideals of a democratic society and how such a society stands apart from other polities or political forms. Like Thucydides, Plutarch shows through numerous anecdotes and examples Pericles' bold and decisive leadership, and how Pericles, his conduct of affairs, and his leadership sharply contrasted with the pandering and bankrupt policies of those who succeeded him.[10]

While Pericles would have learned the art of leadership from aristocratic mentors within his own family, from his own circle came one – Socrates – who would argue that such things as politics, and knowledge generally, should be taught. This foundation would lead most famously to the arguments of Plato who, in the early fourth century BC, would argue that leadership was a highly specialized task requiring skill, training, discipline and the right temperament. Plato's Academy, established c. 387 BC, became a training center for prospective leaders and attracted students not only from Athens itself but from around the Greek world.[11] The skills and attributes of a leader were not seen as natural, but rather the result of instruction and training. Thus in Plato's view, leaders are *made* not *born*, and in his *Republic*, Plato argues that what were needed were "Philosopher Kings".[12] When philosophers were kings, and kings philosophers, all might be right with the leadership world.

A profound critic of democracy, Plato argued that only the "best" in society could become leaders, as the training of the leader was taxing and difficult.[13] While democracy is the litmus test of political legitimacy in the early twenty-first century, it was not always so. The great Peloponnesian War nearly shattered the democratic idea with several oligarchic or right-wing putsches temporarily eclipsing rule of the many in Athens. But in Plato's day, while the Athenian democracy had its critics, it would be foreign enemies, not domestic, that would overthrow it.[14] It remains true, however, that in the classical period, serious thinkers from Socrates to Plato found democracy flawed as a basis of rule. The people sometimes behaved as a mob, as in the illegal trial, a kangaroo court, of the generals held accountable for the disaster at Arginusae in 406 BC.[15] Who in his right mind would advocate mob rule, or the rule of the unwashed rabble? No, only the "best" in society should govern. If the "noble lie" was that these betters were really no better than the rest, then, social stability and order demanded that the illusion be maintained for the good of the state.[16]

Just as his teacher Socrates attacked democracy, so too Plato attacked it on a variety of grounds, but the most telling was the "craft analogy". If one wanted to learn to sail a ship, a skilled, experienced sea captain might be found for instruction. If one were ill, a trained medical professional should be sought: calling a general meeting of "the people" to vote on some diagnosis would be foolish. No, one needs specialized training to perform specialized and exacting tasks with skill. The people were ill-equipped for such a diagnosis. The same applied to political leadership. As a highly specialized skill, it only stands to reason that trained specialists experienced in leadership have the best chance of diagnosing a political disease and finding a cure for the body politic.[17]

Again, this view, like the contemporary embrace of political democracy, is a stark contrast to modern (American) views of leadership. Today, most candidates for president run as "outsiders" and claim as a badge of honor, that they are not Washington DC politicians. In fact, of the past five presidents, four ran and won as outsiders (Carter, Reagan, Clinton, George W. Bush), while only one, George H.W. Bush, had extensive experience as a Washington DC insider.

But how far can/should we take the craft analogy? If I am ill I certainly will go to a medical professional, but I may or may not take his or her advice; I may seek a second opinion; I may weigh cost versus cure. In short, "I" will make the final decision. I will not rely exclusively on a professional who might well benefit (financially) by my taking his advice. Or his cure might be worse than my disease. In Plato's scheme, we are still left with one of the most fundamental questions of political leadership, asked by the Roman poet and social critic Juvenal: *who shall guard the guardians?*[18]

Plato did not ignore this question. He wanted to deny leaders the material advantage so tempting to some leaders.[19] But material wealth is but one temptation that confronts the leader. Ego and the drive for power or control or glory may also motivate the leader to abuse power and overreach. Can we be ruled by anything but a single strong hand? And does this single strong hand invite inevitable danger?

Further, the very premise on which Plato bases his analysis is open to suspicion. Plato insists that leaders need expert knowledge that can best be attained through training and education. But is leadership a specialized knowledge, and can it be taught? Thinkers like Socrates and Plato, as well as many who study modern leadership studies, insist that, yes, leadership can be taught. But is good *judgment* more important than good *training*? Is common sense, a curious nature, a tough personal constitution, high intelligence, a natural skepticism, a burning hunger for knowledge, a good evaluation or talent, a sense of timing, more important than training? Can one teach common sense? Good judgment? Rulers need subtle personal skills and a robust emotional intelligence as well as proper training and experience. Plato's insistence on a type of benevolent dictatorship of the philosophically trained has a surface appeal, but falls short when it meets the harsh reality of politics in practice.

If the rule of one posed a danger, what of that of the many? The Athenian democracy had a different answer to the question regarding who shall rule, as seen metaphorically in the names given to boys that begin to appear after the 460s BC: Demophon, "voice of the people", Demosthenes, "he stands up for the people", which, with other similar names, point to the triumph of democracy or "people power".[20] The Athenians selected magistrates primarily on a lottery basis, rotating citizens through the more than 700 offices of state, though the influential office of *strategos*, general, was popularly and directly elected without term limits. So, for example, Pericles held the post for 15 consecutive years, prompting Thucydides to record that while Athens was a democracy in name, in reality it was the rule of one man, Pericles.[21] Rotation meant that officials would not hold office long enough to reap personal rewards from their positions, though some tried and were punished for their efforts. Moreover, rotating leadership posts among many citizens diffused power and solved the selection dilemma.

The concept of "we, the people" is grounded in this age when the embryo of political democracy emerged briefly in Athens and elsewhere in the Greek world, granting to the citizen the right to self-rule.[22] In the years after Alexander the Great, the era known as the Hellenistic Age (323–31 BC), representative forms of democracy also developed in Greece. The Achaean League and the Aetolian League, both of which would challenge and then fall to the greater power of Rome (by 146 BC), established legislative authority executed by duly elected officials.[23] Compared, however, with the larger "world" states of the Hellenistic kingdoms (Ptolemaic in Egypt, Seleucid in Syria) the idea that "the people" should rule may be seen as a limited experiment, if not a peculiar concept. Moreover, the impact of Alexander the Great, and his achievements as conqueror and leader, gave great force to the idea of the rule of one man, and established norms of political iconography and authority that would be influential for hundreds of years, penetrating even the Roman conquerors of the Hellenistic states.[24] In this context, the idea of "we, the people", no matter what shape or form the idea developed, could only fall by the wayside.

In Rome of the Republic (c. 507–27 BC) another model for governing emerged out of the ancient city-state. For the Romans, the state, what is usually styled the "republic" from the Latin *res publica*, meant more like "things held in common" than a modern state in which power, leadership, and the other attributes of government and rule are equally shared. With its legislative branch (including judicial functions) in the form of popular assemblies and the Senate, its executive branch in its leaders seemingly popularly elected, the Roman Republic appeared "representative" and this was the image shaped by the Greek prisoner-of-war turned historian, Polybius.[25] With careful attention, Polybius described the Roman constitution as a balanced Aristotelian polity composed of monarchy, aristocracy and democracy, yet he was unable to see either the texture of political life in Rome or the power wielded by the elites.[26]

In reality, the Roman Republic was always an oligarchy in which the few ruled for the benefit of the few, and the many received attention only when it suited the elites. While "representatives" in the form of senators would seemingly govern for the community, their interests and needs – not surprisingly – always took priority. As elites, these representatives filtered the views of the many through their "obviously" superior talents, temperaments and experience, and produced a fairly stable government that generally served the interests of the community. Yet the magistrates or executive body in this supposed balanced regime were drawn from the elites and were in fact (at times when not in office) the "representatives" sitting in the Senate or standing in the popular assemblies. Again the interests of only the few were served.

The basis for this form of government is found in the supposed balance it provided. The Romans feared and hated the rule of kings (such a fear would cost Julius Caesar his life) and so the Republic avoided the dangers of one-man rule. Instead of monarchy (equated with tyranny), the Romans established the collective wisdom of society filtered through popular assemblies and elective magistrates, and so diffused power through several constituencies and individuals. This proved successful and Rome grew in power, size and influence, but in its growth the seeds of its own destruction were planted.

As Rome conquered the Mediterranean world (264-60 BC), eventually growing into a state that stretched from the Atlantic to Mesopotamia, republican institutions proved increasing obsolete and inefficient, while the city of Rome itself proved remote from too many problematic frontier regions. It was Julius Caesar's genius to recognize these deficiencies and to seek a solution. Plutarch wrote of Caesar, and while his life of Caesar reveals multiple complexities of character and ambition, it also reveals a strong and dynamic leader of vision. Plutarch's life of Caesar contrasts with his negative portrait of Mark Antony and its clear account of a dissolute character and misguided aspiration.[27]

Born to a prominent yet checkered family, Mark Antony's youth combined personal recklessness and distinguished military service. It is difficult to know which of these attracted Caesar most, though the two also shared a familial relationship that is often overlooked. Antony's service to Caesar as an outstanding officer and then tribune placed him nearly at Caesar's side on the Ides of March, but the assassins turned Liberators decided to spare his life (at Brutus' urging), a decision they would come to regret. Caesar's death brought Antony into the forefront of republican politics and power, but the arrival of Octavian, Caesar's grand-nephew and heir, slowed, then stalled his claim to the Caesarian legacy. Though Antony and Octavian would make peace by forming the Second Triumvirate (with Lepidus) in 43 BC, their alliance was seldom harmonious and hardly more than political convenience.

Antony's eastern command (after 37 BC) took him away from Rome and his wife Octavia (Octavian's sister and the peacemaker), and made possible his affair with Cleopatra of Egypt. Slowly the alliance between Antony and Octavian decayed until 33/32 the two broke completely, with war breaking out soon after. Octavian's great victory at Actium sealed the fates of Antony and Cleopatra, who not long after died at their own hands in Egypt. Much of what is known of Antony comes from Plutarch's life, and it is accepted that the

Plutarchan portrayal – the great general of ability and charm destroyed by his weaknesses – does not miss the mark.[28]

It would be Caesar's adopted son and Antony's brother-in-law, Octavian, later called Augustus, who would exert strong and even-handed leadership and create a new state, what we call today the Roman Empire (27 BC–AD 476), which emerged from the structures of the old Republic.[29] Empire demanded strong central leadership. For a time Augustus and many of the emperors who followed him ruled as princes, maintaining the fiction of governing within the traditions of the Republic and with the endorsement of the Senate (the "democratic" assemblies being increasingly ignored already under Augustus, their judicial and legislative functions ending in the first century AD).[30] In this era of the "Principate" (c. 27 BC–AD 180), the ruler also commanded a powerful professional army which provided all the authority necessary to rule. The militarized imperial Roman state governed with a strong hand, yet in many ways was a benign polity. This would change in the course of the third century AD, an era of terrible crisis as disease and "barbarian" invasions swept the empire and brought change to the imperial structures. In what became known as the "Dominate", Roman emperors no longer ruled as "princes", but now as "lords and gods" who demanded obeisance, if not the worship, due to a god.[31]

Roman autocracy, later augmented by the conversion to Christianity (Constantine's), would influence political life and theory in the West for a thousand years, effacing the ideas both of democracy and republicanism. Ironically, the ancient civilizations of the Near East had thought only savages could live without kings, an idea briefly eclipsed by the Greeks and Romans. In this post-classical era, when asked "who should rule?", the answer would invariably be a strong leader. And yet, the philosophical basis for such rule remained highly suspect.

LEADERSHIP AND FOLLOWERSHIP

On what Basis should they Rule?

How can political power be *legitimately* exercised? On what basis can the state or an individual rule over others?

Today the near universal belief is that the only way a government can legitimately rule is with the consent of the governed. In the classical period the consent of the masses was less significant than it is today. Of course, all systems ultimately depend on the consent of the governed in one way or another, but during the classical era, the will of the people only rarely and exceptionally manifested itself, and "the people" as a political entity seldom existed as it did in democratic Athens of the fifth century BC; it would require the emergence of a constructed popular identity for "the people" to emerge.

In the classical era, legitimacy emerged out of tradition, power, position, religion, myth, and force. Try as political philosophers might to bring a modicum of rationality to the discussion, one must remember that in this period, relatively few people were literate, books were hand-written and precious, and those who "mattered" were few in number and usually wealthy. They governed by a mixture of force and fear, myth and money. As the Roman Juvenal wrote, the people of imperial Rome could be governed merely by giving them "bread and circuses". Public expectations were meager and as little was expected, the politics of resentment were largely absent in the classical era. Class consciousness may have existed, but there was a more fatalistic view of one's lot in life. As expectations were low, legitimacy was more easily maintained, and the few could more easily govern the many.

Was it easier to rule in such an era? Yes. There were lower expectations and fewer demands placed upon the government. Followership was more readily invested in the state and obedience was more intently demanded (and granted). In this way, legitimacy was conferred on the basis of a lower bar of demands as public consciousness was less well developed and a rights culture had yet to be embraced. People more willingly accepted their lot in life and this allowed for the ruler to demand and expect more, and for the individual to give to the state more readily than is the case today.

How should Society be Organized?

Democracy in both its direct and representative forms was tried in Athens and elsewhere in Greece. In Rome "republican" rule emerged but this, as argued above, must not only be qualified but carefully apprised as it was essentially rule of the "haves" over the "have nots". While hierarchy may seem the norm in both ancient Greece and Rome, it was not. Rather it was the condition of freedom or slavery that mattered, yet even here there were opportunities for freedom and upward mobility for the unfree in both societies. Such division was not seen as a negative, but rather the natural order of society. Egalitarian sentiments may be today's norm, but this was not so in the classical era.

Are Leaders Born or Made?

Where were Plato's rulers to be found? Philosophers had to be made into kings and kings into philosophers, of course. Train a class of expert rulers and allow them to rule. But is it safe to give unchecked power even to a well-trained leader? Might that person be too ambitious, too vain, too power hungry to rule in the interests of society? Plato relies on the training to justice (statecraft equaled soulcraft) and too little on checks and balances (institutional or otherwise). But the key here is that Plato believed that leaders were *made*. It was on the basis of training that one developed the skills necessary to rule.

In the classical era, this was not a widely accepted view. In democratic Athens those who led the community did so through force of personality and ambition just as in the modern American political scene. In republican Rome, while most leaders were born to power, there were several, most notably the great orator and statesman Cicero, who climbed to the top through a combination of political or military skills and aptitude, winning fame that was no less than those born to it. Even in Rome of the emperors, while birth did anoint many, there were no fewer who took power by force of arms (usually) and ruled in the same manner as those born to it.

The question: are leaders made, still vexes us in this day. Are there particular skills that can make a leader, or is it temperament, character, emotional intelligence judgment, common sense, a drive or hunger for power, that motivates individuals to seek high office? And if so, are the true seeds of leadership planted in birth (opportunity) or childhood (psychological predispositions and drives)?

Who are "the People"?

As mentioned above, in the classical age "the people" were narrowly defined. It should not surprise us then that discussion and debate regarding questions of power, legitimacy and authority are largely ignored or glossed over, as concerns for the common man or lower classes (who often were not considered as citizens) took a back seat. It would take modern industrial development of society to create class identity and social awareness to bring to life this entity known as "the people".[32]

Who Gets What?

The "who gets what" question is a perennial one in the study of politics. Who benefits from the available resources of a society is a very good measure of who has power – sometimes hidden – in any political system. Who "ought" to get is one question, who "does" get, quite another. How should it be determined who gets what? Merit? Hard work? Status and birth? Power and force?

In general, societies follow the Golden Rule: whoever has the gold makes the rules. The few govern, and take from, the many. In the classical age, the most important social distinction was free and unfree, but it was possible to move from the latter to the former. Probably most people stoically accepted their lot in life, an attitude that Christianity left unchanged. Even those who, for example, saw slavery as unjust and inhumane seldom imagined something different. Plato, in the *Republic*, even went so far as to suggest that the Guardians should perpetuate the myth that those who took no direct role in governing should be content with their place and role in society.[33]

Plato draws a distinction between a true lie and a *noble lie*. Arguing that the public is in need of ennobling fictions, it is the responsibility of philosophers and rulers to convince non-ruling citizens that their station in life is appropriate and just – even though the philosopher knows otherwise. But if the highest goal of the philosopher is to the "truth", how can even a noble lie be justified? For Plato, this noble lie – in order to be truly noble and not merely self-serving – must serve a higher good for the polis. In the case of the noble lie regarding citizen distinctions, Plato believes that in order to maintain order and stability, it is honorable to promote the noble lie. Such fictions (and their intellectual advocates) of course, extend into the modern era (witness Leo Strauss and his followers).[34]

CONCLUSION

Out of the classical period and the emergence of Christianity, an era of one-man rule emerged throughout most of the Western world. Buoyed by a link to the divine, rulers were able to establish a fiction known as the divine right of kings wherein the king was seen as the legitimate power on earth based on the will of God.[35] As long as the king could persuade enough people to accept this fiction, he ruled on rock solid ground. To defy the king was to defy God, and such blasphemy was met with swift and harsh punishment. Such rule was highly personal and had few structural limits.

How is it possible to insure good government in such an era? The great thinkers, following Plato, argued that one must "teach justice" and that the Philosopher King must "act justly". Good soulcraft led to good statecraft. And yet, if that was the goal, it was markedly unsuccessful in getting the ruler to behave in a manner consistently well suited to the long-term interests of the state. More often than not, the ruler acted out of self-interest, greed, ambition, impulse. In practice, teaching justice proved an insufficient tool, a blunt instrument in efforts to produce good government in an absolutist state.

History tells us that teaching justice just was not enough. It would take the realist Machiavelli in his masterpiece the *Prince*, set in the anarchic world of sixteenth-century Italy, to abandon the hopelessly optimistic or conveniently naive view that merely by teaching justice, one would produce justice. Machiavelli divorced soulcraft from statecraft, and in the process earned himself eternal condemnation: first by the Church who banned him, and then from many critics who were unable to recognize the truism that politics is about power – getting it, keeping it, using it.[36] While much of what

Machiavelli wrote and referred to was contemporary, there was also a pronounced classical bent to his work and thoughts. Leaders of ancient Greece and Rome – Alexander the Great, Nabis the Spartan, Caesar and Scipio Africanus – provide the exemplary material illustrating his principles, making clear the connection between Classical past and Renaissance present.[37] Not only did Machiavelli shockingly reveal the nature of politics, his ideas influenced those of later political thinkers, perhaps beginning most notably with James Harrington, who found in Machiavelli's writings the fascination with political conflict as well as the foundations of all political questions.[38]

If the classical era failed to grasp or take full account of the greed and ambition of rulers, or to embrace too optimistic a view of the ability of teaching justice to control the grosser manifestations of abuse by princes, it did provide for us nearly all the questions on which leadership studies are based today. If the classical era failed us in one way, we should not forget that centered in the classical age are the roots and seeds of democracy, republicanism, participation, "the people" and constitutionalism.

NOTES

1. For further discussion see Fuller (2000) and Wren (1995).
2. For example, one session in our course focused on "Leadership and Terror". In examining this subject use was made of the 1966 film *The Battle for Algiers*, which revealed both issues, that is , from the perspective of the nation state – France – and an embattled colonial people – the Algerian.
3. The bibliography on Plutarch is enormous. While classicists and ancient historians give Plutarch high marks for his lives, they seldom call attention to his leadership dimensions. For studies that examine politics and leadership (broadly considered) see, for example, Wardman (1974) and Duff (1999). For additional treatment of Pericles and Antony as leaders see below.
4. Plutarch enjoyed greater popularity in the eighteenth century than the nineteenth. By mid-nineteenth century his scholarly deficiencies began to attract more attention which led to a decline in his popularity. Yet in the later twentieth century, Plutarch found new generations of readers and students. See Russell (1973: 159–63).
5. See Morgan (2001) and Cohn (2002) for further discussion.
6. Herodotus (1998: 204–06 (Book 3, sections 80–87 in the Greek text)).
7. On Herodotus and this debate see Asheri et al. (2007: 471–8), with discussion and references.
8. Plutarch's *Life of Pericles* and Thucydides books 1–2 are basic texts for Pericles' life and career; Stadter (1989) provides a full study of Plutarch's account. See also, for example, Kagan (1991) and Podlecki (1998).
9. The passage is found in Thucydides (1998: 91–7 (Book 2, sections 35–46 in the Greek text)). There are many scholarly discussions of Pericles and the Funeral Oration, but see the authors cited in note 7 for an introduction to the issues.
10. Thucydides (1998: 107 (Book 2, sections 65.7–10)) provides contemporary analysis, noting the bankruptcy of Pericles' followers, how they pandered to popular desires and simply failed to provide leadership.
11. On Plato and the Academy see, for example, Field (1967) and Guthrie (1972). Note in addition to the *Republic*, other Platonic dialogues reveal their didactic and political function: *Statesman*, *Sophist*, *Laws*.

12. Plato's term is "Guardian" (Greek *phulax*), popularized as "Philosopher King". See Plato (1945: 64 (= *Republic* 375a, the conventional arrangement of works in the Platonic corpus).
13. Yet it is clear that Plato's Guardians were not "class" based, but were rather selected from the "best" of all citizens: there is no "caste" of Guardians. See Plato (1945: 107 (= *Republic* 415c)).
14. Democracy in Athens is a vast subject, but see, for example, Ober (1996). Macedon would overthrow democracy in Athens in 322 and, when restored in 318, democratic rule had always to contend with great powers for survival.
15. Athenian and Spartan fleets clashed in a great naval battle, now late in the war. Though victorious over the Spartans, many Athenian sailors were lost after the battle in a sudden storm that blew up and sank a number of damaged ships. The commanding generals were blamed for the loss of life, put on trial where few other than Socrates dared challenge the mob. The generals, including a son of Pericles, were condemned to death and executed. See the account in Xenophon (1966: 45–52 (= 1.7 in the Greek text)).
16. Plato (1945: 106 (= *Republic* 415b)). The Greek *pseudos* (that is, "false") lies at the inspiration of the "noble lie", but is more complex in its meaning than the English "lie". Plato uses *pseudos* widely to refer to works of the imagination as well as myth, fable and allegory. It should not be seen simply as "propaganda".
17. See, for example, Guthrie (1971: 88–94).
18. Juvenal, in Winstedt (1899: 201–5).
19. See Plato (1945: 108 (= *Republic* 417a–b)).
20. Cf. Raaflaub (2004: 209–10, 345, n. 39).
21. Thucydides (1998: 92) (democratic ideal, [=2.37–8]), 107 (Pericles: sole ruler [2.65.9]) bk 2, sections 37–8, 65, in the Greek text. In fourth-century Athens, Phocion would hold the office a record 45 times in a life stretching over eighty years; see Tritle (1990).
22. The evidence is as obscure as it is limited, but forms of democracy did develop outside of Athens. For discussion see Brock and Hodkinson (2000).
23. The starting point for the study of representative government in ancient Greece remains Larsen (1955) and (1968).
24. On Alexander and kingship see Bosworth (2002: 246–78) and Hahm (2005: 457–76).
25. Polybius (1979: 303–18 (= 6.3–18 in the Greek text)) outlines various ancient constitutions including the Roman (at 6.11–18 in the Greek text). For discussion see Walbank (1967: 635–97) and Mackay (2004: 26–31).
26. Cf. Walbank (1972: 130–56, at 155). Rahe (1992: 602) mentions that James Madison's description of the American constitution resembles Polybius' account of the Roman.
27. Pelling (1988) provides a full study of Plutarch's *Life of Antony*.
28. Pelling (2003: 115–16).
29. For discussion see Mackay (2004), pp. 59–99 (Roman expansion), 143–58 (Caesar), 179–209 (Augustus and the founding of the empire).
30. The Roman assemblies were not democratic, certainly as understood in the twenty-first century; their formal existence survived until the third century AD. For further discussion see Staveley (1972) and Momigliano and Cornell (2003: 372–3).
31. Mackay (2004: 263–82) (the later empire and its problems).
32. See Morgan (1988).
33. Plato (1945: 107) (= *Republic* 415c).
34. See Drury (1999).
35. Constantine's conversion to Christianity was only the latest example of the secular combining with the spiritual in the ancient world. Perhaps the first to challenge this combination of divine and secular authority was Thomas Hobbes. Rahe (1992: 385) notes that in *Leviathan* (1651) Hobbes argued for the "absolute sovereignty of infidel rulers hostile to the true faith".
36. See Machiavelli (1992), p. 237 (Machiavelli on the Index), pp. 238–47 (interpreters of Machiavelli).
37. Machiavelli (1992) pp. 12–14, 42, 44 (Alexander), p. 29 (Nabis), Caesar (pp. 42, 44), Scipio (p. 42); also mentioned are Agathocles, the Syracusan tyrant general (pp. 24–5) and the Persian king Cyrus (pp. 42, 44).
38. See, for example, Rahe (1992: 421–4).

REFERENCES

Asheri, D., A. Lloyd and A. Corcella (2007), *A Commentary on Herodotus Books I–IV*, edited by O. Murray and A. Moreno, with a contribution by M. Brosius, Oxford: Oxford University Press.

Bosworth, A.B. (2002), *The Legacy of Alexander: Politics, Warfare, and Propaganda under the Successors*, Oxford: Oxford University Press.

Brock, R. and S. Hodkinson (eds) (2000), *Alternatives to Athens: Varieties of Political Organization and Community in Ancient Greece*, Oxford: Oxford University Press.

Cohn, S.M. (2002), *Classics of Political and Moral Philosophy*, New York: Oxford University Press.

Drury, S.B. (1999), *Leo Strauss and the American Right*, New York: Palgrave Macmillan.

Duff, T.E. (1999), *Plutarch's Lives: Exploring Virtue and Vice*, Oxford: Oxford University Press.

Field, G.C. (1967), *Plato and His Contemporaries*, London: Methuen.

Fuller, T. (2000), *Leading and Leadership*, South Bend, IN: University of Notre Dame Press.

Guthrie, W.K.C. (1971), *Socrates*, Cambridge: Cambridge University Press.

Hahm, D.E. (2005), "Kings and constitutions: Hellenistic theories", in C. Rowe and M. Schofield (eds), *The Cambridge History of Greek and Roman Political Thought*, Cambridge: Cambridge University Press, pp. 457–76.

Herodotus (1998), *The Histories*, translated by R. Waterfield, introduction and notes by C. Dewald, Oxford: Oxford University Press.

Kagan, D. (1991), *Pericles of Athens and the Birth of Democracy*, New York: Simon and Schuster.

Larsen, J.A.O. (1955), *Representative History in Greek and Roman History*, Berkeley, CA: University of California Press.

Larsen, J.A.O. (1968), *Greek Federal States*, Oxford: Clarendon Press.

Machiavelli, N. (1992), *The Prince*, translated and edited by R.M. Adams, 2nd edn, Norton critical edn, New York: W.W. Norton.

Mackay, C.S. (2004), *Ancient Rome: A Military and Political History*, Cambridge: Cambridge University Press.

Momigliano, A. and T.J. Cornell (2003), *S.v.* "*Comitia*", in S. Hornblower and A. Spawforth (eds), *Oxford Classical Dictionary*, Oxford: Oxford University Press, pp. 372–3.

Morgan, E.S. (1988), *Inventing the People*, New York: W.W. Norton.

Morgan, M.L. (ed.) (2001), *Classics of Moral and Political Theory*, 3rd edn, Indianapolis, IN: Hackett Publishing.

Ober, J. (1996), *The Athenian Revolution: Essays on Ancient Greek Democracy and Political Theory*, Princeton, NJ: Princeton University Press.

Pelling, C.B.R. (ed.) (1988), *Plutarch, Life of Antony*, Cambridge: Cambridge University Press.

Pelling, C.B.R. (2003), "*S.v.*, Antonius, Marcus" (2), in S. Hornblower and A. Spawforth (eds), *Oxford Classical Dictionary*, Oxford: Oxford University Press, pp. 115–16.

Plato (1945), *The Republic*, translated with introduction and notes by F.M. Cornford, New York: Oxford University Press.

Plutarch (1960), *The Rise and Fall of Athens: Nine Greek Lives by Plutarch*, translated with introduction by I. Scott-Kilvert. New York: Penguin Books.

Plutarch (1965), *Makers of Rome: Nine Lives by Plutarch*, translated with introduction by I. Scott-Kilvert, New York: Penguin Books.
Podlecki, A.J. (1998), *Perikles and His Circle*, London: Routledge.
Polybius (1979), The Rise of the Roman Empire, translated by I. Scott-Kilvert, introduction by F.W. Walbank, London: Penguin.
Raaflaub, K.A. (2004), *The Discovery of Freedom in Ancient Greece*, Chicago, IL: University of Chicago Press.
Rahe, P.A. (1992), *Republics Ancient and Modern: Classical Republicanism and the American Revolution*, Chapel Hill, NC: University of North Carolina Press.
Russell, D.A. (1973), *Plutarch*, New York: Charles Scribner's Sons.
Stadter, P.A. (1989), *A Commentary on Plutarch's Pericles*, Chapel Hill, NC: University of North Carolina Press.
Staveley, E.S. (1972), *Greek and Roman Voting and Elections*, London: Thames and Hudson.
Thucydides (1998), *The Peloponnesian War*, translated with introduction and notes by S. Lattimore, Indianapolis, IN: Hackett Publishing.
Tritle, L.A. (1990), "Forty-Five or What? The Generalships of Phocion", *Liverpool Classical Monthly*, **17**, 19–23.
Tritle, L.A. (2010), *A New History of the Peloponnesian War*, Oxford: Wiley-Blackwell.
Walbank, F.W. (1967), *A Historical Commentary on Polybius*, Vol. 1: *Commentary on Books I–VI,* Oxford: Clarendon Press.
Walbank, F.W. (1972), *Polybius*, Berkeley, CA: University of California Press.
Wardman, A. (1974), *Plutarch's Lives*, Berkeley, CA: University of California Press.
Winstedt, E.O. (1899), "A Bodleian MS of Juvenal", *Classical Review*, **13**, 201–5.
Wren, J.T. (ed.) (1995), *The Leader's Companion*, New York: Free Press.
Xenophon (1966), *A History of My Time*, translated by R. Warner, Harmondsworth: Penguin.

5. Handmaiden and queen: what philosophers find in the question: "what is a leader?"

Joanne B. Ciulla

The word "philosophy" was born when the Greek philosopher and mathematician Pythagoras of Samos (572-497 BC) was asked if he thought he was a wise man. He answered no, he was merely a lover of wisdom – a *phileo sophia*.[1] The philosophers who came after him were not as humble. Since philosophy was the study of just about everything, they dubbed it the "queen of the sciences". Philosophy reigned supreme until Christian times when the theologian Clement of Alexandria (150–215?AD) demoted philosophy from the "queen" of the sciences to the "handmaid of theology".[2,3] The Enlightenment philosopher John Locke (1632–1704) also regarded philosophy as a "handmaid" – but to the sciences. He said that the job of philosophy is to clarify assumptions, concepts and definitions, and interpret, analyze and synthesize the results of the sciences (Locke, 1961). Locke clearly describes what it means to *do* philosophy; however, he did not think that philosophy consisted of a distinctive body of truth.

Most philosophers agree that philosophy is a handmaiden, yet there are areas in which it still holds claim to the throne, most notably in logic and (despite the best efforts of theologians) ethics.[4] The other classical divisions of philosophy are metaphysics, which is concerned with the character of reality; epistemology, or the study of the nature, origins, and extent of knowledge; and aesthetics, which is about the assumptions behind our judgments about the arts. In addition to traditional philosophic divisions, we now have the "philosophy of" areas, which are obviously interdisciplinary. They include philosophy of law, science, social science, psychology, history, and so on.

In this chapter, we look at how philosophy serves leadership studies as both a handmaid and a queen. Throughout history, philosophers have written about leaders and leadership, yet only a handful of philosophers today identify themselves as writing about leadership in the context of leadership studies. After a brief discussion of the subject matter of philosophy, I will discuss my work and the contributions of philosophers Eva D. Kort and Antonio Marturano on a question about language and leadership: "what is the definition of a leader?"

WHAT IS PHILOSOPHY AND WHAT DOES IT DO?

In ordinary language, we use the word "philosophy" to talk about a person's beliefs, opinions and assumptions about the world. Anyone can have *a* philosophy about anything, but *having* a philosophy differs from *doing* philosophy. Philosopher Mark Woodhouse explains the difference with the question: "are gurus philosophers?" (Woodhouse, 1975: 30). He defines a guru as someone who helps people find enlightenment and serenity. This question is relevant to the study of leadership because the popular literature is replete with books by "leadership gurus." These gurus are usually consultants or leaders who describe what they have learned from their experiences and offer advice to others on how they too can become enlightened. At times these books are motivational – sometimes they make the reader feel good.

According to Woodhouse, there are three ways that philosophers differ from gurus:

1. Gurus seek truth as a means to achieve a state of mind such as serenity. Philosophers seek truth as an end in itself, not as a means to some psychological state such as serenity or happiness. (Philosophy is just as likely to lead to agitation and despair.)
2. Many of the so-called philosophical insights that Gurus express are psychological generalizations about human nature.
3. Gurus often *assert* philosophically interesting themes, but "to join the club" of philosophers, they must *do* philosophy. Philosophers *do* philosophy, which means they develop and defend their claims of truth based on rational arguments (Woodhouse, 1975: 31).

Philosophy consists of a variety of traditions, each with its own emphasis and style of inquiry. Ancient Greek philosophy offers a treasure trove of insights on leadership. For example, Plato and Aristotle both worked with and taught leaders in their lifetimes, so their philosophic insights about leadership are informed by first-hand experience (see Ciulla, 2004a, 2004b). Unlike the sciences, philosophic works tend to have a very long shelf-life. For example, a 4400-year-old philosophic text written on papyrus can be as relevant today is it was in its own time. Consider, some of the maxims about leadership from the Egyptian philosopher and vizier Ptahhotep (2450–2300? BCE). He writes:

> If you are a man who leads,
> Who controls the affairs of the many,
> Seek out every beneficent deed,
> That your conduct may be blameless...
> If you are among the people,
> Gain supporters through being trusted;
> The trusted man who does not vent his belly's speech,
> He will himself become a leader.[5]

Today, two traditions dominate contemporary Western philosophy, Anglo-American analytic philosophy and continental philosophy. Analytic philosophers see themselves as handmaidens. They focus on exposing conceptual confusions, clarifying concepts, and examining the meaning of terms. Their job is to logically sort things out. They pull ideas apart and then put them together with other ideas – an important service for interdisciplinary fields like leadership studies. Since their aim is conceptual clarity and logical soundness, analytic philosophers write in ordinary language, meaning that they try not to create their own terms to talk about concepts. Those who study analytic philosophy tend to say that they are "trained" as analytic philosophers, since the emphasis is on learning how to *do* philosophy.

The continental European philosophers regard philosophy more as a queen than a handmaiden. Instead of focusing primarily on logic and language, they concern themselves with understanding the human condition and the nature of being itself or metaphysics. Philosophers from the continental tradition are not shy about tackling life's big questions about love, death and God, and psychological questions about how the self is related to others. In some ways the subject matter of continental philosophy is more interesting than analytic philosophy, but it also tends to be more difficult to read. Nevertheless, continental philosophy offers a rich body of ideas for leadership scholars. For example, Martin Heidegger's work has entered discussions about authentic leadership[6] in papers by Bruce J. Avolio and William Gardner (2005). One of the most influential continental philosophers today is Jürgen Habermas. Leadership scholars in Europe have taken a particular interest in his theory of communicative action and rationality, which examines how people coordinate what they do through dialogue and how they reach rational agreement on goals and actions (Habermas, 1981; see also Schnebel, 2000).

Postmodernism also hails from continental Europe. It consists of a combination of elements from the analytic and continental traditions. There is no simple way to describe postmodernism except as a critical theory that attempts to reveal or "unmask" how modern ideas of certain knowledge, historical progress, unified notions of meaning, reality and identity are not what they seem. Postmodernists share with analytic philosophers an interest in the nature of meaning and a wariness of positivism (especially in the social sciences). As members of the continental tradition, postmodernists also seek to understand the ways in which humans construct narratives of history, identity and reality.

Scholars have employed some of the ideas in postmodernist literature to leadership studies. In 1988, Marta Calas and Linda Smircich (1988) wrote a postmodernist critique of the field in which they questioned the way that research was done based on who did the research. More recently, Sonia Ospina and Georgia Sorenson (2006) used a postmodernist theory to examine leadership as a social construction in their article "A constructivist lens on leadership: charting new territory". There is plenty of room for postmodern critiques and approaches to the study of leadership, but scholars who take this approach will have to frame their work in language that is accessible to academics from the various disciplines that comprise leadership studies.

One thing that all philosophic traditions have in common is that they all do ethics. The ethics literature is open to a wide range of interpretation. As philosopher Terry L. Price points out (2004), leaders sometimes misuse philosophic texts to rationalize or support their own unethical behavior. What distinguishes philosophic ethics from ethics done in other disciplines is that *doing* ethics requires a solid grasp of other areas of philosophy, such as logic and epistemology (see Fisher and Kirchin, 2006). Another thing that most philosophic traditions possess is an interest in language, because in many ways, our language *is* our world. Hence, it is not surprising that some of the work done by philosophers in leadership studies focuses on the problem of defining leaders and leadership. As we will see, sorting out this kind of conceptual problem sets the stage for work in leadership ethics.

THE DEFINITION PROBLEM

While trained as an analytic philosopher, my approach to doing philosophy is a bricolage of philosophic traditions. When I began reading the leadership literature in 1991, I was struck by the fact that some authors went to great lengths to define the word "leader" (see Ciulla, 1995, 2002). I found this a bit odd. On the one hand, I could understand defining "leader" for the purpose of a particular study – scientists do it so that they can limit the variables in their research. This sort of definition is called a stipulative definition (see Kripke, 1980). Stipulative definitions are similar to, but not the same as, our everyday use of terms. On the other hand, I noticed that writers, most notably the late Joseph Rost, wanted to define the word "leader" for all scholars (and perhaps for everyone else too) (Rost, 1991). This was problematic on two levels. First, it seemed to demonstrate a desire to control the way that leadership scholars work – if you control the definitions, you control the field. Second, Rost's assertion that leadership studies could not progress if leadership scholars failed to agree on one definition seemed at odds with the way that language works.

I began my analysis of the definition problem by turning to the work of Ludwig Wittgenstein. Wittgenstein observed that the meaning of a word comes from how we use it. While people may use a word in a slightly different way – meaning they have slightly different definitions of it – we still understand what they are talking about. This is because the use of a term by one person has a family resemblance to the use of the term by another person speaking the same language (Wittgenstein, 1991). I decided to look for the family resemblance in the 221 definitions of the word "leader" that Rost had collected (1991: 47–102). Since Rost claimed that his definition was the new post-industrial definition, I decided to examine the "industrial" definitions in their historical context. I noted the similarities and differences between definitions and considered how the social and historical context influenced these definitions.

By doing a linguistic analysis of the term "leader" I gained two insights. First, the differences between definitions of the English word "leader" were implicitly or explicitly normative. As a social construction, the American usage of the word "leader" reflected what people in a certain place and at a certain time thought leaders should be. When scholars said things like: "leaders inspire followers toward common goals", they did not mean that all leaders really did this, they meant that leaders ought to do this. The statement also seemed to mean that the writer only wanted to attribute the word "leader" to a person who inspired followers toward a common goal. I was surprised to see how often leadership scholars wrote as if they were *describing* leaders when they were actually *prescribing* what they thought leaders should be like. Describing what leaders should *be like* seemed to beg the question of what they actually *were*. Was this confusion simply a careless use of language or was something else going on in terms of how we understand the word "leader"?

My second related insight was simply that the question "what is a leader?" was really the question, "what is a good leader?" This relationship between what a thing is and what it ought to be has always intrigued philosophers. Plato argued that reality consists of the physical world and the world of forms or ideas, which might also be understood as ideals since they are perfect. The form of a table is like the paradigm of a table. When we judge the quality of a table, we do so against this ideal (Plato, 1961a). We see a similar inclination in leadership scholars who sometimes feel the need to differentiate between people who are called leaders and "real leaders", or "true leaders", or what Kort will call a "leader proper". They write as if some leaders fit the ideal and others are mere shadows of it. For instance, Bernie Bass's distinction between transformational and pseudo-transformational leaders is really an attempt to eliminate leaders who might fit the description of a transformational leader but are not ethical. Such leaders fall short of the ideal transformational leader who transforms people and is ethical. Scholars from Ptahhotep to Bass have an ideal of a leader. Almost all of them either implicitly or explicitly include ethics as part of that ideal. A philosophic examination of the language of leadership yields insights that are similar to those found in attribution and implicit leadership theories of leadership (Yukl, 2006). We all walk around with slightly different ideal leaders in our minds, even if we all use the same word for them.

When I looked at how other scholars talked about good leaders, I discovered a dichotomy between leaders who are morally good and leaders who are effective at exercising leadership. I called this "the Hitler problem" (Ciulla, 1995). This dichotomy is a vestige of the old positivist notion that the social sciences should be untainted by value judgments. Some historians think Hitler was a good leader, but only in the sense of being an effective one, not in the sense of being an ethical one. I used this dichotomy between ethics and effectiveness as a framework for mapping out the ethically distinctive aspects of leadership (Ciulla, 2004a). My first analysis of the definition problem was by no means complete, but I knew that the end goal was to expose the fact that ethics/effectiveness was in part a false dichotomy. The more that I worked on understanding the relationship between ethics and effectiveness, the more I could see the normative complexities behind the very concept of a leader. That is why I was so pleased when Kort and Marturano took up the challenge.

LEADERSHIP AND PLURAL ACTION

Eva D. Kort critiques and builds on my discussion of the definition problem. Kort argues that the best way to understand what the word "leader" means is to analyze the nature of plural actions or the coordinated actions of people in a group (Kort, 2008). She challenges the assertion in Rost's definition that leadership is a mutual influence relationship by showing that it is circular. She shows the circularity in the following statements:

1. "Leadership" means a relationship between leaders and followers.
2. "Leaders" and "followers" mean anyone who is in a leadership relation.

Using a favorite tool for doing philosophy – the thought experiment[7] – Kort explains why acts, not relationships, reveal the features that identify leadership "proper" from other cases of "purported" leadership. Notice how she contrasts the real person who is supposed to be the leader with an ideal leader. She poses two questions: "what kind or kinds of events would result in a social relation in which some people are leaders and others are followers?" and "which objects or people are involved in such events, and what is the nature of that involvement?" (Kort, 2008: 414). Kort provides a number of simple examples to derive a set of defining characteristics for what constitutes a leader and a follower in a particular situation. She says first, members of a group must intend to perform an action and intend to do it in conjunction with other members of the group. And second, in a particular context, a person is only a leader if he or she makes suggestions for initiatives that the group members find worthy of endorsement. For example, a concertmaster holds a formal leadership position. If he conducts the orchestra with instructions that the musicians know are bad, they will follow him because of his position. In this case, Kort says the concertmaster is merely a purported leader, not a leader proper. She writes: "It is only when the concertmaster does lead – participate in the plural action in (generally) the right sort of way – that the concert-master is the leader in the proper sense" (ibid. 422). She sums up her criteria for the definition of leadership proper taking place in an event this way:

(1) A and M participate in a plural action, Φ;
(2) A and B intend to perform Φ;
(3) A and B cooperate in performing Φ;
  (4) A makes suggestions for proceeding either spontaneously or as a matter of course, which are worthy of endorsement in displaying general competence and being ethically neutral or positive;
  (5) A's suggestions are endorsed by A and M, acted upon by M, and thus influence M's contribution;
(6) Φ is endorsed by A and M;
(7) Φ is ethically neutral or positive (ibid. 423).

Notice how Kort's definition includes unavoidable judgments. Leaders are people whom we recognize as competent and, where relevant, ethical. Kort disagrees with my observation that one of the central features of the leader/follower relationship is power and/or influence, mainly because of the coercive implications of these terms. For Kort, leaders are people whose ideas are voluntarily endorsed and acted on by others in various situations. Power is not central to her ideal of leadership. Whether we can say this endorsement is simply the result of being influenced or a defining characteristic of influence or, as Kort claims, something altogether different from influence, is open to discussion. Her analysis demonstrates how a person can lead without necessarily intending to do so, simply because others endorse his or her ideas. Her analysis of actions and events explains how the rational and voluntary consent of followers distinguishes a leader proper from someone who either holds a leadership position and/or someone who simply coordinates activities.[8]

Kort's focus on plural actions also helps us understand the Hitler problem. Once we raise the question of whether Hitler was a good leader in the context of the particular things Hitler did, we end up with statements Kort says are "almost oxymoronic" such as, "Hitler was a leader of the German people in their killing of over six million innocents" (ibid. 424). While one might still argue that Kort's definition is not about what leaders are but what they should be like, she provides compelling argument for why the description of what a leader is cannot and perhaps should not be purely descriptive.

LOGIC AND SEMIOTICS

Italian philosopher Antonio Marturano (2008) applies logic and semiotics, or the interpretation of signs and symbols, to the definition problem. He believes that the definition problem stems from the fact that most leadership scholars are psychologists who approach leadership as a description of psychological processes and relationships. The problem with this is that the language used to describe a relationship is different from the language we use to name an object such as "chair" or a person's title such as "president".

Marturano begins his analysis with the philosopher and mathematician Gottfried Wilhelm Leibniz's work on identity. Leibniz's Law, or "the identity of indiscernibles", states that for two things to be the same, they have to have all of the same properties. Marturano uses the following example to illustrate Leibniz's Law:

1. Silvio Berlusconi is the owner of Mediaset.
2. Silvio Berlusconi is the Italian Prime Minister.

We could logically add a third sentence that states: "The Owner of Mediaset is the Prime Minister of Italy" because the Owner of Mediaset and the Italian Prime Minister refer to the same person. Marturano then shows us a peculiarity of logic when one introduces propositional attitudes (which are words that refer to people's mental states, such as opinions, value judgments, beliefs, etc.) into language. Consider the following sound argument:

A. The Italian Prime Minister is the owner of Mediaset.
B. The owner of Mediaset is a successful leader.
C. The Italian Prime Minister is a successful leader.

According to Leibniz's Law, the property of *being a successful leader* has to be identical in the case of the prime minster and the owner of Mediaset. But in this case we discover that B and C are referentially opaque – meaning we cannot tell if the property of *being a successful leader* applies identically to the Prime Minister and owner of Mediaset, even though they refer to the same person. Marturano shows us that it is possible to draw two contradictory true statements from the argument.

D. Tony believes that the Italian Prime Minister is a successful leader.
E. Tony believes that the Owner of Mediaset is not a successful leader.

This referential opacity of evaluative terms like "successful" also explains why the statements "Hitler was a good leader" and "Hitler was not a good leader" can both be true because we cannot see the properties of the word "good". In the first case, the properties of the word "good" refer to skills and effectiveness. In the second case, the properties of the word "good" refer to moral qualities. While this is a simple distinction, the really interesting question for leadership scholars is how ethics informs our concept of what constitutes success or effectiveness (Ciulla, 2005).

Arguing that culture and history shape what people mean by the word "leader", Marturano draws on Umberto Eco's semiotics to elaborate on how this works. Eco says that the meaning of a word or a symbol in any culture comes from "textual cooperation" between speakers. People derive their understanding of words from a cultural "dictionary" and "encyclopedia" that provide the rules and assumptions for how to use a word. Marturano explains: "in order for a follower to decode the system of meanings a leader is embodying, she needs not only a linguistic competence but also a capacity to manage anything about her culture that enables her to trigger a series of presuppositions, repressing idiosyncrasies, etc."[9] The encyclopedia and dictionary that we use to decode the meaning of the word "leader" is not written by academics or leaders, but by followers in the context of their society's construction of leadership. Marturano suggests that the meaning of leader is and ought to be fluid. Leaders have to give followers latitude to add meaning to their leadership, and followers must do the same for leaders. Marturano's paper illustrates the logical problem with defining leadership and reformulates the question "what is leadership?" into a question about how leaders and followers jointly shape the meaning of the term. Marturano and Kort use different methods of analysis, but ultimately come out with similar positions in regard to the definition of leadership.

CONCLUSION

Kort's and Marturano's analyses of the word "leadership" explain why there are prescriptive definitions of leaders in leadership literature. There is a sense in which "what is a leader?" and "what is a good leader?" are the same question. The words "leader", "lead", and "leadership" cannot be adequately defined without normative criteria. A *one-size-fits-all* definition of leadership is not possible because, as Marturano shows us, the properties of normative terms are referentially opaque. Hence, it makes more sense for leadership scholars to focus on revealing the moral, social and psychological properties of leaders than on trying to come up with the ultimate definition of a leader.

We have been looking at how three philosophers *do* philosophy and analyze the question, "what is the definition of leadership?" This chapter began with the simple idea that the meaning of the word "leader" comes from the way people use it. Kort analyzed various ways that people use the term in the context of a variety of particular actions by groups. For her, a leader is someone who has ideas that people voluntarily endorse and act upon. Marturano then looked at the kind of fluid cultural values, presuppositions and agreements between leaders and followers that determine what people mean when they use the word "leader".

Two conclusions emerge from this discussion. First, to put it glibly, you are only a leader if rational people think you are, and how they identify you as a leader depends on their cultural and historical assumptions. Second, the word "leader" has a built-in normative aspect to it. A leader only leads if he or she meets certain technical and ethical standards of followers. Hence, leadership is not simply about having and using power. These conclusions are compelling precisely because they are not new. Philosophers throughout history have been reiterating similar ethical values in their ideas about leaders, whether it is Plato's (1961b) definition of the philosopher king who is wise and virtuous or Ptahhotep's maxim that leaders should "gain supporters through being trusted". The philosophic literature chronicles the history of human ideals and aspirations. These ideals and aspirations are embedded in the language that we use to make sense of the world around us, which is why leadership studies cannot do without the handmaiden or the queen.

NOTES

1. Johnstone (1965). It is also worth noting that mathematics was also called the queen of the sciences.
2. Titus Flavius Clemens (AD 150–215) *The Stromata* (n.d.). Chapter 5 of the book is titled "Philosophy the handmaid of theology". Other scholars attribute the saying "handmaiden of theology" to St Peter Damian (1007–72) who was an adversary of the liberal arts. In both cases, the term was meant to make philosophy subservient to theological truths. See Toke (1911).
3. The images used to describe philosophy are markedly female. In Plato's *Theaetetus* (150 c–d) Socrates says: "God compels me to be a midwife, but has prevented me from giving birth" (Plato, 1977: 113). Georg Wilhelm Friedrich Hegel (1770–1831) made famous the Owl of Minerva. The goddess Minverva was the Roman version of the Greek Athena, goddess of wisdom, craft and war. Minerva is associated with an owl, which is also a symbol of wisdom. Hegel writes, "The owl of Minerva takes flight only when the shades of night are gathering". (Hegel, 2001: 20).
4. I realize that this is a very contentious assumption.
5. Lichtheim (1973: 61–82) The passages quoted from this book are available online at: http://www.humanistictexts.org/ptahhotep.htm.
6. Heidegger is cited but it looks as if it is because of his influence on the psychologist Erick Erickson. From what I have seen there is still no serious treatment of his work, in part because it would be at odds with some of the work in this area. Jean Paul Sartre also writes extensively on authenticity in a fashion that may be somewhat closer to the authentic leadership literature.
7. A thought experiment is a series of vignettes or examples that help make some common sense conceptual distinctions.
8. Kort also discusses the distinction between leaders and managers in her paper. She depicts

managers as people who coordinate activities. They are in a position to lead, but they don't necessarily do so unless they meet the conditions that she outlines.
9. Here Marturano cites Eco (1979: 42).

REFERENCES

Avolio, Bruce J. and William L. Gardner (2005), "Authentic leadership development: getting to the root of positive forms of leadership", *The Leadership Quarterly*, **16**, 315–38.

Calas, Marta and Linda Smircich (1988), "Reading leadership as a form of cultural analysis", in James G. Hunt, B. Rajaram Baliga, H. Peter Dachler and Chester A. Schriesheim (eds), *Emerging Leadership Vistas*, Lexington, MA: Lexington Books, pp. 222–60.

Ciulla, Joanne B. (1995), "Leadership ethics mapping the territory", *The Business Ethics Quarterly*, **5**(1), 5–24.

Ciulla, Joanne B. (2002), "Trust and the future of leadership", in Norman E. Bowie (ed.), *The Blackwell Guide to Business Ethics*, Oxford: Basil Blackwell, pp. 334–51.

Ciulla, Joanne B. (2004a), "Aristotle", *Encyclopedia of Leadership Studies*, vol. 1, Thousand Oaks, CA: Sage Publications, pp. 43–6.

Ciulla, Joanne B. (2004b), "Plato", *Encyclopedia of Leadership Studies*, vol. 3, Thousand Oaks, CA: Sage Publications, pp. 1202–6.

Ciulla, Joanne B. (2004c), "Ethics and leadership effectiveness", in J. Antonakis, A.T. Cianciolo and R.J. Sternberg (eds), *The Nature of Leadership*, Thousand Oaks, CA: Sage Publications, pp. 302–27.

Ciulla, Joanne B. (2005), "The state of leadership ethics and the work that lies before us", *Business Ethics: a European Review*, **14**(4), 323–35

Clemens, Titus Flavius (n.d.), The Stromata, Book I, accessed at www.newadvent.org/fathers/02101.htm.

Eco, Umberto (1979), *Lector in Fabula, la Cooperazione Interpretativa nel Testi Narrativi*, Milan: Bompiani.

Fisher, Andrew and Simon Kirchin (eds) (2006), *Arguing about Metaethics*, New York: Routledge.

Habermas, Jürgen (1981), *Theory of Communicative Action*, vol. 1, *Reason and Rationalization in Society* and vol. 2, *Lifeworld and System*, translated by T. McCarthy, Boston, MA: Beacon Press.

Hegel, G.W.F. (2001), *Philosophy of Right*, translated by S.W. Dyde, Kitchener, ON: Batoche Books.

Johnstone, Henry W. Jr (1965), *What is Philosophy?*, New York: MacMillan.

Kort, Eva D. (2008), "What, after all, is leadership? 'Leadership' and plural action", *The Leadership Quarterly*, **19**, 411–25.

Kripke, Saul (1980), *Naming and Necessity*, Cambridge, MA: Harvard University Press.

Lichtheim, Miriam (1973), *Ancient Egyptian Literature: a Book of Readings*, vol. 1, *The Old and Middle Kingdoms*, Berkeley, CA: University of California Press.

Locke, John (1961), *An Essay Concerning Human Understanding*, London: Dent.

Marturano, Antonio (2008), "Understanding leadership: is it time for a linguistic turn?", in Joanne B. Ciulla (ed.), *Leadership and the Humanities*, vol. 3 of *Leadership at the Crossroads*, Westport, CT: Praeger, pp. 117–31.

Ospina, Sonia and Georgia L.J.Sorenson (2006), "A constructivist lens on leadership: charting new territory", in George R. Goethals and Georgia L.J. Sorenson (eds), *The Quest for a General Theory of Leadership*, Cheltenham, UK and Northampton, MA, USA: Edward Elgar, pp. 188–204.

Plato (1961a), "Parmenides", in Edith Hamilton and Huntington Cairns (eds), *The Collected Dialogues of Plato*, Princeton, NJ: Princeton University Press.

Plato (1961b), "Republic", in Edith Hamilton and Huntington Cairns (eds), *The Collected Dialogues of Plato*, Princeton, NJ: Princeton University Press.

Price, Terry L. (2004), "Philosophy", in George R. Goethals, Georgia J. Sorenson and James MacGregor Burns (eds), *The Encyclopedia of Leadership Studies*, vol. 3, pp. 1195–7.

Rost, Joseph (1991), *Leadership for the Twenty-first Century*, New York: Praeger.

Schnebel, Eberhard (2000), "Values in decision-making processes: systematic structures of J. Habermas and N.Luhmann for appreciation of responsibility in leadership", *The Journal of Business Ethics*, **27**, 79–88.

Toke, Leslie (1911), "St Peter Damian", *The Catholic Encyclopedia*, vol. 11, New York: Robert Appleton Company, accessed at www.newdavent.org/cathen/11764a.htm.

Wittgenstein, Ludwig (1991), *Philosophical Investigations*, 3rd edn, translated by G.E.M. Anscombe, New York: Blackwell.

Woodhouse, Mark B. (1975), *A Preface to Philosophy*, Encino, CA: Dickenson Publishing.

Yukl, Gary (2006), *Leadership in Organizations*, 6th edn, Upper Saddle River, NJ: Prentice Hall.

6. Of history and leadership: the discipline of history and the understanding of leadership

J. Thomas Wren

Leadership studies has long been dominated by the social sciences, which simplify complex reality by identifying explanatory variables and developing generalizable propositions. Yet there is something to be said for messy reality – and thus there is something to be said for history, and the study of the swirling and dynamic interplay of constantly changing forces, events and people. Like all scholarly approaches, history can take us in dangerous or misleading directions; but if we identify the challenges of historical exploration, we can discern what history's contribution can be to a truly interdisciplinary study of leadership.

THE PROBLEM WITH LEADERSHIP

Historians have long resisted the siren call of leadership studies, and have long been wary of marrying their discipline to it. This is not due to inherent crankiness among historians; they have good reason for their stance. The application of history to the study of leadership threatens the core presumptions of the discipline. This requires elaboration.

There are various strands of the historians' critique. First is that history resists generalization; it is interested in particulars. Richard Ekman, former president of the Council of Independent Colleges and a historian by training, frames this concern well: "The cautionary argument about history," he writes, "is that there is no guarantee that a pattern of the past will remain a pattern in the future. Historians even say that to expect to find patterns is likely to turn a person's approach from a historical perspective into one that is anti-historical." "That is," he continues, "the search for universals of human behavior that may be the goal of the sociologist [or, it may be added, the scholar of leadership] is contrary to the work of an historian, who ought to be looking for the particularities of human events in specific places and times"(Ekman, forthcoming: 3). Ekman's concern is deftly explored in a recent book by the eminent historian.

John Lewis Gaddis' *The Landscape of History: How Historians Map the Past* (2002). In this chapter, I will draw frequently on Gaddis' book to show us "how historians think" (ibid.: x), why this makes historians wary of leadership studies, and yet how it may also suggest what history has to contribute to the field of leadership studies.

We begin with a necessary concession: historians, when they "do history", engage in more generalization and application than they may realize. Gaddis, noting that history shares many methodological similarities with the hard sciences, observes that the sciences are, in their own ways, predictive: "each of these sciences … tells us something about the future". Is it so odd then, he asks, to wonder if historians can do so as well? (ibid.: 72). Indeed, Gaddis observes, historians do frequently make generalizations – they just tend to delimit them carefully to particular times and places. But he suggests that "such generalizations … [can] have wide applicability. Historians are prepared to acknowledge tendencies or patterns: these are certainly not laws applying to all instances, but they're certainly not useless either" (ibid.: 63).

Gaddis goes on to elaborate upon his quest to discover some way of linking the past to the future, something the social sciences do well with their models and theories. Without resorting to what he calls the "reductionism" of the social sciences, Gaddis turns again to the hard sciences as a possible model. In those sciences, he notes, "It's certainly possible to know the direction in which [things] are moving." Although they allow for variations and are not deterministic, "there is a directionality in all of them that allows us to make sense of the past and still in a very general way to anticipate the future" (ibid.: 60–61). It may be possible, then, even on historians' own terms, to contemplate the implications of the past for the present.

At the same time, it is also the case that historians extrapolate the present back into the past. To the extent that they do this, they are, in a sense, applying history to modern problems. A modern historian, R.G. Collingwood, phrases it this way: "Every new generation must rewrite history in its own way" (Collingwood, 1956: 248, quoted in Gaddis, 2002: 104). Or, as our colleague Gaddis puts it,

> The judgments any historian applies to the past can't help but reflect the present the historian inhabits. These will surely shift, as present concerns do. History is constantly being remeasured. … And even in the absence of new answers from the past, the shifting perspectives of the present can cause us to ask new questions about it that will make it look quite different (Gaddis, 2002: 125, 103).

"We're bound to learn from the past," Gaddis argues, "whether or not we make the effort, since it's the only data we have". Given this inevitability, he says,

> we might as well try to do so systematically. … If we can widen the range of experience beyond what we as individuals have encountered, if we can draw upon the experience of others who've had to confront comparable situations in the past, then – although there will be no guarantees – our *chances* of acting wisely should increase proportionately.

"This gets us close to what historians do," Gaddis concludes: "to interpret the past for the purpose of the present with a view to managing the future" (ibid.: 9–10).

Suddenly the gap between the study of history and the study of leadership seems not so wide.

A second concern often expressed by historians who look askance at leadership has to do with how one actually *makes* this link between history and leadership. The historian Patrick Griffin, for instance, began a piece on leadership in the Jamestown colony with an important caveat about using history as a means of gaining insight into leadership:

> [W]e must recognize that searching for anything can often lead us to distort the past, to create narratives too tethered to our assumptions. In the process, we can get it wrong. The same is true of looking for leadership. Leaders, interestingly enough, can look a fair bit like us, what we admire or deplore in what we conceive ourselves. Unfortunately, it's not often right. A bit of caution, in other words, is in order as we assess … the merits of leadership (Griffin, forthcoming, 3–4).

The right response, Griffin says, is not to deny the possibility of historical insights into leadership, but to proceed with caution and humility. The search for leadership, he says, "cannot represent the entry point … into our studies, our points of departure, or the parameters around which we construe context. We are on far firmer ground when we try to place people and processes and events in their proper contexts and then tease out these themes" (ibid.: 4).

In sum, then, the historians who are chary of leadership studies need not be unduly concerned. The approaches of historians are not all that different from those of careful scholars of leadership, and "good" history – done with the appropriate focus on the era under study – can form the basis for substantive learning about leadership.

THE QUESTIONS OF HISTORY

In order to understand how history can shed light on leadership, it is necessary to consider the nature of historical analysis. Historical analysis is just that: *analytical*. Rather than a mere narration of events (although that is also a part of it), good historical analysis seeks to address certain key issues. These I refer to as the five "Cs" of historical analysis: change, causation, context, character, and connections. Each is worthy of brief explanation, together with an example or examples of historical work that exemplify each. In keeping with historian Patrick Griffin's cautions about "presentism", the leadership implications will be addressed subsequently.

Change

While historians study periods of both dramatic change and relative continuity, they recognize the *dynamism* of all human endeavors. The overarching task of the historian – to which the subsequent four "Cs" are subordinate – is to analyze and explain *change*. Historians, in other words, don't so much study still photographs as movies, with all the characters, plots and subplots interweaving themselves together. Gordon Wood's classic *The Radicalism of the American Revolution* (1992), for instance, examines the intellectual and ideological changes that underlay the American war for independence from Great Britain.

Causation

If change is the overarching theme, *causation* is the stuff of historical analysis. Historians want to know *why* particular changes occurred, and resist easy answers. The historian Carl Gustavson has written: "*No single cause ever adequately explains a historical episode. A 'cause' is a convenient figure of speech for any one of a number of factors which helps to explain why a historical event happened*" (1955: 55, emphasis in original). Social scientists typically seek to isolate a single independent or causal variable, but historians, in the words of John Lewis Gaddis, "assume the interdependency of variables" and "trace their interconnections through time" (2002: 53). Hence a good historian trying to uncover the causes of the American Civil War will not be satisfied with an answer of "slavery", but will look further and explore the vast and dynamic web of social, economic, political and even intellectual "causes" of the war. For an example of this, see James McPherson's *Battle Cry of Freedom: The Era of the Civil War* (1988).

Context

Closely related to causation is the role of *context*. Indeed, our friend Gaddis has said: "Causes always have contexts, and to know the former we must understand the latter" (2002: 53). To appreciate the historical context of any event or episode is, indeed, to grasp the impact of multiple sources of causation. In her narrative and analysis, the good historian takes care to identify the social, economic, political and intellectual currents that shape possibilities and results. Any good piece of historical work, such as McPherson's cited above, closely analyzes context.

Characters

By the term "characters" is meant the role of the individual in history. This has long been the subject of debate, with the extremes being Thomas Carlyle's (1902) statement that "The history of the world is but the biography of great men" on one end of the spectrum, with Tolstoy (1933: IX, 1) on the other: "In historical events great men – so called – are but labels that serve to give a name to an event, and like labels, they have the least possible connection to the event itself." The truth is somewhere in the middle, and we will have the opportunity to think more deeply about the relationship of individuals to their historical context when we turn to the leadership implications of historical study.

Connections

We turn now to the last of our "Cs", the notion of *connections*. It is in making connections that historians draw together their analyses of change, causation, context and characters. Discerning patterns is how historians make sense of their subject; it is indeed the essence of historical analysis. Gaddis says that doing history depends on "the recognition of patterns"; it is the historian's task, he says, "to *represent* reality; to smooth over the details, to look for larger patterns" (2002: 2, 7). It is only through the *interpretation* of the vast amounts of information that confront them that historians contribute any "value-added" to our understanding of the past.

Having some sense of the work of historians, let us consider how historical study can contribute to our understanding of leadership.

LINKING LEADERSHIP TO HISTORICAL ANALYSIS

By leadership, I mean a dynamic and context-bound relationship among individuals:

> *[L]eadership* … [is] … a mutual influence process among leaders and followers in which each participant operates as part of a collective in a complicated and ever-shifting environment in an effort to achieve desired goals (Wren and Price, 2007: 215).

This definition suggests that almost *every* good piece of historical analysis can be linked in some way to leadership. Although most historians do not recognize it – and may even actively resist the notion – in the course of their regular research activities they are actually engaged in leadership studies.

One of the best ways to explore the linkage between leadership and history is to study the work of James MacGregor Burns. Burns is both a distinguished historian, with a Pulitzer prize-winning biography of Franklin Delano Roosevelt, and the seminal figure in modern leadership studies, having redefined the field with his 1978 volume, *Leadership*, and his continuing contributions. Burns helps us see that the questions of historians are, in essence, also the questions of leadership. Let us return now to the five "Cs", now from a leadership perspective.

The focus of historical analysis, as we have seen, is *change*. And, Burns argues, the same is true of leadership studies: "Of all the tasks on the work agenda of leadership analysis," he writes, "first and foremost is an understanding of human change, because its nature is the key to the rest" (2003, 17). For Burns, "The essence of leadership ... is ... the governance of change" (1978: 43), and he views the phenomenon of leadership "as the basic process of social change, of causation in a community, an organization, a nation – perhaps even the globe" (2003: 185). Burns's claims for leadership analysis echo closely our depiction of the work of historians. He notes that "I have come to see leadership ... as a field of study ... that illuminates some of the toughest problems of ... social change" (2003: 9), which is accomplished by the analysis of such questions as "who initiates change, in what circumstances, for what reason, proceeding by what means toward what outcome" (2003: 17). Viewed in this light, traditional historical analysis is central to our understanding of leadership.

In the work of historians, the primary analytical task when investigating change is to determine *causation*. Burns's conception of leadership again parallels the historical approach closely. For Burns, "To define leadership ... is to glimpse its central role in the processes of historical causation" (1978: 433). To Burns, "leadership as a causal force" can be found "almost everywhere. At every stage, there will be the need for creative responses to changes in conditions... there will be the need, that is, for leadership" (2003: 222). So, just as is the case in historical analysis, for Burns leadership study is "*the quest for causality*" (2003: 18). But just as historians do, Burns resists overburdening a single factor like leadership as *the* cause of change. Studying leadership in full, he suggests, "enables us to sort out, at least in a preliminary way, the multiple forces at work. ... At the same time it avoids further search for *the* single cause" (1978: 433, 466, emphasis in original). History, Burns suggests, provides the best model for study: "Case studies of attempts at transformation in complex situations illustrate the role of leadership in the causal process of change" (2003: 220). The work of historians, it seems, is central to the exploration of leadership.

Historians study change and causation in *context*, but, surprisingly, most leadership scholars have come only recently to an appreciation for the context of leadership. Burns's sweeping conception of leadership and its study have long urged the importance of context. He poses the question: "What then, in a preliminary way, can be said about the role of … leadership in the process of … social change?" His response is that "this question can be answered only in the context of the conditions of stability, continuity, persistence, and inertia that grip most of humankind." This context would be familiar to historians: "Leaders and followers," Burns writes, "are locked into relationships that are closely influenced by particular local, parochial, regional, and cultural forces." These contextual factors both frame and influence leadership activities. As Burns puts it, "Leadership … is closely influenced by the structures of opportunity and closure around it".

The term *characters*, of course, refers to the role individuals play in history. Although leadership studies has in the past overplayed the role of the individual ("Great Man" theory; trait theory), and remains overly leader-centric, strides have been made to incorporate a broader range of individuals (read: followers) and, to a limited extent, the context. Still, the role of individuals is clearly a central element of leadership. Leadership studies is badly in need of some of the sophistication offered by historical analysis in this realm. And, again, James MacGregor Burns suggests the linkages. First, Burns acknowledges that "characters" embrace more than the common simplistic approaches. "I describe leadership here as no mere game among elitists and no mere populist response but as a structure of actions that engages persons, to varying degrees, throughout the levels and among the interstices of society." Indeed, for Burns, "'One man leadership' is a contradiction in terms. Leaders, in responding to their own motives, appeal to the motive bases of potential followers. As followers respond, a symbiotic relationship develops that binds leader and follower together into a social and political collectivity." Historical analysis brings these added insights to the roles of both leaders and followers.

By *connections* we mean that historians make sense of their subject by seeking to extract patterns that help to interpret the vast amount of available data. It is no large leap to see that for students of leadership this too is their task: to have the capability to confront the enormous complexities created by the dynamic interaction of social forces, institutional structures, and individual acts of initiative and response, and to make sense of them by creating representations of what are believed to be dominant patterns. James MacGregor Burns was among the first to acknowledge this with his expansive conception of leadership. As he frames it, "In the billions of acts that comprise the leadership process, a pattern can be discerned that makes possible generalizations about leadership" (1978: 427).

The questions of history, then, *are* the questions of leadership. It follows that both historical studies themselves and, more broadly, the adoption of a "historical frame of mind" by participants in the leadership process and leadership scholars are essential to its full understanding. This brings us to a final, perhaps somewhat more controversial (among historians, at any rate) theme: the ways in which historical analysis can bring understanding to current leadership challenges.

FROM THE PAST TO THE PRESENT AND FUTURE

Historians are correct to harbor suspicions about "presentist" applications of historical analysis. For one thing, it is not in their job description. For another, it risks contaminating the historical "realities", as historian Patrick Griffin has pointed out. Still, for practitioners and students of leadership, the discipline of history has much to offer. History may not repeat itself, nor even "rhyme" with the present: but it is relevant to the ongoing study and practice of leadership.

Historic Antecedents to the Present

An initial argument for the relevance of historical analysis is simply that our present challenges are outgrowths of what has occurred in the past. We have seen historian Gaddis point out that "the past weighs so heavily upon the present and the future that these last two domains of time hardly have meaning apart from it.... We know the future only by the past we project into it. History, in this sense, is all that we have" (2002: 141, 3). Moreover, as we seek to understand our present, the careful study of its historical antecedents can bring more sophistication to our contemplation of present realities. Leadership scholars Gill Robinson Hickman and Richard Couto have noted that "the less we consider historical and cultural context, the fewer influential events and factors we take into account" (2006: 184). This includes, for instance, the identification of less-obvious stakeholders in the analysis of any given leadership challenge. If we wished to understand and improve community leadership in Richmond, Virginia, we should expect to undertake a careful study of the tortuous and emotion-laden historical backdrop to the institutions, social relations, subcultures, and mindsets of numerous groups and individuals over a long period of time. Not to do so would be to misunderstand both the real and constructed "realities" of the situation.

Developing a Historical Consciousness

In addition to the more substantive contributions historical analysis can make to our full understanding of the leadership context, a familiarity with the historical approach itself can sensitize scholars and participants in the leadership process to the important nuances of the situation confronted. This does not mean that all need to be trained historians; simply that students of leadership and those who engage in it should acquire a "historical mindset", a Herodotean habit of asking "what happened", and seek for complex but comprehensible answers (Ekman, forthcoming: 3).

Through historical study one becomes more sensitized to the existence and complexities of what I have been calling the five "C's": change, causation, context, characters and connections. Indeed one can devise a protocol of questions that are informed by historical analysis but pertain to current challenges. Questions such as: what is the leadership challenge? Why is this a leadership challenge? Who are the stakeholders? What are their interests? How has the surrounding context impacted the stakeholders? How does the context provide opportunities and constraints for action? Each of these questions, I posit, cannot be answered without careful attention to their roots in the historical context. Any leadership scholar or participant in the process who poses such questions and makes a sincere effort to answer them will have achieved the benefits that a "historical consciousness" brings to leadership.

Exploring Values and Moral Dilemmas

I now venture somewhat beyond what most historians probably accept as the proper limit of historical study, to consider what role history can play in exploring the role of values and moral dilemmas in leadership. This role for history – and for leadership – is fraught with controversy for both disciplines.

James MacGregor Burns has defined "values" as "what is right, worthwhile or desirable"; they are "principles and standards" that "serve as criteria for judgment, preference, and choice" (2003: 205). Such a definition immediately raises two related issues. First, such a definition depicts something that is obviously subjective, and, some would say, "constructed". The second, derivative problem is that the choice on any constellation of values inevitably forecloses others. To the extent such values are imposed in a non-consensual manner, it raises moral issues concerning human agency.

Many historians and leadership studies scholars have gotten themselves hopelessly tangled up in this complex web, but in reality the existence of values (especially conflicting ones) makes the study of history fascinating and indeed makes possible leadership itself. The difficulty comes only when scholars and students confuse *analysis* with *normative judgments*. This may require brief explanation.

Some of the best works of history identify and catalogue the various value sets that underpin the activities of various individuals in a particular historical situation. Bernard Bailyn's *The Ideological Origins of the American Revolution* (1967) and Gordon Wood's *The Creation of the American Republic, 1776–1787* (1969) both trace competing and conflicting values during critical phases of American history. The problem for historians arises when the analysis moves from the descriptive to the normative. That is to say, *describing* values should pose no problem, but *prescribing* them does. This sounds simple enough, but, unfortunately for interests of value-neutrality, the two approaches are unavoidably linked.

The initial difficulty lies in the nature of historical *analysis*. John Lewis Gaddis writes that "historians … cannot escape … mak[ing] moral judgments …. No work of history of which I am aware has ever been written without making some sort of statement – explicitly or implicitly, consciously or unconsciously," about the morality of the subject matter. "You can't", concluded Gaddis, "escape thinking about history in moral terms" (2002: 122). And Hayden White would add that "any historical narrative that has ever been written … [has been] … informed not only by the moral awareness but specifically by the moral authority of the narrator" (1987: 24). Such implicit values of the historian are not to be taken lightly, but the professional seeks to recognize and acknowledge them whenever possible.

A second issue is the matter of historical *judgment*. Most historians reject the outright championing of one set of values over another. Historian John Lewis Gaddis notes that "times impose their morality upon lives; there's no point in condemning individuals for the circumstances in which they find themselves" (2002: 127). And fellow historian Marc Bloch rejects the arrogance required to judge others in other times. It is dangerous, said Bloch, to exalt "to the level of eternal, observations necessarily borrowed from our own brief moment in time" (1953, cited in Gaddis, 2002: 106). Yet all historians do not shy away from the explicit consideration of the values and moral choices of the actors of the past. Historian Edward Ayers has argued that "I feel like we need to honestly reckon with these hard parts of our past, not by going out and beating up on dead people", but, rather, "it should be a sort of mirror to ourselves. What kind of injustices are we living with?" (Ayers cited in Biegelsen, 2008).

Scholars of leadership face similar debates over the values implicitly involved in their analysis and judgment. In leadership studies, the role of values is sharply contested. The field tends to be bifurcated between those who hew to the purported value-neutral social science approach and those who reject this claim to objectivity. Perhaps the best articulation of the latter position – and one to which this author subscribes – is made by leadership scholar Ronald Heifetz. "Understandably," he writes, "scholars who have studied 'leadership' have tended to side with the value-free connotation of the term because it lends itself more easily to analytic reasoning and empirical examination. But that will not do …". For Heifetz, "there is no neutral ground from which to construct notions and theories of leadership because leadership terms … carry with them implicit norms and values" (1994: 14).

If one accepts that values are a part of leadership analysis, it is possible to turn a vice into a virtue by embracing the fact that leadership is imbued with values and to turn our energies to identifying and evaluating them – utilizing, of course, historical case studies. Perhaps the two best examples of how this might be accomplished can be found in the work of James MacGregor Burns and Ronald Heifetz. Burns says that "to define leadership in terms of motivation, value, and purpose is to glimpse its central role in the processes of historical causation" (1978: 433). He proceeds to fill two volumes – his *Leadership* (1978) and *Transforming Leadership* (2003) – with historical examples of his thesis of how values, and in particular the conflicts among them, drive leadership. Similarly Heifetz, in his *Leadership without Easy Answers* argues that "leadership … places emphasis on the act of giving clarity and articulation to a community's guiding values" (1994: 23). He, too, makes his case through historical case studies, and embraces the reality of conflicting values.

If historical studies can become the underpinning for claims of the role of values in leadership, such historical cases can also serve the purpose of holding up, as historian Ayers says, "a mirror to ourselves" by contemplating the actions of individuals in the past. Perhaps the most articulate spokesman for this is philosopher and leadership scholar Richard Morrill. According to Morrill, "The study of leadership" – and indeed the study of history – "provides exhibit after exhibit, case after case, and analysis upon analysis, of the ways values are central to one of the fundamental currents of human experience. In leadership studies, values are taken seriously as driving forces of history." Moreover, it is possible to evaluate the extent to which historical actors operate consistently with existing values. "In reckoning with the inauthenticity of leaders who fail to embody the values they claim, in feeling the weight of unresolved conflicts and contradictions on the self and in organizations, or, on the contrary, in finding examples of leaders who display integrity in the midst of crisis, or in tracing the influence of leaders who elevate the values of their society," argues Morrill, "we can learn to use the methods of values criticism." Through such analysis, one can become sensitized to his/her own strengths and weaknesses. The notion of "values criticism does not impose normative answers," Morrill continues, "but asks normative questions. It gives structure to a form of inquiry," and in the process allows individuals to "find the contradictions and inconsistencies, the narrowness or artificiality, the shallowness or ineffectiveness of the systems of values they are studying, including their own" (Morrill, forthcoming, 9, 18–19).

Although we need not treat it in as much detail, the same can be said of the insights that can be gleaned through the careful study of the moral dilemmas confronted by individuals through history. In a fashion similar to values criticism, through careful study and analysis such historical dramas can be the basis for one's own moral growth and development.

Exploring the Dynamics of Structure and Agency

The earlier discussion of "context" and "characters" merits a further exploration of the nexus between the two. It is there that we find a dynamic that is central to leadership: the links between individual action and the surrounding context. Somewhat ironically, while historians perform this sort of analysis constantly, they do not pause to think about the larger implications of what they are finding. For all their great virtues, one thing historians do not do well is to reflect upon their own method, and its implications. This is unfortunate in a sense, since it makes the relevance of historical work for the understanding of something like leadership more opaque. So we are left to borrow from others who have thought this through more thoroughly, in particular sociologists, philosophers, "critical realists" and others who talk in terms of *agency* and *structure*.

These terms can generally be likened to our historical themes of "context" and "characters". *Structure* can be thought of as those institutional and cultural elements that form the essence of the historical context within which historical characters act, while *agency* denotes the motivations, activity, and results of individual action. The central focus for historians is also the dynamic of most interest to scholars of leadership: as James MacGregor Burns depicted in his historical work, it is "the relation between the leader's character and qualities and the social and political context in which they operated, and the role of each in change." He investigates how "questions of historical causation" relate to "the interplay of environmental and personal forces that shaped the actions of leaders" (2003, 25, 9).

Historians, then, explore this dynamic as a matter of course: it essentially describes the essence of historical analysis. Just as clearly, the dynamics of agency and structure inform leadership. In the field of leadership studies, Burns suggests that this has been an area that has been underappreciated. He notes that scholars have "failed to distinguish conclusively the roles played in social change by individual and situation, by human volition and inexorable social processes, by the 'agency' of actors and the 'structure' of systems." Burns poses the question: "Can a course toward meaningful change be plotted that will give due weight both to the intentions and actions of people and to the situations they confront …?" (2003, 15, 17).

As is the case in all historical analysis, each study is bounded by the uniqueness of time, place and actors, so generalization is inadvisable. Nevertheless careful study of historical work can bring insights to the dynamics of structure and agency. Recently two leadership scholars – Elizabeth Faier, an anthropologist and I, a historian – got together to consider this topic. Our resulting dialogue has since been published. I presented the historian's perspective:

> [I]n my work I build up an elaborate historical context within which people operate. … I cannot predict what any one individual will do in response to … their perception of that context, which is their agency. They can choose to be totally conformist, or they can choose to be change agents, or any other level of response to the contextual cues and constraints. That to me is their agency. As a historian I can look back to choices already made and try to explain what people did, and, hopefully, why they did it.

Faier, for her part, attempted to transform this into a proposition useful for leadership studies. "Are you suggesting then," she asked, "that context is not deterministic but creates a framework in which agency occurs and perhaps even agency structures?" To which Wren replied "yes, I think that is exactly right," although at another place he added the caveat that

> I do think that the historical context does make some actions and reactions less likely to occur because it [sic] just doesn't fit the possibilities in that context. But it doesn't deny that any individual could react in a certain way. So I guess my point is that any human agent can do anything he or she wishes, but the context makes some actions more likely, or, perhaps, more "rational" than others (Wren and Faier, 2006: 217, 208).

This gradual transition in focus from the exceptionalism of historical study to the generalizations of the leadership scholar reaches full flower in our final take on the potential links between history and leadership.

Creating Models and Theories

Wren and Faier, in their discussion of the role of context in leadership, posed the essential problem: "an inability to generalize at some level beyond the idiosyncratic and the localistic dooms any pretense of a theoretical statement about the role of context [or, for that matter, historical analysis] in leadership" (ibid.: 220). Their search for some way of generalizing received some help from an unexpected source: historian Gaddis. Gaddis remarked that "it is quite wrong to claim that historians reject the use of theory, for theory is ultimately generalization, and without generalization historians would have nothing whatever to say." He did go on to qualify this by saying that, for historians, "explanation is … our chief priority: therefore we subordinate our generalizations to it", and he went on to say that historians are not comfortable with devising anything that resembles a formal model or theory (2002: 62, 65).

Thus the most controversial (to professional historians) and problematic (in the attempts at implementation) potential linkage between historical study and leadership is the effort to use history as the basis for theorizing about leadership. One voice to the contrary is that of James MacGregor Burns. He allows that "Leadership is an expanding field of study that someday may join the traditional disciplines of history, philosophy, and the social sciences in scholarly recognition. Today, however, it remains in its growing stages; it has as yet no grand, unifying theory to provide common direction to thinkers and researchers." But Burns thinks that such a theory is possible. "In the billions of acts that comprise the leadership process," he asserts, "...a pattern can be discerned that makes possible generalizations about leadership, generalizations that in turn would underlie an effective general theory and serve to guide the successful practice of leadership." This would entail, among other things "a theory of historical causation" (2003: 2; 1978: 427, 4).

Leaving aside the question of whether Burns is correct in his optimism (when he convened scholars to concoct such a theory, they proved to be unsuccessful) (Wren, 2006), the important matter for our purposes is the extent to which historical analysis can lead to theoretical statements about leadership. Certainly desirability of such historically-informed statements is clear. Wren comments that "it is not wise, when we are thinking of theorizing [about leadership], or thinking about predicting leadership, or thinking about integrating ideas about leadership, to ignore those longer-term things that create circumstances within which our actors operate" (Wren and Faier, 2006: 210). Yet, for reasons that should be abundantly clear by now having to do with the dangers of generalizing from discrete historical analysis, the role of historians in the generation of theory remains problematic. Certainly historical analysis has generated theoretical statements in the past. Historian Crane Brinton famously drew upon his studies of the French Revolution to posit a theory about the stages of revolution (1938 [1965]). But such leaps are few and far between.

With respect to leadership, then, the question about the feasibility of theorizing from historical analysis about leadership remains open. Historian Wren gave a cautious overview: "Although we cannot predict with precision how any specific individual will act within a given context," he said,

> we can nevertheless construct a rigorous way in which we can analyze the [historical] context and thereby identify the parameters within which each actor in the leadership relation operates. This doesn't get us to the level of a theoretical statement, but it does give us an organized way to think about context and its effect.

This led to the conclusions of Wren and Faier in their discourse on the theoretical possibilities of context: "Grand deterministic statements about the role of context are not possible," they decided. Scholars, in the end,

> must content themselves, ultimately, with that protocol of structuring questions that help the analyst perceive the dynamic interaction between the individual and his/her context. While falling far short of a theoretical statement in any traditional sense of the term, this nonetheless does provide a technique for understanding the role of context [and history] more thoroughly (Wren and Faier, 2006: 214, 220).

CONCLUSION: THE SIXTH "C"

Perhaps uniquely, the study of history has a difficult relationship with the study of leadership. Historians tend to believe that historical investigations should be treated as such; that is, it is not the role of the historian to generalize beyond the particularistic historical episodes under study. Moreover, to *begin* historical analysis with presentist questions about leadership is to risk perverting the analysis.

Yet historical perspective and insights are essential to a full understanding of leadership. This chapter has explored the many links between traditional historical work and leadership studies. The questions posed by historians – the five "Cs" – are also central questions of leadership, and historical work can generate understanding of leadership.

Historical analysis brings to our understanding of leadership something no other discipline can – at least not in the same way. We might think of this as the sixth "C" of historical study: *complexity*. As opposed to much of the leadership literature, which is, by turns, shallow (the "airport books" on leadership) or narrow (as is the case with the social science approach), historians embrace complexity. The philosopher Michael Oakeshott has pointed out that "historians have a web-like sense of reality in that they see everything as connected in some way to everything else" (1933: 128). Gaddis adds that history concerns itself "with interdependent variables interacting in complicated ways over extended periods of time." It is the purpose of historical narrative," says Gaddis, to "track multiple interrelated processes over time, recounting for others as well as [for the historians] themselves, so that all may benefit" (2002: 72, 69).

It is this comfort with complexity, I believe, that makes historical inquiry the ideal model for thinking about leadership.

REFERENCES

Bailyn, Bernard (1967), *The Ideological Origins of the American Revolution*, Cambridge, MA: Harvard University Press.

Biegelsen, A. (2008), "The recent pleasantness", *Style Weekly*, 2 July, p.16.

Bloch, M. (1953), *The Historian's Craft*, New York: Vintage Books.

Brinton, Crane (1938 [1965]), *The Anatomy of a Revolution*, New York: Vintage Books.

Burns, James MacGregor (1978), *Leadership*, New York: Harper and Row.

Burns, James MacGregor (2003), *Transforming Leadership: A New Pursuit of Happiness*, New York: Atlantic Monthly Press.

Carlyle, Thomas (1902), *On Heroes, Hero Worship, and Heroes in History*, New York: Ginn and Co.

Collingwood, Robin G. (1956), *The Idea of History*, New York: Oxford University Press.

Ekman, R. (forthcoming), "Can the study of the liberal arts prepare both effective leaders and productive citizens?", in J. Thomas Wren, Ronald E. Riggio and Michael A. Genovese (eds), *Leadership and the Liberal Arts: Achieving the Promise of a Liberal Education*, New York: Palgrave Macmillan.

Gaddis, John Lewis (2002), *The Landscape of History: How Historians Map the Past*, Oxford: Oxford University Press.

Griffin, Patrick (forthcoming, 2009), "The perils of searching for leadership and discovery: the case of Jamestown and John Smith", in George R. Goethals and J. Thomas Wren (eds), *Leadership and Discovery*, New York: Palgrave Macmillan.

Gustavson, Carl G. (1955), *A Preface to History*, New York: McGraw-Hill.

Heifetz, Ronald A. (1994), *Leadership without Easy Answers*, Cambridge, MA: Harvard University Press.

Hickman, Gill Robinson and Richard A. Couto (2006), "Causality, change, and leadership", in George R. Goethals and Georgia L.J. Sorenson (eds), *The Quest for a General Theory of Leadership*, Cheltenham, UK and Northampton, MA, USA: Edward Elgar.

McPherson, James M. (1988), *Battle Cry of Freedom: the Era of the Civil War*, New York: Oxford University Press.

Morrill, Richard L. (forthcoming), "Liberal education, leadership, and values", in J. Thomas Wren, Ronald E. Riggio and Michael A. Genovese (eds), *Leadership and the Liberal Arts: Achieving the Promise of a Liberal Education*, New York: Palgrave Macmillan.

Oakeshott, M. (1933), *Experience and its Modes*, Cambridge: Cambridge University Press.

Tolstoy, L. (1933), *War and Peace*, New York: Oxford University Press.

White, Hayden (1987), "Narrative in the representation of reality", in H. White (ed.), *The Content of Form: Narrative Discourse and Historical Representation*, Baltimore, MD: Johns Hopkins Press.

Wood, Gordon S. (1992), *The Radicalism of the American Revolution*, New York: Alfred A. Knopf.

Wood, Gordon S. (1969), *The Creation of the American Republic, 1776–1787*, Chapel Hill, NC: University of North Carolina Press.

Wren, J. Thomas and Terry L. Price (2007), "Conclusion", in Terry L. Price and J. Thomas Wren (eds), *The Values of Presidential Leadership*, New York: Palgrave Macmillan.

Wren, J. Thomas and Elizabeth Faier (2006), "Contemplating context", in George R. Goethals and Georgia L.J. Sorenson (eds), *The Quest for a General Theory of Leadership*, Cheltenham, UK and Northampton, MA, USA: Edward Elgar.

Wren, J. Thomas (2006), "A quest for a grand theory of leadership", in George R. Goethals and Georgia L.J. Sorenson (eds), *The Quest for a General Theory of Leadership*, Cheltenham, UK and Northampton, MA, USA: Edward Elgar.

7. Classic sociology: Weber as an analyst of charisma

Stephen P. Turner

Despite the fact that Max Weber is the original and sole source of the social science concept of charisma (as distinct from the religious concept), and the fact that his discussion of charisma is highly precise, detailed and widely applicable (Adair-Toteff, 2005; Turner, 1993, 2003; Baehr, 2008, for discussions), the literature on charisma rarely uses the details of his ideal-type of charismatic authority, and is largely limited to ritual citation. In what follows I will briefly explain the core ideas that figure in his account of charismatic leadership, and illustrate them with a few well-known public figures. Examples are so plentiful in recent world politics that any of a long list could be chosen. Understanding charisma in the corporate world takes a bit more effort, but Weber himself discussed business charisma, and the examples he gave shed some light on business charisma today.

THE CORE MODEL: BEATING EXPECTATIONS

Weber gives a short list of model charismatic leaders: religious leaders, such as Bhagwans, who must perform miracles, the Herzog, or elected military leader, who must succeed on the field of battle, and a secondary variety, law prophets, who arise in a crisis to lay down law. The key to the two main types is that they must prove themselves – publicly, continuously, and through extraordinary acts or successes (1922 [1978]: 1114). In these model cases, the results are hard to manipulate or fake. Winning a battle is objective, as are miracles.

What are the modern variants of these types? Politicians, religious leaders, moral leaders, revolutionaries, stock market "gurus", and so on. Each of them is faced with the same kind of problem. They must "prove" their charisma to their followers and potential followers. The thing they must prove is that they are exceptional, and exceptional in a way that justifies their claims on the obedience and commitment of their followers. Weber has a phrase for this kind of exceptional quality, "un-everyday-ness" (1922 [1978]: 297), which suggests the uncanny. But mere exceptionality – such as the possession of remarkable talents with card tricks – cannot explain why someone can command a following.

So there must be something more going on here, implicit in Weber's account, and illustrated by his examples. What might it be? One basic element of the model of charisma for Weber is the idea that the charismatic leader believes that he or she has an exceptional, extraordinary mission given by God or in some sense sacred or part of fate. The fact that they have been chosen for this mission is part of what makes them extraordinary. Indeed, the two notions go together: to be given a mission is extraordinary, but it also implies the presence of special powers to fulfill this mission or fate (1922 [1978]: 1114).

People who believe in themselves are, of course, a dime a dozen, not to say a blight on the landscape. So this conviction is not, in itself, enough to qualify a person as charismatic. And this is where proof comes in. There must be evidence of the pair of elements: of the calling to an extraordinary mission and of the extraordinary powers required to fulfill this mission. One must not only imagine oneself to be Joan of Arc, one must do something that validates the idea.

Validation of one's special powers and validation of the mission mutually support one another through a process of feedback and amplification. Consider the case of Osama bin Laden. His Islamist ideas about the restoration of the Caliphate and the restoration of the status of Islam in the world were, both before his successful series of terrorist actions and afterwards, minor political ideas, and would not have commanded even a tiny fraction of a vote in an election or in an opinion poll. Nor do the details of his ideas matter even now. His is not an ideological movement, but a charismatic one.

How did it succeed? The key is expectations. Various attacks on Arab regimes, on Western interests, and on tourists have been made over the years by anti-Western Islamist leaders. They succeeded, in the sense that they were carried out successfully, and in some countries brought the movement close to political power. But in these cases for the most part the successes were within the range of ordinary expectation. Attacking tourists is easy to do. Bombing a well-guarded Embassy in a non-Muslim country and killing hundreds, however, is not easy to do. And this is the kind of success that Bin Laden's movement began to achieve.

VALIDATING THE MISSION

One may reasonably ask what the military point to these bombings was. They did not drive away the Americans, or win friends in the countries in which they were carried out, or gain political power or control of land. They are the paradigm of "senseless violence". They are, nevertheless, extraordinary. But are they extraordinary merely in the sense of card tricks? The answer is clearly that they do something more: they serve an important role in the creation of the charismatic leader and the validation of his mission, and more importantly his personal mission, the mission embodied in him.

How does this work? The ideas of the movement are marginal ideas, the ideas of cranks. The man on the street would dismiss them as such, especially because the goals that are espoused, which might be mildly desirable, appear to be impossible to achieve. This impossibility is a matter of expectations, however. And expectations can be made to change. They may be made to change, specifically, by the successes of leaders. These successes both make them credible as speakers, but more importantly they change our expectations about what is possible.

The changes are not mysterious. We operate with very vague and poorly grounded expectations, rooted in fear, about what is possible politically, in business, and so forth. New events readily shatter these expectations. They are not the kind of ordinary expectations we have about the natural world or about human relations with those we know and are close to. They are expectations about what are, for us, rare events. But they are changed by the experience and evidence of the acts of the leader. For Weber this change is absolutely central: "charisma, if it has any specific effects at all, manifests its revolutionary power from within, from a central *metanoia* [change] of the follower's attitudes" (1922 [1978]: 1117). And it is the exemplary actions of the leaders that produce this change, which is fundamentally a change in expectations about what is possible. The actions of the leader, by exceeding ordinary expectations, change them. But this change is not the normal revision of expectations. The changes are large, and are experienced as, and result from, the "anxiety and enthusiasm of an extraordinary situation" (1922 [1978]: 1117).

But here we get into the realm of illusion – very large illusions as well as small ones. There are many players in the game of setting expectations. The government of the United States seeks to project the expectation that resistance or attack will be met with massive force – that it is better not even to try. And indeed, this expectation is basic to American power. If every dictator or national leader thought that he or she could ignore or defy the threat of the use of American power, and if this power would have to be deployed every time it was challenged, the number of wars would be endless and the power itself would soon disappear, consumed by dozens of minor conflicts. The sparing, occasional, use of power serves to maintain the expectation that the United States can and will act, and this expectation is the real source of influence over the actions of others. This creates an opportunity for challengers – as it did in the time of Jesus and the Roman Empire.

The charismatic leader also plays a game of expectations, in which the dominant powers or adversaries that are often the charismatic leader's enemies play an important role. One can see the same pattern repeatedly in the newspapers. The errant leader does something the dominant power prefers he would not do. The dominant power tries diplomacy. A parade of dignitaries is sent to persuade him to relent. This is done with much publicity, especially on the side of the leader, who is eager to show the great power of the world deferring to and begging him to act their way. For him, the expectation that terrible things might happen if he did not agree, which is also the impression that the representatives of power wish to present, is equally important, because the leader is going to very publically, and repeatedly, "stand up" to power and reject the demands, in the name of the nation, its mission, its sovereignty, and so forth.

The ordinary leader would treat these as bargaining situations in which something might be gained by resistance, but in which the ultimate goal is to seal the best possible bargain. Diplomacy is merely haggling over the price. The charismatic leader treats these situations differently. For him and his audience, each act of resistance in which one survives or succeeds is one in which the ordinary expectations of being crushed by the superior power are surpassed. The very fact that both sides are eager to produce the expectation that he will be forced to give in and if he does not, that he will be crushed, makes any outcome better than being crushed or giving in into a victory – into a surpassing of expectations. This can become routinized. Fidel Castro and Hugo Chavez repeatedly announce the threat of imminent invasion by the United States. When it does not occur, they prove themselves again as having defeated the all-powerful adversary, and thus prove themselves to be special. And this proof of course validates their personal mission as well.

This is why militarily meaningless actions and senseless violence do make sense. They are proofs of the special powers of the leader. But they are more than this. They serve to make the vision of the leader more credible – what the actions say is this: what is possible with me is different, and much grander, than what is possible with ordinary leaders. Follow me in my mission, in my vision of what is possible, and what seemed impossible will happen.

THE LEADER AS THE PATH

Weber repeatedly used the example of Jesus, who said such things as "I am the way, and the truth and the life," which is to say both the source of the vision and the instrument of realizing it, that through me things are possible that are not possible otherwise, and especially, as Weber quoted, "it has been written …, but *I* say unto you" (1922 [1978]: 1115). The key to charisma is precisely the ability to present oneself as the way, as the instrument, and to rise above what is written, in this case the law, and command on the basis of one's personal authority.

But what about the content of the mission? And of the expectations that are changed? Here things get a bit more complicated. One complication comes from the process of raising and altering expectations themselves. As I write this, the ruler of Zimbabwe, Robert Mugabe, a charismatic national liberation politician, is clinging to power at gunpoint as the world watches in horror. His campaign posters cheerily read "All Good Things are Possible", which is the essential idea the charismatic leader trades on – with the implied qualification that it is only through the leaders, so it means "[Only Through Me] All Good Things are Possible". But raising expectations in this way creates debts to the future: a requirement that eventually these good things must arrive.

The moment of reckoning can be put off indefinitely, but not permanently. This is why Weber says that charisma begins to die at the moment of its birth (1922 [1978]: 1120). Eventually the leader must deliver the goods. And what typically occurs in politics as in business contexts is that the leader does two things: delivers some goods, especially to the highest ranking and most loyal followers, but also continues to surpass expectations, especially by beating expectations, usually by manufacturing fake expectations to surpass, and changing expectations by raising them, something that is made plausible by the continued beating of expectations.

In the case of Mugabe, all the ills of Zimbabwe and the failures of the regime to feed the people or bring them wealth are blamed on the powerful British and White interests that are conspiring to take Zimbabwe back, back from the people of Zimbabwe to whom Mugabe delivered it by expelling White rule and then the White landowners and producers themselves. The threats are amped up every time the leader needs a victory against the odds – and predictably the leader succeeds, because the threat is not real. Castro and Chavez, similarly, regularly announced threats of US invasions. Castro advertised these threats on signs in the countryside. And every time the resolute actions of the great leader overcame these terrible threats by the powerful enemy.

This sort of thing can go on for decades. Once the basic image of the world propounded by the leader has been accepted, and the mission of resistance has been identified with the ruler as the only one capable of carrying it out, both leaders and followers are trapped in the logic of charismatic success, in which the overcoming of obstacles reinforces the leader's mission and claim to the mission. But the mission nevertheless has content, and the content is an eventual pay-off. For religious leaders, the pay-off can be in the next world, so the message can be kept alive longer. But for the political and especially for the business leader, there need to be pay-offs sooner.

This need for pay-off spells the death of charisma, because the mechanisms for bringing about rewards are mundane – people need to be paid. Things cost money. Goods need to be secured or produced. In the classical world of

Roman generals and raiders like Genghis Khan or Attila, and even in the time of early modernity, this securing of goods could take the form of looting or extracting tribute. Distributing it fulfilled the promises. In the modern world, however, fulfilling promises means bureaucratic organization and all this implies – rules, offices, schemes by which people are appointed because they can do the jobs, continuity, rationality, predictability – in a word, accountants. And this is the antithesis of the high-flux, ever-changing world of charisma, where inner qualities and a spark of the divine count for everything, and where missions are made by breaking with the predictable and rejecting normal expectations.

SMALL CHARISMA: THE PROBLEM OF LEADER SELECTION

Weber, in his writings on politics, was also concerned with small charisma, not the large world-reshaping charisma of a Jesus or Napoleon, but the kind of charisma that allowed a leader to gain a following that would back him, and whose backing would give him freedom of action on the world stage. The support which enabled the leader to act was of course not enough; the leader needed the inner capacity to act, the energy, the ability to size up and seize opportunities, to see that what people thought was a risk was not a risk, and so forth. So Weber focused on the leader selection process in modern democratic mass societies. He was especially concerned that the usual selection processes selected out or against this kind of leader, and gave little training or experience in taking risks and gaining a following (1922 [1978]: 1441–62). Parties that were highly organized, such as the main German Socialist party of his time, were highly bureaucratized, and to rise to the top in it one needed to be a good organization man: bad training and selection for world leaders who were faced with international threats and opportunities.

Weber had similar points to make about business. He analyzed one example of an American financier, Henry Villard, who raised a vast amount of money from investors for a purpose that he kept secret even from the investors, a "blind pool", on the basis of the investors' belief in his individual power to make money for them (1922 [1978]: 1118). This is the charismatic model. It is the opposite mentality of the accountant, who is for business what the bureaucrat is for government: a slave to rules, to expectations rooted in the past, and to conventional thinking. Business, Weber thought, both required and rewarded (though usually punished) the few businessmen who could rise above the mass of bookkeepers and see opportunities that others could not, or create them.

As one can readily see, the same issues of selection apply: one needs experiences of an entrepreneurial, risk-taking kind in order to become a credible leader. But one is not likely to get these experiences climbing up the corporate ladder. Indeed, the corporate ladder is the place where potential leaders are killed off by the demands of conformity and endless rounds of group-think-producing meetings. So the person who has the most experience of a large enterprise and its business is likely to be the person least capable, on a personal level, of leading it. And this is what motivates the desperate searches for genuine leaders in corporate life.

REFERENCES

Adair-Toteff, Christopher (2005), "Max Weber's charisma", *Journal of Classical Sociology*, **5**, 189–204.

Baehr, Peter (2008), *Caesarism, Charisma and Fate*, New Brunswick, NJ: Transaction Publishers.

Turner, Stephen (1993), "Charisma and obedience: a risk cognition approach", *Leadership Quarterly*, **4**, 235–56.

Turner, Stephen (2003), "Charisma reconsidered", *Journal of Classical Sociology*, **3**(1), 5–26.

Weber, Max (1946), *From Max Weber: Essays in Sociology*, translated by H.H. Gerth and C.W. Mills, New York: Oxford University Press.

Weber, Max (1968), *Max Weber on Charisma and Institution Building*, edited with an introduction by S.N. Eisenstadt, Chicago, IL: University of Chicago Press.

Weber, Max (1922 [1978]), *Economy and Society: An Outline of Interpretive Sociology*, 3 vols, edited by Guenther Roth and Claus Wittich, Berkeley, CA: University of California Press.

8. Thinking sociologically about leadership

Sonia M. Ospina and Margo Hittleman

INTRODUCTION

Sociologists have an ambivalent relationship with leadership as a social phenomenon worth exploring. On the one hand, a search for "leadership" in contemporary sociology journals yields few entries. Yet a sociological perspective has permeated the study of leadership from the field's beginnings (Ayman, 2000). Weber's insights on "charisma", for example, remain key to leadership studies. And social psychologists, along with scholars in applied fields such as management, education and public administration, draw heavily on sociological organization and management theories.

This paradox may arise from the heroic individual-centered approach that dominates the conventional leadership literature with its emphasis on the psychological dynamics of the leader–follower relationship. Sociology is premised on the belief that actors are socially embedded; the idea that meaningful human experience can be understood exclusively from the vantage point of isolated individuals runs counter to sociological thinking. Regardless of researchers' location in a particular epistemic community or where they fall within the quintessential sociological debate about "agency" versus "structure", sociology's goal is to capture how the key features of human agency relate to institutional and structural regularities, as well as the relationships between them. It is, in C. Wright Mills' words, about using "the sociological imagination" by grasping "history and biography and the relations between the two within society" (Mills, [1959] 2000: 5).

Leadership scholars who use a "sociological imagination" may or may not be connected to departments of sociology. Nevertheless they consistently frame research questions and choose methodologies in ways that link individual biography to social structure. In organizational leadership studies, this means looking "beyond personal relations to the larger patterns of institutional development" (Selznick, 1957) and recognizing that the social and historical context in which the work of leadership takes place matters not only to how leadership is carried out, but to how it is constituted and understood.

In this chapter, we explore what thinking sociologically about leadership has offered the field of leadership studies, and more importantly, what integrating a stronger sociological approach could offer. We begin by pointing to two key sociological concepts – context and relationships – that permeate the leadership literature and highlight the ways a limited application of these foundational constructs has constrained their analytical and theoretical value. Next we suggest several ways scholars might bring a stronger sociological lens to the work of understanding leadership. We argue that thinking sociologically broadens attention beyond atomistic "leaders" or dyadic leader–followers engaged in an "influence relationship" to shine light on the social milieu within which relationships, interactions and processes are negotiated and constituted. Doing so challenges scholars to attend more closely to "the work of leadership" as well as to understand that work in new ways. We discuss these ideas first theoretically, then illustrate them by examining some recent empirical research on leadership in social change organizations.

Three caveats set the context for the choices we make here and help bound our reflections. First, our chapter draws predominantly from scholarship about leadership in organizational contexts rather than from studies of political leaders or the normative literature. Even here, we have been highly selective; a short chapter precludes an exhaustive review. Second, our examples come primarily from scholars working from an "interpretivist" perspective as that is the community in which our own work is grounded. This does not represent *all of sociology*, but instead presents a particular viewpoint within the discipline.[1] Finally, while the scholarship we cite draws upon the heritage established by the sociological fathers Emil Durkheim, George Simmel, Max Weber and Karl Marx, we do not explicitly review their work.

SOCIOLOGICAL CONCEPTS IN THE FIELD: LIMITS AND POSSIBILITIES

Influential theories such as situational leadership theory, the contingency approach, and transformational and charismatic leadership draw upon salient sociological concepts. Most notably this is expressed in concerns with how leadership occurs within a social and historical context and in the growing interest in the collective, relational dimensions of leadership. We examine each in turn.

Attending to Context

The desire to identify a universal set of inherent traits, styles or behaviors of "great men" and "great women" still defines much scholarship. Yet scholars also agree that leadership cannot be fully understood apart from the context in which it exists. They argue that the leadership relationship is "embedded in a social setting at a given historical moment" (Biggart and Hamilton, 1987: 439), and that "leaders must be understood in their 'natural' setting" (Kets de Vries, 2001: 8576). A variety of contextual dimensions appear in the organizational leadership literature, including an organization's structure and culture, goals, strategy and mission, demographics, core processes of technology, policy and governance, degree of success and organizational cycle (Jackson and Parry, 2008).

Neo-charismatic and transformational scholars influenced by the "sociologically informed work of Burns" (Pitsis, 2007) highlight the interconnections between the influence relationship and the circumstances and conditions within which it develops (Bryman et al., 1996; Parry and Bryman, 2006).[2] But leadership research has not been fundamentally transformed by these insights. Attention to the "organizational context" remains an "under-researched area" (Porter and McLaughlin, 2006: 206), marginalized in transformational leadership studies (Bryman et al., 1996) and unintegrated in neo-charismatic leadership theories (Beyer, 1999).

Even when context is explicitly considered, most empirical leadership work assumes that it exists independent of leaders, followers, and their relationship. In this "entity" approach (Uhl-Bien, 2006), context is the background environment within which leaders relate to followers, enact their behaviors and make decisions. It is assumed to exist prior to the studied phenomenon and explored primarily to better illuminate the relationship or the behaviors of the engaged actors.

In contrast to this person–situation split, a sociological perspective invites analysts to view the relationship between person and situation, biography and history (or agency and structure) as much more dynamic and reflexive: actions and interactions of social agents are both generative of social structure and constrained by it (Giddens and Turner, 1987). It calls into question both an excessive focus on the leaders (agents) and the unidirectional, deterministic ways in which "context" has been often used.

Attending to Relationships

Leadership scholars are increasingly interested in exploring the relational dimensions of leadership (Uhl-Bien, 2006). Transformational, neo-charismatic and LMX (Leader–Member Exchange Theory) scholars, for example, are now interested in the quality of the leader–follower relationship and the contingencies that surround it. Others have looked beyond the leader–follower dyad to consider collective relationships such as distributed or shared forms of leadership.

In general, however, these are identified as one kind of leadership increasingly necessary in today's complex environment. For example, scholars writing about distributed leadership suggest that the *trend* toward new organizational forms *requires* a type of leader capable of creating the conditions to manage effectively in more flexible organizational forms (Pearce and Conger, 2003). This perspective shifts attention from uni-directional to reciprocal exchanges (theorized as a response to new "contextual" requirements). But the notion of an influence relationship among discrete, independent entities remains unchallenged. In contrast, an explicitly sociological lens interrogates the dominant assumptions of the individual and collective versions of the entity perspective.

BRINGING A SOCIOLOGICAL LENS TO LEADERSHIP STUDIES

A sociological lens invites us to separate "leaders" from "leadership" (for example, Rost, 1991; Vanderslice, 1988). It shifts attention from a nearly exclusive focus on attributes, styles, behaviors and activities of individuals involved in an influence relationship, to inquire about the nature and quality of what social actors do together to construct and advance a common purpose. Consider Drath's (2001) metaphor of the "deep blue sea". Leaders, he suggests, are merely the "sparkling white caps" of ocean waves. We can't understand the ocean merely by studying these caps. Similarly, our grasp of leadership is incomplete unless we consider not only questions about *who* leads, but also about the *what*, *where* and *how* of leadership (Grint, 2005: 18).

Redirecting Attention to "the Work of Leadership"

Organization and management scholars in the late 1970s applied a sociological orientation to argue that leadership emerges from the constructions and actions of people in organizations as they assign each other different roles and functions, including the roles of leadership. Smircich and Morgan (1982) and Tierney (1987), for example, related leadership to shared meanings and stressed the leaders' role of managing meaning for effectiveness. Other scholars pointed to leadership's cognitive and symbolic functions to help people make sense of events (Hunt, 1984) or give legitimacy to organizational realities and decisions (Pfeffer, 1977).

These scholars shared transformational theorists' interest in meaning making and the new concern of leadership theorists with processes of social cognition. But their approach to leadership was fundamentally different. Leadership scholars who took the "cognitive turn" (Lord and Emrich, 2000) overwhelmingly framed cognition as an individual, psychological process occurring solely in people's minds. They attended, for example, to the attributional processes by which followers bestow leaders with authority (Meindl et al., 1985; Hogg, 2001).

In contrast, those using a sociological lens portrayed cognition as "embedded" or grounded in the social world. Because people make sense of the world only through interactions with their environment and the people in it, meaning making is a collective, rather than an individual task. Further, a sociological lens proposes that the material aspects of the settings influence how cognitive processes develop, and that cognition is "embodied", reflected not only in individuals' minds and behaviors, but also in practices, artifacts and institutions. Hence "context" – with identifiable contingencies – affects how people comprehend the world and how they respond to it (Wilson and Keil, 2001).

Very little empirical work on leadership was produced to further develop these powerful ideas in the US.[3] But the renewed interest in context and relational leadership reinforces the value of thinking sociologically. For sociologically oriented scholars, "relational leadership" is neither a "type" of leadership nor a "trend". Rather, leadership is "intrinsically relational and social in nature… the result of shared meaning-making, and …rooted in context and place" (Ospina and Sorenson, 2006: 188).

For these analysts, meaning making and organizing processes that mobilize individuals into collective action are as relevant as interpersonal influence dynamics. "Context" is an emergent space constructed and named by participants in events that draw upon shared agreements, or "knowledge principles" (Drath, 2001) to advance the work. And the emerging, mutually constituted relationships between leaders, followers and context provide the conditions for leadership to happen.

Thus, rather than focusing on "leaders" and "contextual factors" in a foreground–background manner, sociologically-based researchers argue that

> leadership cannot be abstracted from the organizational processes of which it is a part. The study of leadership, properly conceived, is the study of the process in which flexible social order is negotiated and practiced so as to protect and promote the values and interests in which it is grounded. (Hosking, 1997: 315)

Further, this perspective questions the notion of leadership as something that belongs to the individual, suggesting instead that leadership is found in the work of a group, and so it is the property of the group (Dachler and Hosking, 1995), a collective achievement (Drath, 2001) or the emergent property of a social system (Parry and Bryman, 2006).

Leadership, then, is the social and relational processes (meaning-making included) that emerge to address organizing and action. Since structure is not merely a prescribed organizational framework but a negotiated and emergent product of patterned interaction, it is wise to observe the work that helps organizational members construct, through everyday practices, the very "rules" of organizing that they follow. A key question becomes how relational interactions contribute to "the generation and emergence of social order" (Uhl-Bien, 2006: 42).

This has important implications, not just for theorizing about leadership, but for its empirical study as well. It invites us to "deconstruct leadership activities from their embeddedness in institutional hierarchies and structures" (Robnett, 1997: 19); understand the socially constructed roles and relations that contribute to create direct social order, action and systems change; and remember that since relational dynamics occur in a context, the latter is fundamental to understand leadership (Uhl-Bien, 2006: 37).

Analytical attention then naturally shifts to "processes" (Hosking, 1988) and to "the work of leadership, as opposed to the agents through which it is carried out" (Foldy et al., forthcoming). Further, as Alvesson (1996) suggests, tying leadership "to a formal position or defined as a fixed quality" closes the inquiry "prematurely". It is better to think of it, instead, "more openly in relationship to that which goes on in the work organization context and the relations being formed and reformed in processes of sense-making, attribution and negotiation" (Alvesson, 1996: 469). Observing these processes, he argues, will offer more insights about leadership than interviewing leaders about it. Indeed, this approach to empirical research explores the processes and relations that constitute the work of leadership as it is happening.

SEEING LEADERSHIP DIFFERENTLY: AN EMPIRICAL LOOK

To illustrate our argument, we turn to a small, but growing, body of sociological literature about leadership in grassroots social change organizations. We believe this literature is noteworthy not merely to illuminate leadership in these particular contexts, but in its as-yet-unrealized contributions to a richer understanding of insufficiently explored facets of leadership in other settings as well.[4]

These scholars have produced empirical research on how leadership emerges and develops in community-based social change organizations and social movement groups. They bring distinct interests, approaches and contributions to their work. Nevertheless, their sociological lens produces identifiable consequences. First, they draw heavily from social theory – particularly feminist and critical race theory – which challenges assumptions about who is a leader and what is defined as leadership. Second, taken together, their work shifts theorizing from an emphasis on leadership as an "influence relationship" to an understanding of leadership as a process of collective meaning-making, developmental capacity-building and collaborative action. Third, they direct attention to dimensions of leadership rarely examined in other studies. Most notably they elucidate the work involved in building the capacities of people, organizations and communities, and developing, not "followers", but groups of people empowered to act together to bring about change. Fourth, they attend to the processes and practices by which this work is carried out.

In each case, these researchers moved beyond the most visible, formal actors in top organizational positions, to attend to work that included those without formal organizational titles or traditionally recognized leadership roles. The "centerwomen" in Sacks' (1988) study of union organizing, the "bridge leaders" in Robnett's (1997) work on African-American women's leadership in the Civil Rights movement, the "midwife" leaders in Belenky et al.'s (1997) study of grassroots organizations in the US and Germany, or the US social change leaders in Ospina and her colleagues' multi-year study (for example, Ospina and Foldy, 2008), all played important – if often overlooked or unacknowledged – roles in shaping people's consciousness, building organizations, forming networks, and mobilizing people into action.

In contrast to scholars who worry about the dangers of "an overly broad definition of leadership" that devalues organizational hierarchies (Morris and Staggenborg, 2004: 177), we find that these studies demonstrate how examining various types of leaders – and more importantly, their work – sheds a dramatically different light on what "leadership work" is, how it unfolds and how given organizations' goals are accomplished. Indeed, positioned outside the mainstream leadership field, these researchers are less directly concerned with the role of leaders or the nature of leadership itself. Instead, they aim to understand the work of a particular type of group and "the recurrent problems they face" (Selznick, 1957: 23) in their organizing efforts to realize a social change vision. This aim mirrors Selznick's characterization of a sociological interpretation of organizational leadership.

Expanding the typical equation of leadership with activities such as crafting decisions and influencing followers, these researchers highlight the ways leaders and followers collectively and strategically support growth and development in people, organizations and communities. And they demonstrate how, through this work, people (particularly those who have been marginalized or excluded) change their sense of who they are and what they are capable of, form new understandings of themselves and the world in which they live, develop a public voice, and come together to take effective, collective action.

Leaders do not disappear in these studies. But light is shed on the nature of what they do and the logic underlying their work. Thus, for example, Belenky et al. (1997) describe the work of what they came to call "developmental leadership" as follows:

> These leaders want to know each person, what they care about, and where they are trying to go. They also work to articulate the goals that people in the group have in common. They look for each person's strong points, for the things already in place upon which the person could build. They also look for the strengths in people's culture as a building foundation for the whole community. They ask good questions and draw out people's thinking. They listen with care. … Then they look for ways to mirror what they have seen, giving people a chance to take a new look at themselves and see the strengths that have not been well recognized or articulated. (1997: 14).

Then, the authors continue, critical analysis through permanent and deep conversation helps the group to "develop a vision of how things ought to work" (ibid.: 14).

Similarly, Ospina and her colleagues have identified a variety of "leadership practices" that help groups seeking to make social change move their agendas forward. In one study, for example, they identified "bridging leadership practices", that is, purposive interventions that helped diverse groups cross boundaries by creating new bonds or strengthening existing ones. Such practices include prompting cognitive shifts; naming and shaping identity; and engaging dialogue about difference (Ospina and Foldy, 2008).

Finally, this body of research reveals the historical, social, cultural and political character of leadership. Drawing heavily from feminist and critical race theory, and embracing the interpretive turn, scholars like Robnett (1997), Belenky et al. (1997) and Ospina and Su (2008) incorporate an analysis of social location, power, hegemony and oppression into their inquiry. They explore how micro and macro mechanisms that sustain particular systems of oppression and their intersections are weaved through, and influence the work of leadership in significant ways. By challenging dominant assumptions, their gendered and/or critical race analyses deepen and advance our understanding of leadership.

CONCLUSION

In this chapter we offer a way to think sociologically about the complex social phenomenon we call "leadership". We have argued that this allows scholars to incorporate more successfully concepts like context and relationship both in empirical research and in theory. This happens in two ways. First, a sociological lens redirects attention to the work of leadership as collective and relational. Second, it makes evident how this work is embedded in broader processes and institutions, thus highlighting the structures of power and domination that characterize and sustain stratified social systems.

The result is a broader understanding of what counts as leadership, one which challenges the heroic, male, white, positional view that has dominated the field. The studies of leadership in social change organizations illustrate this point. In deconstructing the actual logic of the organizing processes from which leadership emerges (Hosking, 1988), these scholars have drawn attention to how the relationships, interactions and negotiations required for collective action manifest in actual leadership practices in localized contexts (Ospina and Foldy, 2008). They also remind us that leadership emerges in particular contexts characterized by culturally and historically grounded structures of power.

In doing so, they make visible dimensions of leadership vital not only to "social change" organizations, but to leadership in other settings as well. These dimensions are particularly salient given both scholars' and practitioners' concerns with new organizing trends. As people seek models of "multicultural" leadership or expect positional leaders to move beyond "influencing followers" to build collectively the capacity of flattened, flexible and boundary-less organizations, understanding how people can take effective initiative and engage in coordinated action becomes urgent.

In our attention to what sociology has and can bring to the study of leadership, we are not arguing that it offers the only or the best way to understand this phenomenon. For example, we agree with Shamir's claim (1999) that a psychological and a sociological approach to charisma can be complementary, not contradictory. Yet a sociological lens is particularly suited to address the growing concern to expand scholarship beyond individual leaders, followers and their relationship (Uhl-Bien, 2006) to new conceptualizations that enrich understanding of the "work of leadership" and the "interactive … processes" related to it (Gronn, 2002: 4441). Such a lens has been relatively absent from empirical studies of leadership, particularly in the US. Addressing this imbalance can help move the field forward.

NOTES

1. An apparent rift between a US research community dominated by a psychological (and positivist) orientation to the study of leadership and a more sociological (and interpretivist) orientation in Europe, Australia and New Zealand merits turning a sociological eye on the field of leadership itself. That, however, is outside the scope of this chapter. We simply note here that much of the empirical sociological work on leadership is currently taking place outside the US. Other leadership scholars who do not work under the positivist paradigm in the US tend to take a multidisciplinary approach, drawing as needed from the humanities and the social sciences. See Goethals and Sorenson (2006) for examples.
2. Debates triggered around interpretations of charisma are quite educational. See Issue 4 in Volume 9 of *The Leadership Quarterly* (1999), particularly the articles by Bass, Shamir, House and Beyer, respectively.
3. In Europe, scholarly interest in leadership took off at about the same time that the "postmodern turn hit Europe", producing from the start scholarship that was "both sociological and postmodern" (Grint, personal communication, 2008).
4. For studies of social change and leadership within a traditional perspective see *The*

Leadership Quarterly Yearly Review of Leadership, **5**(3–4), pp. 193–317 (1994). For a more extensive review of the study of leadership in social movements, see Morris and Staggenborg (2004). We do not discuss here other sociologists studying social change organizations (for example Polletta, 2002 and Wood, 2002) because their interests are not explicitly on leadership.

REFERENCES

Alvesson, M. (1996), "Leadership studies: from procedure and abstraction to reflexivity and situation", *The Leadership Quarterly*, **7**(4), 55–85.

Ayman, R. (2000), "Leadership", in E.F. Borgatta (ed.), *Encyclopedia of Sociology*, 2nd edn, New York: Macmillan.

Belenky, M.F., L.A. Bond and J.S. Weinstock (1997), *A Tradition That Has No Name: Nurturing the Development of People, Families and Communities,* New York: Basic Books.

Beyer, J.M. (1999), "Taming and promoting charisma to change organizations", *Leadership Quarterly*, **10**(2): 307–30.

Biggart, G. and N.W. Hamilton (1987), "An institutional theory of leadership", *Journal of Applied Behavioral Science*, **23**, 429–41.

Bryman, A., M. Stephens and C. à Campo (1996), "The importance of context: qualitative research and the study of leadership", *Leadership Quarterly*, **7**(3), 353–70.

Dachler, H.P. and D.M. Hosking (1995), "The primacy of relations in socially constructing organizational realities" in D.M. Hosking, H.P. Dachler and K.J. Gergen (eds), *Management and Organization: Relational Alternatives to Individualism.* Brookfield, VT: Avebury.

Drath, W. (2001), *The Deep Blue Sea: Rethinking the Source of Leadership*, San Francisco, CA: Jossey-Bass.

Fletcher, J.K. and K. Kaufer (2003), "Shared leadership: paradox and possibility", in C.L. Pearce and J.A. Conger (eds), *Shared Leadership: Reframing the Hows and Whys of Leadership,* Thousand Oaks, CA: Sage Publications.

Foldy, E., L. Goldman and S. Ospina (forthcoming), "Sensegiving and the role of cognitive shifts in the work of leadership", *Leadership Quarterly.*

Giddens, A. and J. Turner (1987), *Social Theory Today*, Stanford. CA: Stanford University Press.

Goethals, G. and G. Sorenson (eds) (2006), *The Quest for a General Theory of Leadership*, Cheltenham, UK and Northampton, MA, USA: Edward Elgar.

Grint, K. (2005), *Leadership: Limits and Possibilities*, Basingstoke: Palgrave Macmillan.

Gronn, P. (2002), "Distributed leadership as a unit of analysis", *Leadership Quarterly*, **13**, 423–51.

Hogg, M. (2001), "A social identity theory of leadership", *Personality and Social Psychology Review*, **5**(3), 184-200.

Hosking, D.M. (1988), "Organizing, leadership and skillful process", *Journal of Management Studies*, **25**, 147–66.

Hosking, D.M. (1997), "Organizing, leadership and skillful processes", in K. Grint (ed.), *Leadership: Classical, Contemporary and Critical Appraoches*, Oxford: Oxford University Press, pp. 293–318.

Hosking, D. (2007), "Not leaders, not followers: a post-modern discourse of leadership processes", in B. Shamir, R. Pilai, M. Bligh and M. Uhl-Bien (eds), *Follower-*

Centered Perspectives of Leadership: A Tribute to the Memory of James R. Meindl, Greenwich, CT: Information Age Publishing.

Hunt, S. (1984), "The role of leadership in the construction of reality", in B. Kellerman (ed.), *Leadership: Multidisciplinary Perspectives*, Englewood Cliffs, NJ: Prentice-Hall.

Jackson, B. and K. Parry (2008), *A Very Short, Fairly Interesting, and Reasonably Cheap Book About Leadership*, London: Sage.

Kets de Vries, M.F.R. (2001), "The sociology of leadership in organizations", in J. Smelser and P.B. Baltes (eds), *International Encyclopedia of the Social and Behavioral Sciences*, Oxford: Pergamon, pp. 8573–8.

Lord, R.G. and C.G. Emrich, (2000), "Thinking outside the box by looking inside the box: Extending the cognitive revolution in leadership research", *Leadership Quarterly*, **11**(4), 551–79.

Meindl, J.R., S.B. Ehrlich and J.M. Dukerich (1985), "The romance of leadership", *Administrative Science Quarterly*, **30**, 78–102.

Mills, C.W. ([1959] 2000), *The Sociological Imagination*, Oxford: Oxford University Press.

Morris, A. and S. Staggenborg (2004), "Leadership in social movements", in D. Snow, S. Soule and H.P. Kriesi (eds), *The Blackwell Companion to Social Movements*, New York: Blackwell Publishing, 171–196.

Ospina, S. and E. Foldy (2008), "Building bridges from the margins: the work of leadership in social change organizations", paper presented at the 2008 Academy of Management, Anaheim, CA.

Ospina, S. and G.L.J. Sorenson (2006), "A constructionist lens on leadership: charting new territory", in George R. Goethals and Georgia L.J. Sorenson (eds), *The Quest for a General Theory of Leadership*, Cheltenham, UK and Northampton, MA, USA: Edward Elgar.

Ospina, S. and C. Su (2008), "Weaving color lines: race, ethnicity and the work of leadership in social change organizations", paper presented at the APPAM Research Conference, Los Angeles, CA.

Parry, K. and A. Bryman (2006), "Leadership in organizations", in S.C. Clegg, T. Hardy, T. Lawrence and W. Nord (eds), *The Sage Handbook of Organization Studies*, 2nd edn, Thousand Oaks, CA: Sage, pp. 448–68.

Pearce, C.L. and J.A. Conger (eds) (2003), *Shared Leadership: Reframing the Hows and Whys of Leadership*, Thousand Oaks, CA: Sage Publications.

Pfeffer, J. (1977), "The ambiguity of leadership", *Academy of Management Review*, **2**, 104–12.

Pitsis, T. (2007), "Leadership", in G. Ritzer (ed), *Blackwell Encyclopedia of Sociology*, Malden, MA: Blackwell Publishing.

Polleta, F. (2002), *Freedom is an Endless Meeting: Democracy in American Social Movements*, Chicago, IL and London: Chicago University Press.

Porter, L.W. and G.B. McLaughlin (2006), "Leadership and the organizational context: like the weather?", *The Leadership Quarterly*, **17**, 559–76.

Robnett, Belinda (1997), *How Long? How Long? African American Women in the Struggle for Civil Rights*, New York: Oxford University Press, pp. 12–35.

Rost, J. (1991), *Leadership for the Twenty-first Century*, Westport, CT: Greenwood.

Sacks, K. (1988), *Caring By the Hour*, Chicago, IL: University of Illinois Press.

Selznick, P. (1957), *Leadership in Administration: A Sociological Interpretation*, Berkeley, CA: University of California Press.

Shamir, B. (1999), "Taming charisma for better understanding and greater usefulness: a response to Beyer", *Leadership Quarterly*, **10**(4), 555–62.

Smircich, L. and G. Morgan (1982), "Leadership: the management of meaning", *Journal of Applied Behavioral Science*, **18**(3), 257–73.
Tierney, W. (1987), "The semiotic aspects of leadership: an ethnographic perspective", *American Journal of Semiotics*, **5**, 223–50.
Uhl-Bien, M. (2006), "Relational leadership theory: exploring the social processes of leadership and organizing", *The Leadership Quarterly*, **17**, 654–76.
Vanderslice, V. (1988), "Separating leadership from leaders: an assessment of the effect of leader and follower roles in organizations", *Human Relations*, **41**(9), 677–96.
Wilson, R. and F. Keil (eds) (2001), *The MIT Encyclopedia of Cognitive Sciences*, Cambridge, MA: The MIT Press.
Wood, R. (2002), *Faith in Action: Religion, Race and Democratic Organizing in America*, Chicago, IL: The University of Chicago Press.

9. What makes leadership necessary, possible and effective: the psychological dimensions

George R. Goethals and Crystal L. Hoyt

In 1914 British explorer Ernest Shackleton, along with 27 other men, embarked on an expedition to cross the continent of Antarctica. They would go by dog sled from one side to the other, passing through the South Pole. In early December, as the southern summer solstice drew near, the expedition left a whaling station on tiny South Georgia Island on the ship *Endurance*. *Endurance* was to sail through ice floes to the Antarctic, disembark a small party to cross the continent, and return to South Georgia, and then to England. Another ship would meet the crossing party on the other side of the continent, and bring it home to England.

Things didn't go as planned. The ice floes were unusually thick that summer, and in mid-January, they trapped *Endurance*. She was stuck fast. Shackleton ordered the crew to make winter quarters in the ship, and on the ice. Crossing the Antarctic was now out of the question. Survival would have to do. Shackleton hoped that in the spring, roughly the next November, the floe would break up enough to set *Endurance* free. However, when the ice eventually began to move, it simply crushed the *Endurance*. All 28 men barely managed to get into three small lifeboats, escape the floe before they were also trapped and crushed, and row and sail through wind and waves for days to Elephant Island, a small speck of land at the end of a peninsula stretching into the South Atlantic. They were fortunate to locate Elephant Island. They could easily have missed it, and been blown into the fiercely stormy South Atlantic and certain death.

Shackleton decided that the only hope of rescue was to sail before winter set in again with five other men in the largest of the lifeboats, 800 miles across the South Atlantic to the whaling station they had left more than a year before. Then he would hire a ship to return to rescue the other 22 men. Sailing through icy hurricanes in April, the six miraculously found South Georgia. Shackleton and two others immediately set out on a dangerous march across the island to the whaling station. Once there, Shackleton sailed a ship back to rescue the three others at the landing site. Finally, after several frustrated attempts, Shackleton sailed another ship from Chile that rescued all 22 men on Elephant Island just before that vessel too was trapped in the ice.

Leadership was necessary to survive the first winter on the ice, to guide three small boats to Elephant Island, to cross the South Atlantic in one of them, and eventually to rescue the remaining crew at the end of the second winter. While few groups face the challenges that the crew of *Endurance* overcame, most require leadership to coordinate action and address the interpersonal needs and emotions that arise whenever people work together. Very often, leadership is necessary. Shackleton provided it magnificently. None of the expedition would have survived if he hadn't. We will describe Shackleton's leadership later. For now, his story simply underlines the fact that human achievement, even survival, generally requires leadership.

In 1918, when she was 34 years old, Eleanor Roosevelt, mother of five, and wife of Franklin Roosevelt, Assistant Secretary of the Navy, discovered that her husband had been having an affair with another woman. She decided that she would not divorce Franklin, but that she would lead an independent life, concerning herself with the social issues that had engaged her for many years. Then in 1921, Franklin contracted polio. He never fully regained use of his legs. Eleanor pushed Franklin to continue with his political career, despite his severe disability, and committed herself to helping him. Both the affair and the polio had steeled Eleanor, and she became both an aid to her husband and an independent political and social agent for the causes she believed in.

Thanks to Eleanor's backing, Franklin recovered enough to return to public life. He became Governor of New York, and then in 1932 was elected, for the first of four times, President of the United States. He served until he died in 1945.

Eleanor was a leader for her causes both before and after Franklin died. Before, she pushed for equal rights for women, blacks and the poor, famously resigning from the Daughters of the American Revolution, the DAR, when they refused to let the African-American Marian Anderson sing at Constitution Hall in 1939. After Franklin's death she was a force for human rights during the early days of the United Nations, and she was an influential figure in the Democratic Party until her own death in 1962.

The leadership Eleanor Roosevelt exerted was not necessary in the same way that Shackleton's leadership was so obviously necessary to the survival of the men of the *Endurance*. The people Eleanor led and fought for had been ignored, or worse, for decades. But she showed that leading them, and leading others on their behalf, was possible. Human beings are prepared by both their evolution and their experience to respond to leadership. In this chapter we will explore just what it is about the human condition that makes leadership possible.

When Abraham Lincoln became President in 1861, seven southern states had already seceded from the Union, and four more would quickly follow. Lincoln was committed publicly and privately to preserving the Union. But he faced immense obstacles. The states had divided over slavery, the South's "peculiar institution". Lincoln personally opposed slavery, but he did not set out at first to abolish it. If he had, crucial border states like Maryland and Kentucky would have seceded, and the Union could never have survived. It is said that when an abolitionist told Lincoln that he would have God on his side if he emancipated the slaves, he replied, "It would be good to have God on my side, but I must have Kentucky." Lincoln knew that he had to worry about the hard realities of politics in his government and in the country as a whole if he were to save the Union.

After more than a year of war Lincoln understood that the country needed a more powerful moral purpose to continue the fight. Emancipation would provide that moral purpose. But he must tread carefully in order to keep on his side those who wanted to save the Union but not disturb slavery. Lincoln's skill in navigating the dangerous waters of the Emancipation Proclamation is a marvelous case study in effective leadership. He held enough of the country together to make the decree stick, and ultimately won the war and abolished slavery. Using Lincoln as one powerful example, we will consider how men and women exercise effective leadership, even in the most challenging times.

In this chapter we explore leadership from a psychological perspective. We consider the three questions raised by the examples discussed above. What about the human condition makes leadership necessary, what makes leadership possible, and what makes leadership effective? Considering leadership from these vantage points will allow us to organize a wealth of psychological knowledge about leading and following, and about doing them both well or not well.

WHAT MAKES LEADERSHIP NECESSARY

The case of the *Endurance* underlines the necessity of leadership. The lesson *Endurance* teaches us is best captured by the inroads that evolutionary psychology has made in integrating our understanding of leadership. Van Vugt (2006) argues that in both human and animal groups, decisions need to be made about "what to do and when and where to do it" (p. 355). Someone needs to decide on the timing and type of activity. Where should the group look for food, water and protection from other groups or from predators. The group is best served if some kind of leader/follower structure evolves. Using a game theory analysis, Van Vugt shows that if a group has either too many leaders or not enough, it will not fare well. The groups that find the right mix will be selected for over time. In short, leadership is necessary, and groups that evolve to produce optimal proportions of leaders and followers will succeed.

The *Endurance* expedition had, fortunately, the right mix of leaders and followers. Shackleton himself was at the top of a leadership hierarchy. He made tough decisions about where and when to move, what provisions would be needed at various times and places, and how the larger group should be divided for sleeping in tents, for manning the three lifeboats, and, finally, for the dangerous journey sailing the lifeboat *James Caird* from Elephant Island to South Georgia. In each subgroup there was another leader, one whom Shackleton could absolutely depend on. Most important was Frank Wild, who stayed on Elephant Island with the 21 others left to wait for, and hope for, ultimate rescue. Wild needed to lead that large group, which had to survive for over four winter months on a small beach, converting the remaining two lifeboats into a shelter. He was remarkably successful. In short, as evolutionary theory has emphasized, leadership is often necessary. Consequently, we have evolved so that leadership is also possible.

WHAT MAKES LEADERSHIP POSSIBLE

Evolutionary Theory

Human beings are social animals. As discussed above, that fundamental feature of the human condition makes leadership necessary. Human evolution, in turn, has made us fit for leadership. It has made leadership possible. The universal patterns of leadership and followership that are evidenced across both human and non-human social groups (ranging from honey bees and migratory birds to chimpanzees) support the contention that both leadership and followership are evolved psychological mechanisms. They have persisted through the process of natural selection precisely because they allowed our ancestors to successfully navigate environmental problems (Van Vugt, 2006; De Waal, 1996). According to evolutionary psychologists, the processes of both leadership and followership emerged together over years of human evolution in order to deal effectively with coordination problems associated with group life, such as problems of group movement, and conflict and competition both within and between groups (Tooby and Cosmides, 1992; Van Vugt, 2006; Van Vugt et al., 2008a, 2008b).

As noted above, the social coordination approach to understanding the evolution of both leadership and followership can be nicely illustrated using evolutionary game theory (Van Vugt, 2006). In an example of a simple two-person game, the players find themselves thirsty and looking for a watering hole. For mutual protection, they must travel together. To do so, they must decide whether to lead or follow. If both choose to follow, nothing happens, and they don't achieve their goal. If they both choose to lead, they risk separation and death. Thus the best outcome occurs when one chooses to lead and the other to follow. The leader may get better outcomes than the follower, but even the follower is better off than he or she would be if both tried to lead or both waited to follow. Everyone in the group benefits from coordinating so that there is a leader and a follower, though the leader benefits more. How does evolution help produce the outcome where one person leads and one person follows? Some selection theories suggest that most people are flexible enough to be either a leader or follower, and they make their choices based on the situation. Others suggest that evolution produces an optimal and stable ratio of leaders and followers in a population (Maynard Smith, 1982; West-Eberhard, 2003; Wilson et al., 1996).

This evolutionary framework has important implications for a psychological understanding of leadership. First, it maintains that both leadership and followership emerged together and are complementary strategies. Thus any psychological examination of leadership must consider followership. Also, Van Vugt and colleagues offer a 'mismatch' hypothesis such that processes that were adaptive in ancestral times may no longer work so well in contemporary society. For example, in hunter-gatherer times leadership 'roles', per se, did not exist. Consequently, when a person led, his or her behavior was attributed, appropriately, to their personality. However, in modern society when people lead because of their specific roles, evolutionary adaptation may lead people to be too quick to attribute their behaviors to their personality as opposed to their role, making the fundamental attribution error (Tetlock, 1985).

Terror Management Theory

Another theoretical approach to understanding what makes leadership possible maintains that our need to identify with and follow leaders stems from our attempts to cope with our unique existential dilemma. According to Terror Management Theory (TMT), humans are predisposed to face an existential dilemma because (1) we, like other animals, have an inborn desire for self-preservation, and (2) we, unlike other animals, have an advanced cognitive capacity for abstract thinking and self-reflection which renders us aware of our ultimate mortality (Greenberg et al., 1986; Solomon et al., 1991). This awareness of our impending death is potentially terrifying. Consequently, humans have developed ways of coping with this prospective terror. We have developed cultural worldviews that give us shared conceptions of reality that offer structure, permanence and meaning to life. These worldviews not only can provide us with symbolic and literal immortality (for example, fame or a promised afterlife), but also confer self-esteem, which buffers us from death-related anxiety. If we live up to the standards of our worldview, we can feel good about being a positive member of our group (Pyszczynski et al., 2005).

One way humans manage their fear of death is to identify and support leaders who confirm their worldview and make them feel they are a part of something larger than themselves (Pyszczynski et al., 2003). When faced with near certain death, the men in Shackleton's crew surrendered even more fully to his leadership in order to cope with their death-related anxiety. Shackleton made them feel a worthy part of a meaningful and important venture. Research has demonstrated that this desire to identify with and support a leader is not indiscriminate. Cohen et al. (2004) found that mortality salience led to more positive evaluations of charismatic gubernatorial candidates and less positive evaluations of relationship-oriented candidates. In addition to showing a preference for charismatic leaders under mortality salience, people also evidence increased support for leaders with masculine rather than feminine qualities (Hoyt et al., 2009). In sum, terror management theory provides a motivational account of what makes leadership possible. It helps us cope with the potentially terrifying thoughts of our own mortality.

Obedience to Authority

The evolutionary approach and the terror management perspective on leadership both contend that seeking a leader and the need to follow that leader are more or less hard-wired in humans. This argument is bolstered by a long line of research in social psychology demonstrating a startling human propensity to obey authority figures. This proclivity was clearly demonstrated by the men on the *Endurance* who readily obeyed the directives of "the boss". It was observed more dramatically in Stanley Milgram's well-known learning and shock studies (1973). Participants were brought to a laboratory under the guise of participating in an experiment examining the impact of punishment on learning. The participants were assigned the role of "teacher", and their job was to administer increasingly strong and painful shocks to the "learner", an experimental confederate, when he incorrectly identified previously learned word pairs. In the initial experiments, "stark authority was pitted against the subjects' strongest moral imperatives against hurting others, and, with the subjects' ears ringing with the screams of the victims, authority won more often than not" (Milgram, 1973). In the best-known version of Milgram's studies, nearly two-thirds of participants obeyed the authority figure to the end. These studies and others reveal the powerful situational influence of authority figures and the robust tendency of humans to obey – even when there is no pre-existing relationship between the follower and leader and even if the leader has questionable authority. Importantly, Milgram's initial findings have been replicated using a range of different paradigms (Blass, 2000; Burger, 2009). According to Milgram, this inclination for obedience "flows from the logical necessities of social organization … if we are to have society – then we must have members of society amenable to organizational imperatives" (Blass, 2002: 74). We can see then that both evolution and social necessity have made leadership possible.

Social Perception

One result of having evolved from primates, according to Gardner (1995), is that we expect leadership. Our expectations regarding leadership are part of human beings' complex cognitive capacities. They are essential to understanding what makes leadership possible. A social cognitive approach to understanding leadership asserts that leadership emerges from various cognitive and attributional processes. Social cognitive perspectives range from acknowledging that followers' perceptual processes play an important role in leadership processes to an extreme social constructionist view in which leadership is construed as existing solely in the eye, or the mind, of the beholder (Forsyth and Nye, 2008). On the social constructionist end of the spectrum, Meindl's (1995) work on the "romance of leadership" suggests that leadership has extraordinary explanatory power for people, such that people tend to discount or underweight the causal impact of factors other than leadership on group processes and outcomes. They attribute the group's success or failure to the leader.

Besides believing that group outcomes are attributable to the leader, people have preconceptions regarding the traits, characteristics and behaviors that make for a good leader (Lord et al., 1984). These tacit beliefs, or implicit leadership theories, describe prototypical leadership focusing around both task and people skills and include qualities such as sensitivity, intelligence, dedication and dynamism (Eden and Leviatan, 1975; Epitropaki and Martin, 2004; Kenney et al., 1996; Offerman et al., 1994). According to the prototype matching hypothesis, followers categorize people as being a leader or not a leader to the extent that their traits and behaviors match these prototypical leadership characteristics (Lord, 2005; Lord and Maher, 1991). Once categorized as leaders, the leader schema is activated and leads people to perceive, encode and recall information about the leader and the leaders' effectiveness that fits the leader schema (Lord, 1985; Lord et al., 1982).

While these implicit leadership theories and leader schemas can facilitate information-processing, they can also result in biased perceptions and evaluations, thereby making leadership more or *less* possible for certain individuals. For example, rather unimportant traits, such as attractiveness, are often part of our implicit theories, thus rendering us vulnerable to the "Warren Harding

Effect", or perceiving an attractive, but incompetent individual as having leadership potential (Gladwell, 2005). Also, ratings of leaders often reflect people's leader schemas more so than the qualities of the particular leader they are evaluating (Foti and Lord, 1987). In addition, leader schemas are widely associated with certain social identities, such as being white and male. Thus people of color and women generally don't fit the schema, making it difficult for them to be seen as leaders. Role congruity theory explains that the traits embraced in most leader schemas are inconsistent with the stereotypic traits of women (for example, sensitivity, helpfulness) but are consistent with the stereotypic traits of men (for example, assertiveness, competitiveness; Eagly and Karau, 2002). This incongruity between our preconceptions of leaders and our preconceptions of women initially stood in the way of Eleanor Roosevelt being a successful leader. While she overcame these prejudices, they have made it difficult for many other women to attain top leadership positions and also to be perceived as effective in them.

Social Identity Theory of Leadership

Social identity theory provides a cognitive approach to understanding what makes leadership possible, viewing it as emerging from normal social-cognitive processes associated with group life (Hogg, 2001; 2008). The foundations of this approach lie in social identity theory's basic principles that people's self-concepts and self-esteem are strongly influenced by the groups to which they belong (Tajfel and Turner, 1979). The part of an individual's self-concept that derives from membership in social groups is referred to as a social identity (Tajfel, 1981). These social identities consist of prototypes, or a general set of attributes that characterize a particular group one belongs to and distinguish it from other groups. According to social identity theory, individuals automatically place people, including themselves, into social categories, and derive a sense of self-esteem from their group memberships. Thus their self-concept is, in part, dependent on their evaluation of their own group (ingroup) in comparison to other groups (outgroups).

According to the social identity theory of leadership, as group members identity more strongly with their group, the perception, evaluation and effectiveness of the leader is increasingly based on the followers perceiving the leader to possess prototypical properties of the group (Fielding and Hogg, 1997; Hains et al., 1997; Hogg et al., 2006). This social identity approach acknowledges that leader schemas also play a role in the perception of leaders. However, they play a lesser role to the extent that group membership is valued and salient.

According to the social identity perspective, highly prototypical group members are more influential than less prototypical members for a number of reasons: they are consensually popular and liked, through their status they can gain compliance from other group members, and they are likely to behave in group-serving manners, thus cultivating trust from the other group members (Hogg, 2008). This social attraction and perceived legitimacy gives the prototypical members the latitude to be innovative and non-conformist (see idiosyncrasy credits below) and the sum of these attributions imbues prototypical members with perceived charismatic personalities. The role of social identity can be seen in responses to Lincoln's leadership. In 1860 Lincoln was a prototypical member of the Republican Party. This helped him win the party's presidential nomination. In office, Lincoln was well-liked and was perceived to be consistently acting in the best interest of the country. Through the trust those perceptions cultivated, he earned the latitude to announce his Emancipation Proclamation in 1862, and later endorse the passage of the Thirteenth Amendment to the Constitution.

Legitimacy and Idiosyncrasy Credit

Both the research on perceptions of leaders and the social identity approach emphasize that leadership is both constrained by and made possible by followers. Leadership is a process in which followers are as integral as leaders. Followers' perceptions, expectations and attributions influence who is seen as appropriate for the leader role and how leaders are evaluated. One of the most important attribution followers make about any leader is his or her legitimacy. Hollander (1993) emphasizes that the leader's legitimacy is accorded or withdrawn by followers, and that legitimacy functions "as the latitude followers provide a leader to bring about change" (p. 33). By conferring legitimacy upon a leader, followers strongly impact the leader's behaviors, social influence and ultimately group performance (Hollander, 1993).

Attributions of legitimacy empower leaders to exercise both influence and power in large part through what Hollander (1958, 1993) called idiosyncrasy credits. According to the idiosyncrasy credit model, leaders earn "credits" from followers over time by demonstrating competence in achieving group goals and loyalty in conforming to the group. Followers allow leaders to spend down some of their accumulation of attributed credits by tolerating later innovation or non-conformity from the leader. Indeed, another term for idiosyncrasy credit is "the credit to deviate". The determination of competence and loyalty stems from many factors, some of which may or may not actually signal those attributes, such as seniority in a group or quantity of participation. Followers are particularly unlikely to give credits to people who are perceived to be different, that is, group members with low prototypicality, or who have characteristics that are not valued in society, such as those with lower socioeconomic status. In this way we see some of the common themes in the social identity and idiosyncrasy credit approaches to leadership. Although the idiosyncrasy credit model suggests that leaders spend down credit when they deviate, leaders are expected to deviate to some degree and thus successful innovations can increase, as opposed to deplete, credit.

WHAT MAKES LEADERSHIP EFFECTIVE?

When we think about the leadership of Shackleton, Eleanor Roosevelt and Lincoln, we see two aspects of their effectiveness. First, they were successful in getting others to follow them. Second, they led their followers in ways that accomplished goals that were important for both themselves and their followers. In this section we focus on both these aspects of leader effectiveness.

How Leaders Induce Others to Follow

The initial success of inducing others to follow depends on both personal and situational qualities. As discussed above, crisis situations and threats, particularly those that remind us of our mortality, make people more likely to follow leaders. But the characteristics of leaders probably contribute more to the equation. Roughly coordinated to our schemas or implicit theories about the traits and behaviors of leaders, there are actual traits and behaviors associated with leading, and successfully inducing others to follow.

Emergent leaders typically have personal qualities that are captured by trait research that has identified the so-called Big Five (Hogan and Hogan, 2004, encyclopedia article). Factor analytic studies show that people differ on five major traits. These are Surgency (also called Extraversion); Stability (also called its opposite, Neuroticism); Agreeableness; Conscientiousness; and Openness (also called Intellectance). Surgency is best illustrated with Ernest Shackleton. He was outgoing and forceful, and could dominate when he had to. Eleanor Roosevelt may be the best example of Stability. Through many crises and challenges she kept her emotions in check. She knew how to steadily persist and maintain her self-control. Perhaps Lincoln is the best example of Agreeableness. He was certainly more agreeable that the brusque Shackleton. His sense of humor not only helped him, it engaged others and made them feel comfortable. Both Lincoln and Roosevelt were Conscientious. Perhaps Roosevelt was the better organized of the two, a hallmark of conscientiousness. All three were open and intellectually alive. Roosevelt may have been the most open, then Lincoln, and third, Shackleton. They were sensitive to others' thoughts and feelings, and to different ideas about how to achieve their goals. Importantly, their Openness did not mean that they were not decisive. All of them were unwavering in their principles and stood by their choices.

Another trait that is closely tied to getting others to follow is emotional intelligence (Lopes and Salovey, 2008). People who can perceive, understand, use and manage emotions – both their own and others' – have an advantage in leading. Lincoln had uncanny talent for these skills.

In many situations, a personal quality that is important in attracting followers is charisma. As noted above, crisis is one circumstance where people are especially prone to look for charismatic leadership. Charisma has been defined in many ways, including Max Weber's idea of the individual who is perceived to have superhuman traits and Bass's (1997) idea of the person who is worthy of emulation or identification. Perhaps charisma is one of those qualities that is hard to define but easy to identify. President John F. Kennedy was widely perceived as having charisma. He was handsome, suave and articulate, and he moved with grace and self-assurance. Many people had a positive emotional reaction to seeing and hearing him. Whatever charisma is, he had it. Not surprisingly, charisma is associated with greatness ratings of US Presidents (Emrich et al., 2001) and inspiring leadership more generally (Riggio and Riggio, 2008). It's an important quality in inducing followers to go along with a leader.

While traits are important, and the pure personal qualities of a leader have much to do with liking and then following, behavior is equally important. Many years ago Stogdill (1974) identified two major categories of leader behavior, "initiating structure" and "showing consideration". Bales (1958; 1970) and others correspondingly discussed task-related vs. socioemotional behaviors and roles. More recently Bass has discussed intellectual stimulation and individualized consideration as behaviors that effective leaders perform in order to induce following. This pair of behaviors, whatever they are called, are central to people's implicit leadership theories and are most relevant to understanding leadership in small groups. Shackleton was most focused on tasks and structure in leading the men of *Endurance*, but he acted to address individual emotional challenges as well, notably by taking the men most likely to make trouble into his own tent to absorb their grievances and keep them from spreading their discontents.

Another set of behaviors that is relevant in both large and small groups is one comprising persuasion or, as Howard Gardner discusses it, storytelling or narrative. Leaders must provide a vision or narrative that frames past experience and points the way toward future behavior. They must provide rationales and arguments for group action. Abraham Lincoln's second inaugural address provides a good example of such framing. He suggested that the Civil War was visited on both north and south as God's punishment for the "offense" of slavery: it was easy to believe, he argued, "that American Slavery was one of those offenses which, in the providence of God, must needs come, but which … He now wills to remove". Thus Lincoln initially provided an interpretive framework for the past and present. In his conclusion Lincoln went beyond framing the past and pointed the way for the future: "With malice toward none; with charity for all; with firmness in the right as God gives to see the right, let us strive on to finish the work we are in". Leaders persuade using both reason and "peripheral cues", such as their own credibility, rhetorical flourishes, or a long list of arguments, that signal to an audience that the leader is to be believed (Petty and Cacioppo, 1986).

Related to persuasion is a behavioral aspect of charisma. Charismatic leaders not only persuade, they also provide a compelling vision, and followers increasingly define themselves in terms of the work they do toward making that vision a reality. This behavior is called "inspirational motivation" by Bass. It is well illustrated in memorable phrases from Kennedy's speeches such as:

> In the long history of the world, only a few generations have been granted the role of defending freedom in its hour of maximum danger. I do not shrink from this responsibility – I welcome it.... The energy, the faith, the devotion which we bring to this endeavor will light our country and all who serve it – and the glow from that fire can truly light the world.

Part of charisma then is a certain kind of persuasion. Researchers have demonstrated the importance of both images and metaphors in charismatic persuasion (Emrich et al., 2001; Riggio and Riggio, 2008).

In addition to engaging in both task-related and socioemotionally-oriented behaviors, and in persuasion, leaders also employ various kinds of power. French and Raven (1959) distinguished reward and coercive power, by which leaders control followers' outcomes, and also legitimate, referent, expert, and informational power by which leaders use their position, their attractiveness or similarity to group members, and their knowledge to try to engage followers voluntarily. Eleanor Roosevelt had little or no reward or coercive power, so used her expertise and to some extent her referent power, as a woman, to move her followers. Shackleton used reward, coercive, legitimate and expert power. Lincoln used them all.

Another important element related to the exercise of power concerns how authorities use legitimate power. Leaders gain much more voluntary compliance with their decisions and their urgings if they seem to be based on fair decision-making procedures (Tyler and Lind, 1992; Tyler, 2005). Such compliance turns out to be based considerably more on whether the leader's decision uses fair procedures, or "procedural justice", than whether it gives followers what they want. Followers trust that they will get fair outcomes over time if the leader uses fair procedures. Thus it is important for leaders to employ unbiased, ethical and respectful procedures in making decisions.

In sum, leaders who are effective in mobilizing followers have certain personal characteristics and employ a certain set of behaviors. We should remember, however, that leadership is only meaningful with respect to followers, and followers' traits and behaviors interact with those of leaders. This fact means that traits like openness and behaviors such as procedural justice occupy a special place in effective leadership.

What Helps Leaders Successfully Achieve their Goals?

Getting people to follow is one thing. Leading them toward successful goal achievement is another. Kaiser et al. (2008) point out that the qualities that allow leaders to emerge are not the same as those that make them effective. Effective leadership rests on a combination and interaction of personal and situational attributes.

Ronald Heifetz's (1994) approach to leadership emphasizes leaders helping followers do adaptive work, which in turn means facing reality and thinking about how group goals and values can best be advanced, given that reality. Shackleton worked hard to get his sometimes reluctant followers to face hard facts: crossing the Antarctic was out of the question; the only hope for survival was for a small group to manage an extremely dangerous crossing of 800 miles of the South Atlantic. The leader who can best help followers assess and adapt to reality is a leader with high degrees of intelligence, or, more elusively, judgment. Intellectual brilliance is a predictor of rated presidential greatness (Simonton, 1987) and brain power is acknowledged as an important component in leadership effectiveness by researchers (for example, Goleman, 1998) who focus on other qualities. Abraham Lincoln was clearly gifted intellectually, and his judgment in knowing just how far to push the Union toward emancipation at any given time was key to saving the Union. In addition to general intelligence, specific competencies are important for effective leadership. In line with Hollander's idiosyncrasy credit model whereby followers grant credits on the basis of competencies relevant to the group, Van Vugt notes that followers "process task relevant skills quickly" (2006: 362).

While leader attributes are important for group success, one of the most intriguing lines of psychological research on leadership effectiveness points to combinations of leadership style and situational condition as being determinative. This approach is captured in Fiedler's (1993) contingency model of leadership effectiveness. Fiedler's early research distinguished leaders who primarily value interpersonal relations from people who primarily value successful task completion. However, at first Fiedler was unable to correlate leadership style with group effectiveness. After puzzling over his data he discovered that each style is effective in different situations. Every situation has more or less situational control for the leader, and is therefore more or less favorable for leadership. Decades of research have basically supported a model in which the task-oriented leader is more effective in very favorable or very unfavorable situations, while the more interpersonally-oriented leaders are more effective in moderately favorable situations. The demands of high, medium and low favorability or control situations seem to match the proclivities of either task- or relationship-oriented leaders, producing the main findings. Taken together, the research on what makes leadership effective shows that personal leader qualities are important, but that there has to be a match or mesh of the leader's qualities with what the situation demands.

Effective decision-making is critical to leadership success. There are a number of group processes that can undermine good decision-making such as biases in the way information is shared within the group (Stasser and Titus, 1985), the tendency toward making extreme decisions (Levine and Moreland, 1998), and extremely strong desires for group consensus. All of these tendencies can be seen in perhaps the best known example of flawed decision-making, *groupthink*, a distorted mode of information processing resulting in poor decisions (Janis, 1972). A number of causes of groupthink have been identified including extremely cohesive groups, being isolated from outside scrutiny, lacking procedures to evaluate alternatives, having a leader with a strong, directive leadership style, and high levels of stress or external threat. As a result, group members rationalize their group's actions and invoke stereotypes of opposing groups, maintain an illusion of invulnerability and an exaggerated belief in their group's morality, and feel extreme pressure to conform to the group and sustain group cohesiveness. Lincoln implicitly understood these factors associated with poor decision-making. His construction of a "team of rivals" by bringing together his defeated opponents for the presidential nomination (Kearns Goodwin, 2005) ensured that his cabinet would not be overly cohesive or isolated from outside scrutiny, and would include multiple viewpoints and adequate evaluation of alternatives.

CONCLUSION

The psychological perspective on leadership begins with recognizing that the human condition makes leadership and coordination necessary for group success, and that human evolution has responded to this reality by making us prepared for leadership. We are prepared, to different degrees, to lead or to follow, to both command and obey. We are also prepared to think about what it means to lead and follow. We have implicit theories, probably both learned and evolutionarily based, about what leaders do and what they are like. Sometimes the way we think about leaders or respond to them is not entirely rational or adaptive, as we see with some of the terror management research. For better or worse, we are leading and following as well as social animals.

Our schemas about what leaders are like fit quite well the characteristics of people who emerge as leaders. Those with traits such as charisma and extraversion get others to follow. We think that a somewhat different set of individual characteristics and group processes make for the most effective leadership, judged by whether groups achieve their goals. Overall the psychological approach to leadership alerts us to both learned and evolutionarily based influences on how people think and act in groups, and whether they lead, and are led, effectively.

REFERENCES

Bales, R.F. (1958), "Role and role conflict", in E.E. Maccoby, T.M. Newcomb and E.L. Hartley (eds), *Readings in Social Psychology*, New York: Holt.

Bales, R.F. (1970), *Personality and Interpersonal Behavior*, New York: Holt, Rinehart, and Winston.

Bass, B.M. (1997), "Does the transactional–transformational leadership paradigm transcend organizational and national boundaries?", *American Psychologist*, **52**, 130–39.

Blass, T. (ed.) (2000), *Obedience to Authority: Current Perspectives on the Milgram Paradigm*, Mahwah, NJ: Lawrence Erlbaum.

Blass, T. (2002), "The man who shocked the world", *Psychology Today*, March/April, pp. 68–74.

Burger, J.M. (2009), "Replicating Milgram: would people still obey today?", *American Psychologist*, 1–11.

Cohen, F., S. Solomon, M. Maxfield, T. Pyszczynski and J. Greenberg (2004), "Fatal attraction: the effects of mortality salience on evaluations of charismatic, task-oriented, and relationship-oriented leaders", *Psychological Science*, **15**(12), 846–51.

de Waal, F.B.M. (1996), *Good Natured: The Origins of Right and Wrong in Human and Other Animals*, Cambridge, MA: Harvard University Press.

Eagly, A.H. and S.J. Karau (2002), "Role congruity theory of prejudice toward female leaders", *Psychological Review*, **109**, 573–98.

Eden, D. and U. Leviatan (1975), "Implicit leadership theory as a determinant of the factor structure underlying supervisory behavior scales", *Journal of Applied Psychology*, **60**, 736–41.

Emrich, C.G., H.H. Brower, J.M. Feldman and H. Garland (2001), "Images in words: presidential rhetoric, charisma, and greatness", *Administrative Science Quarterly*, **46**, 527–57.

Epitropaki, O. and R. Martin (2004), "Implicit leadership theories in applied settings: factor structure, generalizability, and stability over time", *Journal of Applied Psychology*, **89**, 293–310.

Fiedler, F.E. (1993), "The leadership situation and the black box in contingency theories", in M.M. Chemers and R. Ayman (eds), *Leadership Theory and Research: Perspectives and Directions,* San Diego, CA: Academic Press, pp. 1–28.

Fielding, K.S. and Hogg, M.A. (1997), "Social identity, self categorization, and leadership: a field study of small interactive groups", *Group Dynamics: Theory, Research, and Practice*, **1**, 39–51.

Forsyth, D.R. and J.L. Nye (2008), "Seeing and being a leader: the perceptual, cognitive, and interpersonal roots of conferred influence", in C.L. Hoyt, G.R. Goethals and D.R. Forsyth (eds), *Leadership at the Crossroads: Leadership and Psychology*, vol.1, Westport, CT: Praeger.

Foti, R.J. and R.G. Lord (1987), "Prototypes and scripts: the effects of alternative methods of processing information on rating accuracy", *Organizational Behavior and Human Decision Processes*, **39**, 318–40.

French, J.R.P. and B. Raven (1959), "The bases of social power", in D. Cartwright (ed.), *Studies in Social Power*, Ann Arbor. MI: Institute for Social Research, pp. 150–67.

Gardner, H. (1995), *Leading Minds: An Anatomy of Leadership,* New York: Basic Books.

Gaulin, S.J.C. and D.H. McBurney (2001), *Psychology: An Evolutionary Approach*, Upper Saddle River, NJ: Prentice-Hall.

Gladwell, M. (2005), *Blink: The Power of Thinking Without Thinking*, New York: Little, Brown and Co.

Goleman, D. (1998), "What makes a leader?", *Harvard Business Review*, November–December, pp. 93–102.

Greenberg, J., T. Pyszczynski and S. Solomon (1986), "The causes and consequences of a need for self-esteem: a terror management theory", in R.F. Baumeister (ed.), *Public Self and Private Self*, New York: Springer-Verlag, pp. 189–212.

Hains, S.C., M.A. Hogg, and J.M. Duck (1997), "Self-categorization and leadership: effects of group prototypicality and leader stereotypicality", *Personality and Social Psychology Bulletin*, **23**, 1087–100.

Heifetz, R.A. (1994), *Leadership Without Easy Answers*, Cambridge, MA: Harvard.

Hogan, R. and J. Hogan (2004), "Big five personality traits", in G.R. Goethals, G.J. Sorenson and J.M. Burns (eds), *Encyclopedia of Leadership*, London: Sage Publications.

Hogg, M.A. (2001), "A social identity theory of leadership", *Personality and Social Psychology Review*, **5**, 184–200.

Hogg, M.A. (2008), "Social identity theory of leadership", in C.L. Hoyt, G.R. Goethals and D.R. Forsyth (eds), *Leadership at the Crossroads: Leadership and Psychology*, vol.1, Westport, CT: Praeger.

Hogg, M.A., K.S. Fielding, D. Johnson, B. Masser, E. Russell, E. and A. Svensson (2006), "Demographic category membership and leadership in small groups: a social identity analysis", *The Leadership Quarterly*, **17**, 335–50.

Hollander, E.P. (1958), "Conformity, status, and idiosyncracy credit", *Psychological Review*, **65**, 117–27.

Hollander, E.P. (1993), "Legitimacy, power and influence: a perspective on relational features of leadership", in M.M. Chemers and R. Ayman (eds), *Leadership Theory and Research: Perspectives and Directions,* San Diego, CA: Academic Press, pp. 29–47.

Hoyt, C.L., S. Simon and L. Reid (2009), "Choosing the best (wo)man for the job: the effects of mortality, salience, sex, and gender stereotypes on leader evaluations", *Leadership Quarterly*, **20**, 233–46.

Janis, I. (1972), *Victims of Groupthink*, Boston, MA: Houghton-Mifflin.

Kaiser, R.B., R. Hogan and S.B. Craig (2008), "Leadership and the fate of organizations", *American Psychologist*, **63**, 96–110.

Kearns Goodwin, D. (2005), *Team of Rivals: The Political Genius of Abraham Lincoln*, New York: Simon and Schuster.

Kenney, R.A., B.M. Schwartz-Kenney and J. Blascovich (1996), "Implicit leadership theories: defining leaders described as worthy of influence", *Personality and Social Psychology Bulletin*, **22**, 1128–43.
Levine, J.M. and R.L. Moreland (1998), "Small groups", in D. Gilbert, S. Fiske and G. Lindzey (eds), *The Handbook of Social Psychology*, vol. 2, 4th edn, Boston, MA: McGraw-Hill, pp. 415–69.
Lopes, P.N. and P. Salovey (2008), "Emotional intelligence and leadership: implications for leader development", in C.L. Hoyt, G.R. Goethals and D.R. Forsyth (eds), *Leadership at the Crossroads: Leadership and Psychology*, vol. 1, Westport, CT: Praeger.
Lord, R.G. (1985), "An information processing approach to social perceptions, leadership, and behavioral measurement in organizations", *Research in Organizational Behavior*, **7**, 87–128.
Lord, R.G. (2005), "Preface: implicit leadership theory", in B. Schyns and J.R. Meindl (eds), *Implicit Leadership Theories: Essays and Explorations*, Greenwich, CT: Information Age Publishing, pp. ix–xiv.
Lord, R.G., and K.J. Maher (1991), *Leadership and Information Processing: Linking Perceptions and Performance*, Boston, MA: Unwin Hyman, Inc.
Lord, R.G., R.J. Foti and C.L. De Vader (1984), "A test of leadership categorization theory: internal structure, information processing, and leadership perceptions", *Organizational Behavior and Human Performance*, **34**, 343–78.
Lord, R.G., R.J. Foti and J.S. Phillips (1982), "A theory of leadership categorization", in H.G. Hunt, U. Sekaran and C. Schriescheim (eds), *Leadership: Beyond Establishment Views*, Carbondale, IL: Southern Illinois University Press, pp. 104–21.
Maynard Smith, J. (1982), *Evolution and the Theory of Games*, Cambridge: Cambridge University Press.
Meindl, J.R. (1995), "The romance of leadership as a follower-centric theory: a social constructionist approach", *Leadership Quarterly*, **6**, 329–41.
Milgram, S. (1973), 'Obedience to authority: an experimental view', *Harpers Magazine* (December), 62–77.
Offerman, L.R., J.K. Kennedy Jr and P.W. Wirtz (1994), "Implicit leadership theories: content, structure, and generalizability", *Leadership Quarterly*, **5**, 43–58.
Petty, R.E. and J.T. Cacioppo (1986), "The elaboration likelihood model of persuasion", in L. Berkowitz (ed.), *Advances in Experimental Social Psychology*, **19**, New York: Academic, pp. 123–205.
Pyszczynski, T., J. Greenberg and S. Solomon (2005), "The machine in the ghost: a dual process model of defense against conscious and unconscious death-related thought", in J.P. Forgas, K.D. Williams and S.M. Laham (eds), *Social Motivation: Conscious and Unconscious Processes*, New York: Cambridge University Press, pp. 40–54.
Pyszczynski, T., S. Solomon and J. Greenberg (2003), *In the Wake of 9/11: The Psychology of Terror*, Washington, DC: American Psychological Association.
Riggio, R.E. and H. Riggio (2008), "Social psychology and charismatic leadership", in C.L. Hoyt, G.R. Goethals, and D.R. Forsyth (eds), *Leadership at the Crossroads: Leadership and Psychology*, vol.1, Westport, CT: Praeger.
Simonton, D.K. (1987), *Why Presidents Succeed: A Political Psychology of Leadership*, New Haven: Yale.
Solomon, S., J. Greenberg and T. Pyszczynski (1991), "A terror management theory of social behavior: the psychological functions of self-esteem and cultural worldviews", in M. Zanna (ed.), *Advances in Experimental Social Psychology*, vol. 24, Orlando, FL: Academic Press, pp. 93–159.

Stasser, G. and W. Titus (1985), "Pooling and unshared information in group decision making: biased information sampling during discussion", *Journal of Personality and Social Psychology*, **48**, 1467–78.

Stogdill, R. (1974), *Handbook of Leadership*, New York: Free Press.

Tajfel, H. (1981), *Human Groups and Social Categories*, Cambridge University Press, Cambridge.

Tajfel, H. and J.C. Turner (1979), "An integrative theory of intergroup conflict", in W.G. Austin and S. Worchel (eds), *The Social Psychology of Intergroup Relations*, Monterey, CA: Brooks-Cole.

Tetlock, P.E. (1985), "Accountability: a social check on the fundamental attribution error", *Social Psychology Quarterly*, **48**, 227–36.

Tooby, J. and L. Cosmides (1992), "The psychological foundations of culture", in J. Barkow, L. Cosmides and J. Tooby (eds), *The Adapted Mind: Evolutionary Psychology and the Generation of Culture*, New York: Oxford University Press, pp. 19–136.

Tyler, T.R. (2005), "Process based leadership: fair procedures, identification, and the acceptance of change", *Leadership Quarterly*, **16**, 121–53.

Tyler, T.R. and E.A. Lind (1992), "A relational model of authority in groups", in M.P. Zanna (ed.), *Advances in Experimental Social Psychology*, vol. **25,** San Diego, CA: Academic Press, pp. 115–91.

Van Vugt, M. (2006), "The evolutionary origins of leadership and followership", *Personality and Social Psychology Review*, **10**, 354–72.

Van Vugt, M., R. Hogan, and R. Kaiser (2008), "Leadership, followership, and evolution: some lessons from the past", *American Psychologist*, **63**, 182–96.

Van Vugt, M., D. Johnson, R.B. Kaiser and R. O'Gorman (2008), "Evolution and the social psychology of leadership: the mismatch hypothesis", in C.L. Hoyt, G.R. Goethals and D.R. Forsyth (eds), *Leadership at the Crossroads: Leadership and Psychology*, vol.1, Westport, CT: Praeger.

West-Eberhard, M.J. (2003), *Developmental Plasticity and Evolution*, Oxford: Oxford University Press.

Wilson, D.S., D. Near and R. Miller (1996), "Machiavellianism: a synthesis of the evolutionary and psychological literatures", *Psychological Bulletin*, **119**, 285–99.

10. The management perspective: engineering effective leadership in organizations

Ronald E. Riggio

The commonly held belief about business schools, particularly by our colleagues in the humanities and social sciences, is that the work done in B-schools is primarily applied and not very scientific. When it comes to the management perspective on leadership, however, nothing could be further from the truth. In fact, one argument that can be made about the management/organizational behavior approach to leadership is that it was overly scientific for many decades, and not very practitioner-oriented. As a result, concepts and theories of leadership by management scholars were quite theoretical, with some being very difficult or nearly impossible to translate for the practice of leadership. The approaches to applying management and leadership theories taken by management scholars from the 1950s through to the 1970s were very leader-centric and involved manipulations of leader/manager behavior in order to "engineer" effectiveness. That orientation, one that we believe is passing, is represented in the chapter title.

It is also impossible to discuss management's contributions to leadership studies without acknowledging the contributions that psychology made in influencing the thought and research of management scholars. In many ways, management and psychology are inextricably linked and will likely continue to be so because of the many psychologically trained scholars in departments of management. As a result, many of the key leadership theories that have influenced the study of leadership in business schools have psychological origins, or are "hybrids" of theories emanating from management and psychology.

MANAGEMENT VS. LEADERSHIP

Before we look at theories of leadership popular in management circles, it is critical to discuss this core question discussed in business circles – the distinction (if there is any) between management and leadership. Typically, *leadership* refers to the higher-level functions of a person with authority or influence in a group – providing strategic direction, overseeing the decision-making process, initiating and managing change. *Management* is usually used to describe the administrative functions of persons with authority or influence – monitoring and controlling process, budgeting, focusing on standards. Although this issue is not exclusive to the business world, it is given greater consideration here than in other disciplines. In fact, some disciplines may avoid the term *management* altogether, associating it exclusively with the world of business.

The distinction between management and leadership from the business/management perspective is more than just semantics. It represents a fundamental shift in how management scholars have looked at managers and leaders in organizations, as we shall see later in our discussion of theories of leadership. Kotter (1990) sees a major difference between management and leadership. For example, managers plan, organize, and provide structure. Leaders strategize, provide a vision, and try to build commitment to the vision and common purpose. These are essentially different "lenses" through which to view the process of moving a collective forward. Similarly, managers use incentives and disciplinary actions to encourage desirable behavior and discourage the undesirable (or the inert). Leaders energize, inspire and empower followers in order to get positive results.

When the field of management began to make the shift from viewing those in positions of power and control as mere "managers" to viewing them as taking on the higher-level "leadership" activities (for example, *visioning* as opposed to *planning*; *strategizing* as opposed to *allocating resources*), it caused a fundamental shift in both the theories of leadership emanating from the business schools, and in management scholars' thinking about management/leadership.

EARLY INFLUENCES ON MANAGEMENT AND LEADERSHIP

Two divergent perspectives represent the roots of modern management. The first can be seen in the writings of Adam Smith. In the *Wealth of Nations*, Smith (1776) discusses the management of industrial operations with the goal of increasing manufacturing productivity. This line of thinking is later championed by Frederick Taylor (1911) and continues throughout the majority of the twentieth century. The focus here is the manager as the engineer of human performance, structuring the work situation to coordinate the efforts of subordinates to maximize output.

The second perspective was championed by Mary Parker Follett (1949), and involves a focus on the harnessing of followers, including their input and initiative, with the leader and followers together following the common purpose – the shared goals and purpose of the organization. This perspective was carried forward by Elton Mayo (1933), and later by Peter Drucker (1954). In the 1980s this focus on the follower reappears and is still strong in the management research literature, although a focus on more complex theories of leadership is coming to the front in the twenty-first century.

These two themes of focus on production and focus on people re-emerge in the psychological literature from the behavioral studies of leadership conducted in the 1950s and 1960s at Ohio State University and the University of Michigan (Kahn and Katz, 1960; Stogdill and Coons, 1957; see Riggio, 2007, for an overview). In both research programs, the dichotomy between the leader's focus on the task/productivity and the leader's focus on the followers/relationships is the major finding. The task versus relationship focus of these behavioral studies of leadership had a significant impact as a starting point for management-based theories of leadership emerging in the 1960s, 1970s, and beyond. Most recently, a meta-analysis determined that these two behavioral constructs are both significantly related to leader effectiveness, with behaviors focusing on followers and relationships having a slightly stronger impact (Judge et al., 2004)

SITUATIONAL THEORIES OF LEADERSHIP

Once it became clear that leader behaviors/style could be dichotomized as task-focused vs. follower-focused, it was necessary to explain how two nearly diametrically opposed styles of behavior could both be related to effective leadership. The answer was that different styles are effective in different types of leadership situations. This realization led to a generation of leadership theories that are collectively referred to as situational, or contingency, theories. Historically, the first contingency theory was proposed by a psychologist, Fred Fiedler. Trained as a clinical psychologist, Fiedler's theory (1964, 1967) asserted that the task vs. follower orientation of leaders was relatively fixed and represented a core motivation on the part of the leader. Leaders were either motivated primarily by the task or motivated by interacting with people on the job. As a result, managers/leaders tend to have this preferred style of leading that focuses primarily on the task or on the people/relationships. According to Fiedler, this style is quite difficult to change. Fiedler therefore focused on developing a continuum of leadership situations that ranged from situations that were highly "favorable" for the leader (that is, where the leader has a great deal of situational control) to situations that are highly "unfavorable" for the leader (situations where the leader has little work-related knowledge and influence over followers). Although this theory is quite complex and makes fine distinctions between different types of leadership situations, the general findings suggest that leaders who are task-oriented (Fiedler prefers the term "task-motivated") do best in situations that are either highly favorable to the leader or highly unfavorable – the extremes of the continuum. Relationship-motivated leaders do better in situations that are neither particularly favorable nor unfavorable in terms of the leader's situational control. Fiedler's research with the contingency model, as well as his program for improving leadership in organizations (termed "Leader Match"; Fiedler and Chemers, 1984) flourished for decades, but like many situational leadership theories, has fallen out of favor in recent decades.

One of the most popular leadership theories taught in management is known as Situational Leadership Theory (SLT; Hersey and Blanchard, 1977). Taking the opposite perspective of Fiedler, SLT presumes that leaders are flexible and can alter their task-focused and follower-focused behaviors in order to meet the demands of the situation. The "situation" for SLT is the "developmental level" of the followers – ranging from followers who are self-directed and self-motivated (highly developed) to followers who are low on development and need constant direction. Leaders then adapt their leadership behaviors to fit the developmental level of each follower or group of followers. This results in the four combinations of high–low directive (task-focused) and supportive (follower-focused) leadership styles, ranging from *directing* (high-task, low-follower); to *coaching* (high–high); to *supporting* (low-task, high-follower); to *delegating* (low–low). Successful leadership depends on the leader's ability to recognize the developmental needs of any particular follower or group and to be able to alter his or her behavior to provide the most appropriate and effective leadership style.

Over the years, Situational Leadership Theory has undergone several iterations, but was wildly popular as a leadership training approach. Hersey and Blanchard (1993) claim that the vast majority of Fortune 500 companies have used SLT training. This widespread use as a leadership training model has been tempered, however, by a lack of supporting research to appropriately validate the theory (see Northouse, 2010, for a brief review of criticisms of SLT).

The predominant theme illustrated by these situational or interactionist approaches to leadership is creating the appropriate application of leader behaviors to fit situational factors – in essence, "engineering" effective leadership. A theory that to our minds epitomizes this approach is the Decision-Making Model of leadership proposed by Vroom and his colleagues (Vroom and Jago, 1988; Vroom and Yetton, 1973). This model suggests that the critical element of leadership is decision-making. Moreover, a leader can be effective by simply choosing the appropriate decision-making strategy when faced with an important decision. Using the theory, the leader asks a series of yes–no questions designed to analyze the decision-making situation. Then, based on the pattern of responses to the questions (and on empirical research validating the model), the leader is told which decision-making styles to use, ranging from purely autocratic decision-making to strategies of consulting with followers, to purely democratic decision-making. The result is a "programmed" method that is something like a recipe for effective leadership.

As mentioned, these situational theories of leadership, and several others, dominated management research and practice for several decades. As with most leadership theories emanating from management and psychology, the situational theories, and their predecessors (for example, trait theories, behavioral theories), are all very leader-centric. The leader is the lever that operates on the follower, taking into account situational factors (including the characteristics of the followers themselves). Management scholars, in particular James Meindl and his colleagues (Meindl et al., 1985) challenged this assumption and argued that scholars have suffered from a "Romance of Leadership" that puts leaders at the center and gives little attention to the critical role of followers. We will return to this theme later.

A SHIFT FROM LEADER AS STRATEGIST TO LEADER AS MENTOR

A fundamental transformation (pun intended) occurred in management approaches to leadership in the late 1970s and 1980s, moving away from the idea that leadership is about "engineering" outcomes, to a more relationship-based approach. With the advent of new theories such as Path–Goal Theory (House, 1971), Leader–Member Exchange (LMX; Dansereau et al., 1975; Graen and Uhl-Bien, 1995), and particularly Transformational Leadership Theory (Bass, 1985; Bass and Riggio, 2006), leaders became viewed as catalysts for organizational outcomes through the care, coaching and development of followers.

Path–Goal Theory (House and Mitchell, 1974) views the leader as a facilitator or "coach" who must adopt particular leadership roles in order to help the group navigate the difficult path to attaining their shared goals. In the Path–Goal model, the leader still displays behaviors focused on the task and production or focused on fostering good relationships, but the leader is not dictating the process. The leader is a coach or mentor helping the groups to reach goals – goals to which the group of followers has become committed.

Leader–Member Exchange (LMX) Theory (Graen and Uhl-Bien, 1995) asserts that effective leadership is determined by the quality of the interaction between the leader and particular group members/followers. According to LMX, the leader develops different types of dyadic relationships with followers, some of which are high-quality while others are low-quality relationships. The goal of the successful leader is to try to improve the quality of these dyadic relationships as much as possible, and harness the power of the high-quality follower relationships to achieve goals.

While Path–Goal and LMX theories are still strictly contingency models, with the leader's behavior regulated by situational conditions, they are different from their predecessors because the "situation" is now the followers (and the relationship between the leader and followers). The next stage in the evolution of management approaches and theories of leadership had perhaps the largest impact in stimulating research on managerial leaders, and that was the development of transformational leadership theory, along with instruments to measure transformational leadership,

Beginning with Burns's (1978) notion of *transforming* (versus *transactional*) leaders, and continuing with Bass's operationalization of the theory (Bass, 1985), transformational leadership focuses on the qualities of particularly effective leaders who are able to inspire, challenge and develop followers in order to obtain extraordinary levels of follower commitment and performance. An extension of charismatic leadership theories, transformational leadership views successful leaders as inspirational and able to motivate followers, and as positive role models – leaders who followers try to emulate. However, the theory goes beyond this and suggests that transformational leaders are concerned with and sensitive to each follower's individual needs and stimulates followers to be creative, resourceful, and strive for excellent performance. As a result, transformational leaders are very focused on the individual development of each follower – attempting to "transform" followers into nascent leaders.

No doubt, transformational leadership and LMX theory are particularly attractive because of the leader focus on the follower, and the emphasis on the positive and productive relationships between leader–mentor and follower–protégé. In fact, there has been a surge of interest in *positive organizational scholarship* and much research on transformational leadership theory is included in this category. With its emphasis on the leader as a positive role model and as mentor to followers, transformational leadership certainly fits. (A corresponding and parallel movement is also occurring in psychology – the positive psychology movement.) Transformational and LMX theories were (and are) quite popular with management scholars and have spurred a near-explosion in leadership research. Indeed, unlike the previous contingency models, research on these theories continues currently unabated.

LEADER-CENTRIC VS. FOLLOWER-CENTRIC APPROACHES (AND BEYOND)

In the 1980s and 1990s, theories such as transformational leadership and LMX suggested that leaders are still "engineering" outcomes, but now through the development of positive relationships with followers. Despite their orientation toward the follower, these are still very leader-centric in nature. The past decade has seen the beginning of a shift in how management views leadership. The leader-centric approach is being highly criticized, but in the Western world, it is very hard for us to break from our romance of leaders.

One recent approach involves a primary focus on followers and the nature of followership (Chaleff, 2009; Kellerman, 2008). The idea is that in today's organizations, with flatter, hierarchical structures and technologically-savvy and knowledgeable workers, leadership is a joint venture between those in positions of authority and those doing the work. Another approach is focused on shared leadership (Pearce and Conger, 2003), where leadership is a collective, group-level process. In these perspectives, leadership can be exercised by any member of a group or organization.

These more follower-centric approaches to leadership have moved forward, hand-in-hand with a more humanistic approach to management/leadership. Post-World War II, and into the 1980s, leadership had involved the leader's cognitive processes – processing information from the environment, making decisions, creating action plans, and the like. With the greater focus on the relational aspects of the leader–follower bond, there was a corresponding emphasis on the emotional aspects of leadership. From these perspectives, effective leaders need to have good "people skills", be empathic, and be what has been labeled "emotionally intelligent" (Goleman, 1995; see Cherniss, 2010 for a recent overview). In fact, the emphasis on the emotional aspects of management has become so pronounced that the theme of the 2010 Academy of Management meeting was "Dare to Care: Passion and Compassion in Management Practice and Research".

Of course, leadership involves *both* the leader and the follower. It is partly cognitive and partly emotional in nature. Leadership can be engineered, in part, by the leader using transactional or transformational means, but it can also bubble up from even the lowest ranks, through followers taking initiative and engaging in leadership behaviors. Moreover, effective group and organizational processes do not only involve leaders and followers and their dynamic interplay, all are embedded in a complex and ever-changing external environment. It is this broader picture that has led leadership theorists in management to widen their lens and explore complexity theories of leadership.

Based on the idea of complex adaptive systems (CAS), Complexity Leadership Theory (Uhl-Bien et al., 2007), views leadership as emerging from the complex interplay of individuals in a group or organization, taking into account the unique context/situation, which leads to adaptive outcomes. In other words, leadership is a complex process that does not involve programmed, or "engineered", leadership. Instead, it involves the collective efforts of multiple individuals to learn, adapt and innovate in response to changing conditions. It is a form of shared leadership, and like shared or team leadership, more commonly occurs in knowledge-based, as opposed to production-based, organizations.

MANAGEMENT PERSPECTIVES ON LEADERSHIP IN THE CONTEXT OF OTHER DISCIPLINES

It is important to place the management/business approach to leadership studies in the context of other disciplines that have contributed to our knowledge of leadership. In many ways, management, interconnected with psychology, has done a great deal of the "heavy lifting" in leadership research. What I mean by this is that the sheer volume of leadership research and theorizing that has emanated from business schools (and business oriented psychologically-trained researchers) is immense. In fact, the top journals publishing leadership research are in the management/business area (Academy of Management publications; *The Leadership Quarterly*; *Journal of Management*) and psychology (*Journal of Applied Psychology*).

In many ways, however, leadership scholars in departments of management have been in an ivory tower, not connecting regularly with other disciplines (except for psychology). Yet, the influence of other disciplinary perspectives on leadership research in management was there in the early days (for example, the work of sociologists on how organizational structure impacts leadership). However, as leadership/management research broadens its reach, there is greater influence of other disciplinary perspectives on management scholars. The ethical crises in business leadership, coming to a head in the Enron and WorldCom scandals and the more recent economic meltdown, have led to an exploding growth on ethical management/leadership, with roots in ancient (and more recent) philosophical perspectives. The awareness that leadership is more than just cognitive processes, has led to the study of emotions in leadership, and management scholars are becoming increasingly interested in the neuroscience of human behavior.

In a recent review of the future of leadership research, Avolio et al. (2009) suggested that the future directions for leadership research needs to involve broader perspectives. They argue that greater attention needs to be paid to the *process* of leadership. That would require greater understanding of leader (and follower) cognitive processes, knowledge of the role that culture plays, understanding how emotions and cognitions interact, and understanding the situational/environmental processes involved in all their complexity. Leadership, more than any other topic, may play a critical part in taking management from its ivory tower and placing it in the midst of the interplay of academic disciplines.

REFERENCES

Avolio, B.J., F.O. Walumbwa and T.J. Weber (2009), "Leadership: current theories, research, and future directions", *Annual Review of Psychology*, **60**, 421–49.

Bass, B.M. (1985). *Leadership and Performance Beyond Expectations*, New York: Free Press.

Bass, B.M. and R.E. Riggio (2006), *Transformational Leadership*, 2nd edn, Mahwah, NJ: Lawrence Erlbaum.

Burns, J.M. (1978), *Leadership*, New York: Harper & Row.

Chaleff, I. (2009), *The Courageous Follower: Standing Up To and For Our Leaders*, San Francisco, CA: Berrett-Koehler.

Cherniss, C. (2010), "Emotional intelligence: toward clarification of a concept", *Industrial and Organizational Psychology*, **3**(2), 110–26.

Dansereau, F., G. Graen and B. Haga (1975), "A vertical dyad linkage approach to leadership within formal organizations: a longitudinal investigation of the role making process", *Organizational Behavior and Human Performance*, **13**, 46–78.

Drucker, P.F. (1954), *The Practice of Management*, New York: Harper & Row.

Fiedler, F.E. (1964), "A contingency model of leader effectiveness", in L. Berkowitz (ed.), *Advances in Experimental Social Psychology*, vol. 1, New York: Academic Press.

Fiedler, F.E. (1967), *A Theory of Leadership Effectiveness*, New York: McGraw-Hill.

Fiedler, F.E. and M.M. Chemers (1984), *Improving Leader Effectiveness: The Leader Match Concept*, revised edn, New York: Wiley.

Follett, M.P. (1949), *Freedom and Co-ordination: Lectures in Business Organization*, London: Management Publications Trust.

Goleman, D. (1995), *Emotional Intelligence*, New York: Bantam.

Graen, G.B. and M. Uhl-Bien, M. (1995), "Relationship-based approach to leadership: development of leader-member exchange (LMX) theory of leadership over 25 years: applying a multi-level multi-domain perspective", *The Leadership Quarterly*, **6**, 219–47.

Hersey, P. and K.H. Blanchard (1977), *Management of Organizational Behavior: Utilizing Human Resources*, Englewood Cliffs, NJ: Prentice Hall.

Hersey, P. and K.H. Blanchard (1993), *Management of Organizational Behavior: Utilizing Human Resources*, 6th edn, Englewood Cliffs, NJ: Prentice Hall.

House, R.J. (1971), "A path–goal theory of leader effectiveness", *Administrative Science Quarterly*, **16**, 321–8.

House, R.J. and T.R. Mitchell (1974), "Path–goal theory of leadership", *Journal of Contemporary Business*, **3**, 81–97.

Judge, T.A., R.F. Piccolo and R. Ilies (2004), "The forgotten ones? The validity of consideration and initiating structure in leadership research", *Journal of Applied Psychology*, **89**(1), 36–51.

Kahn, R. and D. Katz (1960), "Leadership practices in relation to productivity and morale", in D. Cartwright and A. Zander (eds), *Group Dynamics: Research and Theory*, 2nd edn, Elmsford, NY: Row, Peterson and Co.

Kellerman, B. (2008), *Followership*, Boston, MA: Harvard Business Press.

Kotter, J.P. (1990), *A Force for Change: How Leadership Differs from Management*, New York: Free Press.

Mayo, E. (1933), *The Human Problems of an Industrial Civilization*, Cambridge, MA: Harvard University Press.

Meindl, J.R., S.B. Ehrlich and J.M. Dukerich (1985), "The romance of leadership", *Administrative Science Quarterly*, **30**(1), 78–102.

Northouse, P.G. (2010), *Leadership: Theory and Practice*, 5th edn, Thousand Oaks, CA: Sage.

Pearce, C.L. and J.A. Conger (eds) (2003), *Shared Leadership: Reframing the Hows and Whys of Leadership*, Thousand Oaks, CA: Sage.

Riggio, R.E. (2007), "Behavioral approach to leadership", in S. Rogelberg (ed.), *Encyclopedia of Industrial/Organizational Psychology*, Thousand Oaks, CA: Sage, pp. 48–50.

Smith, A. (1776), *The Wealth of Nations,* London: W. Strahan and T. Cadell.

Stogdill, R.M. and A.E. Coons (eds) (1957), *Leader Behavior: Its Description and Measurement*, Columbus, OH: Ohio State University, Bureau of Business Research.

Taylor, F.W. (1911), *The Principles of Scientific Management*, New York: Harper.

Uhl-Bien, M., R. Marion and B. McKelvey (2007), "Complexity leadership theory: shifting leadership from the industrial age to the knowledge era", *The Leadership Quarterly*, **18**(4), 298–318.

Vroom, V.H. and A.G. Jago (1988), *The New Leadership: Managing Participation in Organizations*, Englewood Cliffs, NJ: Prentice-Hall.

Vroom, V.H. and P.W. Yetton (1973), *Leadership and Decision-making*, Pittsburgh, PA: University of Pittsburgh Press.

11. Leadership research and education: how business schools approach the concept of leadership

Susan Elaine Murphy and Stefanie K. Johnson

Today's organizational leaders, whether in the for-profit or not-for-profit world, are under increased pressure from various constituents to perform well. Direct pressure emanates from shareholders, boards of directors, customers, government regulators and the courts. Indirectly, business magazines put pressure on CEOs whose successes are celebrated with cover stories and whose failures are dissected with long, detailed exposés. Moreover, in times of crisis, many pundits point to corporate leaders as the source of good or evil, and the salaries and bonuses commanded by these leaders often take center stage. Beginning in fall 2008, an increasing number of leaders were blamed, and subsequently removed, to underscore to the US stock markets and the world that leaders were the source of many of the problems facing companies such as Chrysler, Merrill Lynch, Lehman Brothers, Countrywide and Bank of America.

Throughout US industrial history, for better or for worse, organizational leaders have enjoyed a type of celebrity status. Because of this emphasis, leaders' actions, both positive and negative, have been offered as exemplars of what leaders should and should not do to succeed, and are discussed in business schools across the US and abroad. Learning from CEOs who have turned a company around, or who have enjoyed years of increasing stock prices, is part and parcel of how management is understood in business schools and how business students are educated.

After the business scandals of 2000 and those of fall 2008 shook the financial markets, many articles questioned whether the education of MBAs was lacking, and therefore partially to blame for ineffective and unethical leadership (Feldman, 2005; Holland, 2009; Mintzberg, 2004). It was estimated that 40 per cent of the CEOs in the S&P 500 possessed an MBA (Spencer Stuart, 2006). Both what is taught and how it is taught in business schools have been criticized severely since the scandals of 2000. Likewise, business school research and scholarship did not escape the criticism. According to Bennis and O'Toole (2005):

> During the past several decades, many leading B schools have quietly adopted an inappropriate – and ultimately self-defeating – model of academic excellence instead of measuring themselves in terms of the competence of their graduates, or by how well their faculties understand important drivers of business performance, they measure themselves almost solely by the rigor of their scientific research (p. 1).

They were not the sole voice of criticism, as others joined in and suggested that business school research is so abstract and far removed from real-life practices that practitioners see no relevance to their issues (Ghoshal, 2005; Lorange, 2008; Pffefer and Fong, 2002). In fact, finance is the only discipline within business schools that is thought to be producing the type of research that can be applied to help improve organizations (AACSB, 2008; Harris, 2008). Where does the topic of leadership as researched by business school faculty fall within these criticisms? With business schools under attack by scholars and by their own accrediting body, the AACSB (Association to Advance Collegiate Schools of Business), for the way in which they understand, research, and teach management to the next generation of business leaders, it may be implied that schools are falling short with respect to leadership research as well.

In this chapter we explore the ways in which leadership research and education is approached within business schools in the US. In the first section we begin with a brief summary of a general conceptualization of leadership within business schools, using writings from pre-eminent business thinkers of the twentieth and twenty-first centuries to understand the role of leadership within the practice of management. We also provide a cursory review of research publications in an attempt to shed light on whether or not leadership research can be criticized in the same manner as other areas of management scholarship. In other words, is leadership research lacking in its applicability to real world business leadership problems? In addition, we also review the way in which leadership is developed and taught within business schools. Throughout the chapter we recommend methods for improving both leadership research and education within business schools.

LEADERSHIP RESEARCH IN BUSINESS SCHOOLS

The Distinction Between Leadership and Management

To lead organizations, managers need a prerequisite set of skills to accomplish the organization's objectives. In many ways, the objectives have remained relatively unchanged since the first business school, Wharton, opened its doors in 1881 at the University of Pennsylvania to help educate business leaders. Whether it was a focus on profitability, or long-term sustainability for the organization, the main emphasis of professional training was to educate individuals to understand the fundamentals of how to run a business. Although the roots of business management and leadership as conceptualized in the twentieth and twenty-first centuries came from many different areas including philosophy, economics and psychology, business schools have provided a unique perspective on leadership within business management. However, not all faculty within business schools agree on the role of leadership within the broader topics of management.

Early writings by management theorists such as Frederick Taylor (known as the Father of Scientific Management), Mary Parker Follet (known as the Mother of Scientific Management, and the first to study the softer side of management), and Elton Mayo (who studied groups at the Hawthorne Electric plant in the 1930s) discussed their thoughts on the tasks of management in the new forms of organizations at the turn of the twentieth century (see Riggio, Chapter 10, this volume, for more discussion of the contributions of these writers). One expert, Chester Barnard, was not a management scholar, but a former executive. In his book, *The Functions of the Executive* (1938), Barnard explored the many tasks of leaders and managers, focusing on both the hard and soft sides of leadership. In his mind, the three main functions for an executive were:

1. Develop and maintain a system of communication (both formal and informal);
2. Gain cooperation and motivation of employees; and
3. Formulate and define the purposes, objectives, ends, of the organizations.

Barnard did not list managing day-to-day activities, but instead focused on communication, motivation, and the larger, more forward-looking activities that are the responsibility of the organization's leaders.

In considering the role of leadership in management, business school faculty have focused on what leaders do and heeded Peter Drucker's (1954) words, "managers do things right, leaders do the right things". Drucker, who is considered by some as the "father of modern management", initially believed that management was synonymous with leadership, and there was no need to talk about leadership as a separate issue. In later years, he did, however, acknowledge the important responsibilities unique to leaders including setting strategy and motivating employees (Cohen, 2009).

A useful description of leadership as distinct from management came from

Henry Mintzberg, who has been writing about management since he published *The Nature of Managerial Work* (1973). Within that work he provided a detailed list of the roles managers enact including those associated with interpersonal contact, information processing, and decision-making. His research, based on his Ph.D. thesis at MIT Sloan School of Management, analyzed the actual work and time management of CEOs. He found these ten roles included: Figurehead, Leader, Liaison, Monitor, Disseminator, Spokesperson, Entrepreneur, Disturbance Handler, Resource Allocator, and Negotiator. According to Mintzberg, then, leadership represents only a portion of what a manager must do in an organization. He defines the leader role as when a manager fosters a proper work atmosphere and motivates and develops subordinates. Another role related to leadership as we think of it today is the role of figurehead, as evidenced by the ceremonial and symbolic duties a manager performs as head of the organization. Mintzberg's work is often included in the discussion of the difference between leadership and management and reflects the idea that "leader" is merely one facet of the role a manager, at any level, must play.

Some of the important distinctions between managers and leaders are further captured in transformational (Bass, 1985) and charismatic (Conger and Kanungo, 1987) theories of leadership as applied to business organizations. Both theories focus on what the leader does to introduce and manage change within the organization. For example, the charismatic leadership process begins with a leader realizing the current inadequacy of the status quo. The leader's sensitivity to the environment, coupled with his or her ability to develop and articulate a compelling vision of the organization's future, and motivate followers, sometimes through unconventional means, describes the process. Transformational leaders work at the dyadic, as well as organizational level, to transform followers' motivation, and therefore move the organization to higher levels of performance than what would be possible under non-transformational leadership.

In this chapter, we consider leadership as a major component of management as evidenced by the types of decisions that managers make for their organizations. In other words, most headhunting firms are not out searching for people to manage large organizations, they are looking for leaders to lead these organizations. Furthermore, organizations do not structure themselves. Leaders, often with help from their top management teams, reorganize and restructure organizations. Therefore, leadership is one of the major activities of managers.

What is the General Focus of Leadership Scholarship in Business Schools?

The "what" question in regard to managers and leaders has changed somewhat over the years and has been influenced by scandals and ethical infractions by business leaders. For example, in the 1980s, leadership was assumed to be the missing element in US business, as Japanese management style and its emphasis on long-term vision, organization culture, and quality seemed to eclipse US dominance. In the 1990s, bloated organizations were in need of re-engineering and were downsized to make them more profitable. As layers of middle management were eliminated, the leaders who remained needed to be skilled in team management and empowerment. In the 2000s, the increased reliance on new working relationships such as virtual teams, diversity and globalization, required other leadership skills. Other more subtle changes in the competitive environment also brought changes to the demands of leaders, while business scandals highlighted the importance of ethical leadership. All of these areas have appeared as topics of research in many of the management research journals.

Even with the many so-called "fads" in leadership, much of the focus on what leaders do can be categorized at three organizational levels: the individual, the group, and the organization. At the individual level, this means identifying the specific tasks, skills and necessary individual characteristics of effective leaders to inform the selection, development and compensation of leaders. There are several related areas of research, including the use of power and influence, emotional intelligence and the effectiveness of leader decision-making (Bass and Bass, 2008).

At the dyadic level, we would see interest in the way in which a leader handles individual relationships, through softer skills such as communication, conflict resolution, empowerment and employee motivation (Khurana and Nohria, 2008). Most of the time this research focuses on the leader's behavior as it affects followers. Research over the years has waxed and waned regarding the extent to which followers influence the dyadic relational model of leadership. Theories such as Leader Member Exchange (Graen and Scandura, 1987) or Situational Leadership (Hersey and Blanchard, 1993) focus on this dyadic relationship (both of these theories are explained in more detail in Riggio, Chapter 10, this volume).

At the group level, much research has been devoted to ways in which leaders design, manage and implement effective groups. For example, Richard Hackman, who is a Harvard psychologist, has written extensively on what makes effective teams and the leader's role in improving team effectiveness (for example, Hackman, 2002). Indeed, although much of our understanding of leadership at the group level has been influenced by the psychology of group processes, more recent research has begun to study the dynamics of self-managing work teams (Thompson, 2007).

At the top level of the organization, leaders are responsible for activities that affect the organization's strategic direction, culture, structure and reputation.

Although the required skills to carry out these tasks at the top level of an organization may be similar to the skills necessary at the individual, dyad and group level of manager, there are additional unique activities that take place at the top echelon of the organization. Strategic management research highlights the role of the CEO in determining strategic direction for the organization, a vision for the organization's success, and the design of the organization's structure (formal and informal). For example, John Kotter, a Harvard Business School Professor, is best known for his research on what leaders actually do to facilitate change within an organization. His book *Leading Change* (1996), which outlined an actionable, eight-step process for implementing successful transformations, has become the change bible for managers around the world. Michael Porter, a strategy scholar, also from Harvard, writes about strategic leadership in organizations, focusing on the firm as a decision-making entity (Porter, 1985). In both cases, the leader is seen as making decisions as to the direction of the organization.

At Stanford Business School, management professor Jeffrey Pfeffer has spent a portion of his career focused on the macro analysis of leadership effectiveness. He makes the point that leaders' decisions with respect to various management practices in the organization have a large impact on the success of the organization. These practices can include participative management or worker empowerment. In his book, *The Human Equation: Building Profits by Putting People First* (1998), he shows research evidence that many of these practices produce real results for the organization which can translate to multiple measures of effectiveness including shareholder return, customer satisfaction, or employee morale.

There are three broad ways in which leadership is understood at the three levels of analysis. The first is through case method research. A particular leader in a particular situation, at a particular point in time is analyzed. What was his or her background, his or her leadership style, and the obstacles he or she overcame in order to be effective? The lessons from these cases may be tied to existing knowledge about best practices in organizational leadership. Another method, systematic qualitative research, focuses on interviews or other research evidence of particular phenomena within an organization and generates testable hypotheses from theory. For example, the early research on organizational culture looked at manager and employee perceptions of the unique culture of their organization and the role that leaders played in establishing or changing an organization's culture (Schein, 1996).

Qualitative data is rich and gives concrete examples of phenomena, although it too can be less generalizable to other organizations if the sample is small or homogeneous. Alternatively, empirical research studies using laboratory or field experiments and survey methodologies are used to identify the personality characteristics and behaviors of effective leaders as they relate to employee and organizational outcomes. Often this research may include large sample sizes with experimental or statistical controls to attempt to explain relationships among leader actions and outcomes.

We offer two caveats here with respect to leadership research. First, leadership is not an agreed-upon category of research in business schools. One reason is that it is faulted for its lack of a coherent overall theory of leadership and for focusing on relatively unimportant aspects of the leadership process (Khurana, 2007). Second, there is an ongoing debate regarding whether or not leadership actually makes a difference in organizations. According to some researchers (both inside and outside of business schools), the success or failure of an organization can be attributed to a plethora of other factors unrelated to leadership (Meindl, 1995; see also Goethals and Hoyt, Chapter 9, this volume for a discussion of leadership and social perception). However, most would argue that leadership is in fact a "researchable" phenomenon that has generated findings that are important to organizations.

A Cursory Examination of Leadership Research in Business Schools

As mentioned previously, business schools have faced a maelstrom of criticism for not producing the type of research that translates into usable ideas for today's managers and leaders (AACSB, 2008). In fact, many of the "A" list publications produced by the top business schools appear to enhance academic reputation only, and do little to help inform management practices used in businesses today (Adler and Harzing, 2009; Pfeffer and Fong, 2002). However, there has been no study that pinpoints the extent to which this is a problem in the publications of leadership research. To understand where leadership falls in the coverage of management as a research topic, we chose to examine leadership research in the top discipline-based management journal, *Academy of Management Journal*, the top practitioner management journal, *Harvard Business Review*, and the top leadership journal, *The Leadership Quarterly*. There would be no disagreement that the first two journals are the top business publications where one would find leadership research. The third journal, *The Leadership Quarterly*, is the oldest journal with respect to specific research around leadership although many of the publications have a social psychology emphasis.

Within the *Academy of Management Journal* we searched article titles for the words "leader", "leadership", "supervisor", "supervisory", "CEO", and "executive", resulting in 113 articles since 1992. If we expanded our search to look for articles that had an indexed subject of "leadership", there were 247 articles during the same time period, but we decided that because some were outside the field of typical leadership study, we examined our first set of 113 articles more carefully. We then looked at some of the terms separately to get an overall picture of the type of research in these journals. With respect to topics using the term "leader" and "leadership" in the title (n=44), almost 33 per cent of the articles focused on the behavior of the leader. In the 2000s there was some emphasis on Bass's (1985) transformational leadership theory, and in the 1990s some focus on the theory of Leader–Member Exchange (Graen and Scandura, 1987). However, a fair number of articles focused on employee outcomes that were affected by leadership. These included employee empowerment, justice perceptions, motivation, voice, performance, and organizational citizenship behaviors. A handful of articles focused on other aspects of leader behavior including impression management, leader emotional displays, and influence tactics. A small group of studies looked at the aspects just described in an international or cross-cultural context.

Other articles with the term "leader" or "leadership" in the title focused more on the group as the unit of measure with some study of top management teams. Only nine articles (8 per cent) used the term "supervisor" (or "supervisory") in the title. The focus here was on the lower-level dyadic relationships in organizations and about half focused on support and fairness. Searching on the term "executive" showed 22 articles (19 per cent), of which nine focused on determinants of executive compensation, while another large number were focused on turnover of CEOs. Two articles looked at executives as modeling either ethics or sensitivity to work–family issues. Using the word "CEO" (not leadership or executive) pulled up 44 articles (39 per cent) dealing with a range of leadership issues as well. Again, many of the articles (n=25; 22 per cent) focused on CEO compensation.

We used a similar methodology to examine articles published by the *Harvard Business Review* (HBR). For this search we chose to use only the term "leadership", which revealed 317 articles published since 1992. These articles did not necessarily contain "leadership" in the title, but it was a topic of the article. Using the HBR search engine to look at a breakdown of topics in the last two years, the 114 publications on leadership included: Crisis management (25); Power and influence (22); Leadership qualities (19); Leadership transitions (15); Management styles (13); Leadership development (10); and Vision (6). (These numbers add up to more than 114, as articles had multiple topics.)

The topics discussed in the articles were broad, but captured the role that leaders play in many aspects of the management of business. Many topics were related to some of the management and leadership emphases mentioned earlier in this chapter, including quality, culture and teams, as well as customer focus. More recent articles focus on the leader's role in innovation, creativity or the application of technology. Many of the articles focused on various aspects of management, but most were related to the leadership of the organization as it related to employees, direction and design.

We examined one additional journal that receives submissions from business school and organizational psychology faculty, *The Leadership Quarterly*. This journal focuses exclusively on leadership studies, and although it accepts papers from a wide range of disciplines, most research is from the organizational behavior, organizational psychology, and/or social psychology perspectives. A superficial review of articles published from January 2010 to October 2010 shows many leadership studies attempting to uncover some of the underlying processes of leadership as outlined by some of the other chapters in this volume (Goethals and Hoyt, Chapter 9; Riggio, Chapter 10). As business schools have become more populated with organizational psychologists, especially in the areas of organizational behavior and leadership, laboratory and field experiments have once again become a common form of research in business schools (Thompson et al., 2004). However, this research must be translated for leaders to use in organizations or for leadership development specialists to design leadership education programs.

Summary

In contrasting the contents of the *Academy of Management Journal* and *Harvard Business Review* (HBR), there is a vivid disconnect between rigorous discipline-based scholarship and contributions to practice summarized in HBR. The first summarizes research that is very complex, or perhaps after-the-fact, and corroborates the disconnect that Pfeffer and Fong described in 2002 and other critics have noted (Adler and Harzing, 2009; Khurana, 2007). However, for the *Harvard Business Review* publications, a cursory review reveals that there are a fair number of articles that are based on assorted data collection practices such as convenience sampling, or small interview populations with homogeneous demographics. Although many of these articles are compelling, they raise the question as to whether or not these lessons in leadership can be applied generally to different types of organizations in different situations. The articles and empirical studies reported in *The Leadership Quarterly* provided mixed evidence of applicable leadership knowledge. Some articles attempted to test small portions of leadership theory with only a cursory mention of larger, actionable implications, while other submissions critiqued the applicability of theories and made concrete recommendations.

Through our analysis of research publications, it appears that business schools seem to agree what leadership is, but disagree about the centrality and importance of leadership in management. As a result, business school curricula and research seem to reflect this differential emphasis. In the next section of this chapter, we specifically address what is taught with respect to leadership, by whom, and how.

LEADERSHIP EDUCATION

Similar to the popularity of leadership research in business schools, leadership has become a hot topic in business education, and a small body of research has begun to examine the extent to which, and methods by which, leadership can be taught as part of the business curriculum. In this section we examine the teaching of leadership in business schools in terms of the best practices put forth by business scholars and in terms of what business schools are actually doing to teach their students leadership. Specifically, we examined the education practices of the top 10 business schools in the country, based on *US News and World Report*'s rankings. We found that all ten business schools that we examined offered at least one course in leadership. Although our sample was small, it is consistent with other research findings on the topic. For example, Doh (2003) found that 32 of the top 50 business schools had at least one course in leadership as part of the business curriculum. Navarro (2008) found that 34 of the top 50 business schools actually required a course in leadership.

Yet, despite the ubiquity of leadership education in business schools, educators (and researchers and practitioners) continue to ask the question of whether leadership can even be taught. In his article in *Academy of Management Learning & Education* entitled "Can leadership be taught? Perspectives from management educators", Doh (2003) interviewed six top leadership educators and scholars to address this question of whether and how leadership should be taught in business schools. Not surprisingly, all of the scholars agreed that leadership can and should be taught in business schools, but there was some disagreement on how leadership should be taught (Doh, 2003). Two main questions emerged from this study: what methods should be used to teach leadership and who should do the teaching? We address the findings and bring in the work of other scholars in the area to address these questions.

What Methods Should be Used to Teach Leadership?

Based on his interviews, Doh (2003) found that leadership education should be very practical, including reliance on feedback and coaching, utilization of experiential activities to practice leadership, and case analysis of leader successes and failures. Although it sounds like all of the participants acknowledge the importance of learning theory as well, they all agreed that leadership cannot be learned by reading textbooks. Interviewee Stephen Stumph said,

> Book knowledge is only a small part of effective leadership – just as reading a tennis book is only a small part of being an exceptional tennis player. Leadership is a performance sport. Leadership requires both thinking and doing – to the satisfaction

> of many others with diverse expectations. Hence, most of what is taught as "best practice" is only best practice for a specific audience – one that the particular learner may not encounter (Doh, 2003: p. 59).

The focus on experiential and practical learning is consistent with the suggestions of other business scholars who have been critical of the reliance on theory in teaching business students. For example, De Dea Roglio and Light (2009) highlight the importance of teaching reflection skills to business students. Given that most business students already have work experience, the focus should be on them re-learning or making sense of their experiences, rather than learning a whole new language about business (De Dea Roglio and Light, 2009).

Further, Navarro's (2008) *Academy of Management Learning & Education* article entitled, "The MBA core curricula of top-ranked US business schools: a study in failure?" contrasts the ideal teaching methods with the current practices commonly used in business schools. Among other things, Navarro (2008) argues that business schools should focus on experiential learning, soft skill development, and ethics/corporate social responsibility. Similarly, in Pfeffer and Fong's (2002) controversial *Academy of Management Learning & Education* article entitled, "The end of business schools? Less success than meets the eye", the authors advocate for the importance of an experiential component to business education. Likewise, Bennis and O'Toole's (2005) *Harvard Business Review* article entitled, "How business schools lost their way", notes that business schools are professional schools, and the requisite outcome of a business education is business skill, rather than knowledge of business theory. In sum, there is a great deal of agreement that the teaching of business in general, and leadership in particular, should involve skill-learning, acquired through experiential activities.

Who Should Teach Leadership?

Although there appears to be a fair amount of agreement over how leadership should be taught, there is less agreement over who should do the teaching. Doh (2003) found that some of the scholars interviewed believed that top-level executives should teach leadership, because they were leaders themselves. Other scholars disagreed, noting that those individuals know what worked for them, but do not necessarily know what works in general. For example, Kim Cameron said,

> One would normally say that leaders would be the best teachers of leadership. Jack Welch ought to be the best teacher in the business. He's not, because he describes idiosyncratic events and experiences. I can't do what he does in my role, my organization, and facing my problems. Instead, I need some frameworks, some sense-making

> devices, and some tools to help me behave effectively in a variety of circumstances. That means the best teachers are those who can provide me with the theoretical frameworks, the models, and the foundation tools that allow me to succeed as a leader. (Doh, 2003: 63–4).

Who should teach in business schools has also come under scrutiny by other scholars. Bennis and O'Toole (2005) note the disconnect between the "scientific model" and the "practical model" of business education. Under the scientific model, business scholars are rewarded for publishing in top academic journals, rather than for teaching real-world skills and knowledge.

Likewise, Clinebell and Clinebell's (2008) *Academy of Management Learning & Education* article entitled, "The tension in business education between academic rigor and real-world relevance: the role of executive professors" highlights the need to examine who should be teaching business students. They support the use of "Executive Professors" to teach business students but recommend that these professors should be taught how to teach and suggest that executive professors could be used as guest speakers in classes to supplement the traditional academic's course content. Jay Conger also suggests combining executives with academics to teach leadership; he says (quoted in Doh, 2003: 62),

> In terms of "faculty", the ideal leadership development program would include three groups of "instructors". The first would be a small group of faculty who have a depth of knowledge about leadership and possess the capacity to teach using a broad range of pedagogies (plus a keen interest in developing an individual's potential). The second set would be a very small handful of company executives who possess teaching skills, are accepted role models for leadership, and are capable of conveying simple but powerful frameworks about leadership that are derived from their work experiences. The final group would include professional trainers and would include individuals most familiar with using experiential and feedback methods extensively.

In sum, most of the scholars believe that executives and practitioners are useful sources by which to learn the lessons of leadership. Whether they are the main instructors, or whether they are used to augment the traditional academic model, there are lessons that can be learned from actual leaders. In the next section, we will explore the practices that actual business schools use to teach leadership, considering the lessons learned above.

Leadership Education in the Top Ten

Each year, *US News and World Report* rates all of the MBA programs accredited by AACSB (433 in 2010). According to the 2010 *US News and World Report*, the top ten business schools according to their ranking criteria, which include: quality (peer assessment scores, recruiter assessment scores); placement success (mean starting salary and bonus, employment rates); and student selectivity (mean Graduate Management Admissions Test (GMAT) scores, mean undergraduate Graduate Point Average (GPA), acceptance rate). The list of the top ten appears below (*US News & World Report*, 2010).

1. Harvard
1. Stanford
3. MIT (Sloan)
4. Northwestern (Kellogg)
5. University of Chicago (Booth)
5. University of Pennsylvania (Wharton)
7. Dartmouth (Tuck)
7. University of California, Berkeley (Haas)
9. Columbia University
9. New York University (Stern)

In order to better understand if, how, and by whom leadership is taught at these schools, a small-scale study was conducted using the webpages at each school. To the extent possible, all leadership courses, leadership faculty, and other leadership experiences at each school were researched. It should also be noted that these data were collected in the fall of 2010, and we acknowledge that the courses, faculty, quotes and even the ranking of the top ten may have changed by the time this chapter is published. These data only represent a snapshot in time in terms of what is being offered at the top ten. Yet the information summarized in the sections that follow does offer some insight into the current state of leadership education in business schools.

Centrality of leadership

Possibly in response to the question of relevance of business schools, there was a strong component of leadership emphasized on all of the top ten business schools' webpages. For example, Harvard Business School's homepage displays the quote "For two years. And a lifetime of leadership." Also at Harvard, the webpage says, "At HBS, every decision you make is a priceless lesson in leadership." At the Haas School we found, "BILD [Berkeley Innovative Leader Development] is the connective theme that runs through the entire Berkeley MBA curriculum to ensure that every student develops the skills required of innovative leaders." At Kellogg we found, "At the heart of the Kellogg experience is a strong focus on leadership development. From team projects to school-wide governance, you'll exercise your leadership skills." On the Tuck webpage, they say, "At Tuck leadership development is a material part of the curriculum. This is the direct result of our long-standing focus on individuals, interpersonal relationships, and productive collaboration."

All of the schools examined offered at least one course in leadership. Some of these were core classes such as Harvard's "Leadership and Organizational Behavior" and "Leadership and Corporate Accountability" courses, which are both required of first year students. Similarly, Wharton requires two core courses in leadership: "Leadership Communication in Groups" and "Foundation of Teamwork and Leadership". Haas requires three core leadership classes: "Leading People", "Leadership Communication", and "Strategic Leadership". At Tuck, all first year students are required to take a leadership course focused on personal leader development. At Booth, all students take a "Leadership Effectiveness and Development – LEAD" course which is actually the only required course at Booth. There was also a wealth of leadership electives offered at these schools. Some of these seemed particularly novel and interesting, such as Harvard's "Authentic Leadership Development" and "Moral Leadership" electives. Columbia offers electives in "High Performance Leadership" and "Nonprofit Leadership". Sloan offers a course in "Practical Leadership" and "Leadership Lab for Corporate Social Innovation".

Some of the schools also offer minors or concentrations focused on leadership. Kellogg offers a minor in Leadership. Stern offers a specialization in "Leadership and Change Management". Columbia offers an emphasis on "Leadership and Ethics". Many of the top ten schools also have centers for leadership. For example, Stanford hosts the Center for Leadership Development and Research. Sloan has the MIT Leadership Center. Wharton has the Center for Leadership and Change Management and The Leadership Center. At Harvard there is the Leadership Initiative. Haas has the Center for Nonprofit and Public Leadership. Stern offers a specialization called the "Citi Leadership and Ethics Program".

Which methods are actually used to teach leadership?

All schools highlighted diverse teaching methods for the MBA in general, and for leadership in particular. Teaching methods include: learning from leader speaker series, case studies, coaching, feedback sessions, simulations, problem-solving sessions, action-learning, team projects, in-class lectures, and experiential activities. All of the business schools included some leadership classes that focused on "book learning" and "leadership theory", but we were more interested in the extent to which these schools have adopted an experiential, hands-on approach to teaching leadership. Although we are only basing our analysis on what is included on the business school webpages, we assume that this information is accurate.

Experiential learning A quote from the Sloan page reflects the belief that learning about leadership must involve an experiential component. They say,

"We believe that the development of skilled, thoughtful, passionate leaders must be rooted in real world experience." Sloan offers a variety of experiential programs including a course in leadership called "Tiger Teams" in which teams of three to five students conduct a six-week consulting project for local organizational businesses. Indeed, most of the school described some type of experiential learning related to leadership. These hands-on learning opportunities range from interactive case analysis to outdoor experiences. For example, Haas requires an experiential course to "practice leadership" in which students work with executives or non-profits to address real-world business problems. Stanford also offers "Leadership Labs", which are experiential courses in which students complete simulations and then analyze their decisions in order to enhance self-awareness.

Booth requires first year students to complete a three-day leadership outdoor experience, which involves low ropes courses, high ropes courses, and a climbing tower. Kellogg offers "KWEST" (Kellogg Worldwide Experiences and Service Trips) which are student-organized global adventures. Wharton offers several extreme outdoor adventures as well. They have mountain climbing trips to Kilimanjaro and Alaska, as well as trekking adventures in Antarctica and sailing adventures in Patagonia, among others. Other schools offer voluntary conferences and coursework aimed at developing leadership. For example, Wharton and Haas offer non-credit leadership development workshops. Kellogg offers a leadership workshop specifically aimed at women. Many of the above activities involve the use of teams, including the "Tiger Teams" at Sloan, "KWEST teams" at Kellogg, and "BILD teams" at Haas.

Coaching, feedback and self-analysis Some schools also offer coaching activities and feedback aimed at enhancing self-awareness. Wharton offers a leadership development coaching program which involves assessment, experiential and classroom leadership, professional executive coaches, communication workshops, and alumni mentoring. Tuck also relies on feedback for developing leaders. They say, "Rigorous self-analysis is at the heart of Tuck's approach to leadership development. Combining feedback from coworkers and fellow students with instruction and peer coaching, our students gain insights that the traditional case method can't produce." The "Authentic Leadership Development" course at Harvard involves reflection, discussion and feedback in one-on-one sessions with peer mentors and the professor. Sloan's "Practical Leadership" class involves coaching and real-time feedback from peers and the instructor. The course also involves a great deal of self-reflection, brought about through readings, role plays and experiential exercises. Stern's "Developing Managerial Skills" focuses on developing personal skills such as self-awareness in additional to developing interpersonal skills and group skills. Likewise, Stern's "Leadership Models" class includes a heavy emphasis on developing self-reflection skills needed for leadership.

Focus on ethics

It is also noteworthy that most of the schools mention a focus on ethics, and ethics were strongly highlighted in relation to leadership. For example, Stern hosts the "Citi Leadership and Ethics Program", and Haas has the "Center for Nonprofit and Public Leadership". Even the schools that do not offer "ethics programs" still highlight the importance of ethical leadership in their marketing materials. Sloan states that they are "Dedicated to developing leaders who can improve their organizations and the world." Stanford notes that they highlight a "path to principled leadership and a life of impact." Moreover, many of the schools offer courses focused on social responsibility such as Haas' "Corporate Social Responsibility" course. Kellogg's KWEST trips also involve a service component. Similarly, Wharton's "Nonprofit Board Leadership Program" matches Harvard students with local non-profits to help solve organizational problems.

In sum, it appears that the topics and methods by which leadership is taught at the top ten closely mirror the suggestions by the scholars in this area. The extent to which these experiential activities are used, in comparison to classroom learning and lecture, cannot really be determined in a cursory examination such as this one. However, it appears that all schools value experiential activities to teach leadership or at least espouse this value on their webpages. Either way, from our perspective, this is a step in the right direction in terms of leadership education.

By whom is leadership actually taught?

The majority of the teachers at all of the top ten schools were academic faculty, possibly because the top ten business schools strongly adhere to the academic model of business education. Many schools also had some professionals who serve as lecturers. In the Organizational Behavior group at Harvard, there were two lecturers among the 25 faculty. One, Anthony Mayo, is a former CEO who earned his MBA from Harvard and serves as the Director of the Leadership Initiative. The other, Scott Snook, is a former army colonel and consultant and earned his Ph.D. from Harvard. At Stanford, among the faculty affiliated with the Center for Leadership Development and Research were four lecturers and 14 professors. Among the lecturers is Joel Peterson, an MBA from Harvard who had a very successful business career and now serves as the Director of the Center for Leadership Development and Research. Also, Evelyn Williams serves as the Director of the Leadership Laboratories of the Center for Leadership Development and Research and has over 15 years of experience as a leader development expert in Fortune 500 companies, and was a former professor at Booth.

In addition to the lecturer positions, all of the business schools highlighted speakers who were coming to the university to talk about their experiences as leaders. For example, Sloan notes that they bring in 400 of the "world's finest leaders to campus each year", many of whom are part of the Dean's Innovative Leader Series. Harvard offers the "Leadership and Values Speaker Series". Kellogg offers the "Executive Leader in Residence Series". In sum, it appears that many of the business schools were making efforts to connect business students with real-world leaders, despite the predominance of the academic model of having research professors at these schools. At least when it comes to teaching leadership, it appears that many of the schools recognize the value of leadership experience.

WHO SHOULD CARE ABOUT LEADERSHIP AS CONCEPTUALIZED, RESEARCHED AND TAUGHT BY BUSINESS SCHOOLS?

Essentially everyone should care about the way in which leadership is researched and taught in business schools, including company shareholders, employees and governments. Good, if not great leadership, is expected in our organizations. Even if it is difficult to quantify as measured in terms of return on investment (ROI), it still remains very important. Leadership research and scholarship in business schools can be criticized simultaneously on two fronts. On the one hand, it can be criticized for focusing on esoteric theory-building coupled with complicated empirically derived models of behavior that are unusable to the practicing organizational leaders. On the other hand, some of the practical advice offered by management professors on leadership is not based on academically rigorous research and can in fact do harm in organizations. Faddish management solutions can disillusion employees and cause eventual organizational problems.

One solution to improve the way leadership is researched and taught comes from the push led by Stanford School of Business Professor Jeffrey Pfeffer and others (for example, Denise Rousseau at Carnegie Mellon) to use what is called *Evidence-based Management* (EBMgt). EBMgt is an emerging movement to explicitly use the current, best evidence in management decision-making. While its roots are in evidence-based medicine, there are other applications such as evidence-based education, all of which emphasize applying the scientific method to a field of practice. Contemporary managers and management educators make limited use of the vast behavioral science evidence base relevant to effective management practice (Pfeffer and Sutton,

2006; Rousseau, 2006a, 2006b). In fact, Drucker (as cited by Reay et al., 2009) long ago advised that "management science" research should be applied as "general methodology, a synthesizing and integrating logic" (1955: 124). EBMgt though is not without critics. As noted by Reay et al. (2009) more emphasis on the appropriate type of evidence will help increase effective application to improve management practices.

In conclusion, leadership, as approached in business schools, will continue to be an important topic, although greater effort needs to be made to demystify the topic. The recent emphasis on the gap between how leadership is understood by scholars and how leadership is performed in organizations is causing scholars to rethink how leadership is taught and studied in business schools. Efforts to close this gap create greater potential for a symbiotic relationship between scholarship and practice and will be key in developing research-based solutions to help educate the CEOs of tomorrow.

REFERENCES

AACSB (2008), *Impact of Research Task Force*, Tampa, FL: AACSB International.

Adler, N.J. and A. Harzing (2009), "When knowledge wins: transcending the sense and nonsense of academic rankings", *Academy of Management Learning & Education*, **8**(1), 72–95.

Barnard, C. (1938), *The Functions of the Executive*, Cambridge, MA: Harvard University Press.

Bass, B.M. (1985), *Leadership and Performance Beyond Expectations*, New York: Free Press.

Bass, B.M. and R. Bass (2008), *The Bass Handbook of Leadership: Theory, Research, and Managerial Applications*, New York: Free Press.

Bennis, W.G. and J. O'Toole (2005), "How business schools lost their way", *Harvard Business Review*, **83**, 96–104.

Clinebell, S.K. and J.M. Clinebell (2008), "The tension in business education between academic rigor and real-world relevance: the role of executive professors", *Academy of Management Learning & Education*, **7**, 99–107.

Cohen, W.A. (2009), *Drucker on Leadership: New Lessons from the Father of Modern Management*, San Francisco, CA: Jossey Bass.

Conger, J.A. and R.N. Kanungo (1987), "Toward a behavioral theory of charismatic leadership in organizational settings", *The Academy of Management Review*, **12**(4), 637–47.

De Dea Roglio, K. and G. Light (2009), "Executive MBA programs: the development of the reflective executive", *Academy of Management Learning & Education*, **8**, 156–73.

Doh, J.P. (2003), "Can leadership be taught? Perspectives from management educators", *Academy of Management Learning & Education*, **2**, 54–67.

Drucker, P.F. (1954), *The Practice of Management*, New York: Harper and Row.

Drucker, P. (1955), "Management science and the manager", *Management Science*, **1**, 115–26.

Feldman, D. (2005), "The food is no good and they don't give us enough: reflections

on Mintzberg's critique of MBA education", *Academy of Management Journal of Learning & Education*, **4**(2), 217–20.
Ghoshal, S. (2005), "Bad management theories are destroying good management practices", *Academy of Management Learning & Education*, **4**(1), 75–91.
Graen, G. and T.A. Scandura (1987), "Toward a theory of dyadic organizing", *Research in Organizational Behavior*, **9**, 175–208.
Hackman, J.R. (2002), *Leading Teams: Setting the Stage for Great Performances – The Five Keys to Successful Teams*, Cambridge, MA: Harvard Business Press.
Harris, R. (2008), "The 'bright star' of B-school research: finance", *CFO.com* (March 27), accessed 12 March 2010 at www.cfo.com/article.cfm/10927537?f=search.
Hersey, P. and K.H. Blanchard (1993), *Management of Organizational Behavior: Utilizing Human Resources*, 6th edn, Englewood Cliffs, NJ: Prentice-Hall.
Holland, K. (2009), "Is it time to retrain business schools?", *New York Times*, 14 March, accessed 15 October 2010 at www.nytimes.com/2009/03/15/business/15school.html?fta=y.
Khurana, R. (2007), *From Higher Aims to Hired Hands*, Princeton, NJ: Princeton University Press.
Khurana, R. and N. Nohria (2008), "It's time to make management a true profession", *Harvard Business Review*, October, pp. 70–77.
Kotter, J. (1996), *Leading Change*, Cambridge, MA: Harvard Publishing.
Lorange, P. (2008), *Thought Leadership Meets Business*, New York: Cambridge University Press.
Meindl, J.R. (1995), "The romance of leadership as a follower-centric theory: a social constructionist approach", *The Leadership Quarterly*, **6**(3), 329–41.
Mintzberg, H. (1973), *The Nature of Managerial Work*, New York: HarperCollins, College Division.
Mintzberg, H. (2004), *Managers not MBAs: A Hard Look at the Soft Practice of Managing and Management Development*, San Francisco, CA: Berrett-Koehler.
Navarro, P. (2008), "The MBA core curricula of top-ranked business schools: a study in failure?", *Academy of Management Learning & Education*, **8,** 108–23.
Pfeffer, J. (1998), *The Human Equation: Building Profits by Putting People First*, Cambridge, MA: Harvard Business School Press.
Pfeffer, J. and C.T. Fong (2002), "The end of business schools? Less success than meets the eye", *Academy of Management Learning & Education*, **1**, 78–95.
Pfeffer, J. and R.I. Sutton (2006), *Hard Facts, Dangerous Half-truths, and Total Nonsense: Profiting from Evidence-based Management*, Boston, MA: Harvard Business School Press.
Porter, M.E. (1985), *Competitive Advantage,* New York: Free Press.
Reay, T., W. Berta, W. and M.K. Kohn (2009), "What's the evidence on evidence-based management", *Academy of Management Perspectives*, **31**, 5–19.
Rousseau, D.M. (2006a), "Is there such a thing as evidence-based management?", *Academy of Management Review*, **31**, 256–69.
Rousseau, D.M. (2006b), "Keeping an open mind about evidence-based management", *Academy of Management Review*, **31**, 1091–3.
Schein, E. (1996), *Organizational Culture and Leadership*, 2nd edn, San Francisco, CA: Jossey Bass.
Spencer Stuart (2006), "Leading CEOs: a statistical snapshot of S&P 500 leaders", accessed 12 November 2010 at http://content.spencerstuart.com/sswebsite/pdf/lib/2005_CEO_Study_JS.pdf.
Thompson, L. (2007), *Making the Team*, 3rd edn, Saddle River, NJ: Prentice-Hall.

Thompson, L., M. Kern and D.L. Loyd (2004), "Research methods of micro organizational behavior", in C. Sansone, C. Morf and A.T. Panter (eds), *The Sage Handbook of Methods in Social Psychology*, Thousand Oaks, CA: Sage, pp. 427–42.

US News and World Report (2010), "Best business schools", accessed 1 November 2010 at http://grad-schools.usnews.rankingsandreviews.com/best-graduate-schools/top-business-schools/mba-rankings.

12. Political science and the study of leadership: where have you gone, *homo politicus*?

Norman W. Provizer

Back in 1972, Glenn Paige edited a volume simply titled *Political Leadership*. In his introduction to the 19 essays collected in the book, Paige laments the lack of attention paid to the study of leadership in political science. To illustrate the point, he notes that of the 2614 articles appearing in the *American Political Science Review* from 1906 through to 1963, a mere 17, using Kenneth Janda's computerized keyword index, contained references to leaders or leadership and only one of those (Lester Seligman's 1950 essay on "The Study of Political Leadership") actually focused on a "generic" examination of the subject (Paige, 1972: 5).

Though Paige recognized the discipline's limited effort "to conceptualize the study of leadership in a general way", he also saw hopeful signs. Signs produced by the increased interest in leadership generated by World War II, as well as by the post-war revolutionary movements and the emergence of what would be called "the third world" (Paige, 1972: 5–6). After all, as Montesquieu reminded us, "at the birth of societies, it is the leaders of the commonwealth who create the institutions; afterwards it is the institutions that shape the leaders" (Rustow, 1967: 135).

Additionally, Paige argues that despite the neglect of leadership in political science "it would be a mistake to begin the study of political leadership with the idea that little of relevance previously has been accomplished". Quite to the contrary, there is, in his words, "an abundant literature that can serve as a foundation for such a field". What is lacking is "a coherent field of knowledge with organized potential for sustained advancement" (Paige, 1972: 8). Together with "an accompanying monograph and bibliography", his book of "readings for an emerging field" aimed to take a giant step in that direction (Paige, 1972: v).

EXPLORING POLITICAL LEADERSHIP

The promised monograph and bibliography, *The Scientific Study of Political Leadership*, described as forthcoming in 1972 did not appear until 1977. But when it was finally published, students of political leadership possessed a comprehensive, if not always elegantly fashioned, guide for creating a "*trans*-disciplinary scientific field of global significance" (Paige, 1977: 1), a field based on the principle that "*political leaders constitute a source of enormous creative potential*" – potential "inadequately appreciated by modern political science" (Paige, 1977: 4). In other words, while societies are "not pliant clay to be molded into any form by a master sculptor", leadership does have a role in their shaping. Whatever limiting parameters exist, choices have to be made; and "even constricted choice remains choice nonetheless" (Provizer, 1978: 385). And the choices that political leaders "make or fail to make", according to Paige, "seemingly affects everything" (Paige, 1977: 3).

Importantly, along with the explanation of his basic orientation and an extensive review of the literature, Paige strikes several notes that would emerge as leading themes in leadership studies. For example, during his examination of a number of key works, Paige writes, "While we will be seeking to discover how these approaches explicitly deal with the concept of 'political leadership', we need to be aware that this implies the need for a similar exploration of the treatment of the idea of 'followership'" (Paige, 1977: 16). There is certainly no shortage of work on that subject today.

Additionally, Paige concludes his study by asking, "Can we gain enough understanding of the creative potential of political leadership that will enable us purposively not only to avoid barbarous conditions of global poverty, violence, and repression but also to proceed intelligently toward economic justice, nonviolence, and the further liberation of human potential?" That conclusion (Paige, 1977: 236) comports well with James MacGregor Burns's later emphasis on the global "pursuit of happiness" aimed at eliminating poverty and powerlessness as the "touchstone" of leadership (Burns, 2003, pp. 2; 214–15).

NOTHING MUCH TO SAY

Paige, of course, understood that "The study of political leadership is not all of political science" (Paige, 1977: 7). Still, Paige's emphasis on the relevance of the subject has led others to note that since he "focused attention on the crucial role of leadership, scholars have regularly addressed its role in shaping political events" (Post, 2004: 12). Yet, while Paige discussed the interest generated by Burns's paper "Toward the conceptualization of political leadership" during a pioneering panel at the American Political Science chaired by Betty Glad in 1973, Paige's own efforts to reassert the significance of leadership in politics are nowhere to be found in Burns's important 1978 book, *Leadership* (Paige, 1977: 53).

Ironically, Burns was the Woodrow Wilson Professor of Government at Williams College and a past president of the American Political Science Association when *Leadership* appeared. Despite that background and his role as the co-author of a leading textbook on American government (which was first published in 1950 and is still widely used in updated form), Burns found that the discipline of political science contributed little of value when it came to the study of leadership. "I didn't think," Burns would later say, "political scientists had much to say about leadership" (Sorenson, 2002: 3).

That point is clearly illustrated in the index to his 530-page treatise on leadership. The index contains exactly one entry under political science, concerning the general approach followed by political scientists regarding the subject. As he puts it, they "emphasize the social and political institutions impinging on developing leaders, changes in political leaders as they learn from their experience, the eventual impact of leadership on policy and on history" (Burns, 1978: 27). And underlying all of this is the discipline's emphasis on power, which, according to Burns, is the source of an extremely serious problem.

Early on in *Leadership*, its author confesses:

> As a political scientist I have belonged to a 'power school' that analyzed the interrelationships of persons on the basis only of power. Perhaps this was fitting for an era of two world wars and scores of lesser ones, the murder of entire cities, bloody revolutions, the unleashing of the inhuman force of the atom (Burns, 1978: 11).

Then, continuing along that path, he writes, "I fear, however, that we are paying a steep intellectual and political price for our preoccupation with power. Viewing politics *as* power has blinded us to the role of power *in* politics and hence to the pivotal role of leadership" (Burns, 1978: 11).

That conclusion leads Burns to write:

> Our main hope for disenthralling ourselves from our overemphasis on power lies more in a theoretical, or at least conceptual, effort, than in an empirical one. It lies not only in recognizing that not all human influences are necessarily coercive and exploitive, and not all transactions among persons are mechanical, impersonal, ephemeral. It lies in seeing that the most powerful influences consist of deeply human relationships in which two or more persons engage with one another. It lies in a more realistic, a more sophisticated understanding of power, and of the often far more consequential exercise of mutual persuasion, exchange, elevation, and transformation – in short, of leadership (Burns, 1978: 11).

"We must see power – and leadership – as not things," he goes on to say, "but as *relationships*. We must analyze power in the context of human motives and physical constraints. If we can come to grips with these aspects of power, we can hope to comprehend the true nature of leadership – a venture far more intellectually daunting than the study of naked power" (Burns, 1978: 11).

Burns's call to liberate leadership from the controlling influence of the power concept so attractive to political scientists is reminiscent of Abraham Lincoln's comment near the end of his second annual address to Congress. There, under far more dire circumstances, Lincoln noted, "As our case is new, so we must think anew and act anew. We must disenthrall ourselves, and then we shall save our country" (Lincoln, 1862: 17). For Burns, we must think and act anew to deliver the study of leadership from the bondage imposed by power. That deliverance would not come from political science. Rather, its source would be psychology, and, to borrow the introductory words to a *Psychology Today* interview with Burns conducted by Doris Kearns Goodwin, psychology's "line of research into the psychosocial and moral development of the individual" (Goodwin, 1987: 214).

POWER AND THE MASTER SCIENCE REVISITED

Obviously, in the realm of leadership, Burns was not at all impressed by the view expressed by Aristotle (in *Nicomachean Ethics*) that politics is "the master science". As Victor Wiseman explains, Aristotle's master-science designation did not mean that politics explained all the other sciences existing in a society. Rather, its importance came from the idea that politics is the activity which establishes ordered priorities among competing claims regarding the allocation of values and limited resources in a defined community (an idea later followed by David Easton's well-known 1953 definition of politics as "the authoritative allocation of values for a society"). And by doing this, it is politics that establishes the framework within which "the various 'sciences' could demonstrate their actual importance in the task of making life, and then the 'good life' possible" (Wiseman, 1969: 1). From this perspective, "Politics was the queen of the sciences and the most important of human activities in the days of Plato and Aristotle, the founders of political science" – and those who practiced it were the architects and master builders charged with the construction of well-being and happiness in society (Spiro, 1970: 4 and Lord, 2003: 28–9).

Leaving aside the debate over the primacy of the political, this orientation highlights the notion that the foundation of politics is located in "the exercise of choice" (Shively, 2008: 9). Or, as Charles Anderson writes, "Politics is always a matter of making choices from the possibilities offered by a given historical situation and cultural context" (Anderson, 1971: 121). Viewed in this manner, doesn't the question of politics as choice, involving the selection or non-selection of direction in a given situation and defined context, along with the implementation, adjustment, and impact of the choices made, lie at the heart of leadership as well? To change Harold Lasswell's noted formulation of politics as "who gets what, when, how" just a tad: politics is all about who chooses what, when, how and why (Lasswell, 1936). And is it so strange to make a similar statement about leadership?

The discussion of choice, in turn, leads directly to the question of power. Power, after all, is used to implement choice, while choice itself takes place within the context of power. While there is a vast body of literature concerning the issue of power, the focus here is limited to two basic points. The first is the connection between power and political science. "The concept of power", Lasswell and Abraham Kaplan write, "is perhaps the most fundamental in the whole of political science; the political process is the shaping, distribution and exercise of power". It is "the deference value with which political science is especially concerned" (Lasswell and Kaplan, 1968: 75, 74). In this sense, political science distinguishes itself from other disciplines by making power its central concept. As one of the great proponents of power politics and political realism, Hans Morgenthau, argues, power serves as "a kind of rational outline of politics, a map of the political scene" (Morgenthau, 1971: 31).

From Burns's perspective, that idea explains why political science offers so little to leadership studies. But that's not really the case. Again, in the words of Morgenthau, "By making power its central concept, a theory of politics does not presume that none but power relations control political actions" (Morgenthau, 1971: 3). Power is, as Lasswell and Kaplan note, "a value, and an extremely important one" but that is not to say that it is "always and everywhere more important than other values" (Lasswell and Kaplan, 1968: 77).

POWER AND LEADERSHIP

This raises the second point to consider: what is this thing called power? While numerous variations on the power theme exist, there are certain fundamentals that have particular significance when it comes to leadership, beginning with the now standard refrain that power is a relationship rather than a property. That relationship is multilayered (think, for example, of John French and Bertram Raven's frequently cited 1959 listing of rewards, coercion, legitimacy, expertise and reference as "bases" of power, to which Raven added information in 1965) and can be conducted in a direct, situation-specific context or indirectly, embedded, as Michel Foucault argues, in a vast network that covers all of society (Harvey, 2006).

Because power is a relationship, the concept is much more accommodating than it is constricting. Just as Thomas Friedman informs us that *The World is Flat*, there are numerous voices in leadership studies who remind us of the emergence a "flattened hierarchy" in which collaboration, not command and control, matters most (Kellerman, 2008: 67). But the acceptance of that idea causes no problem for power given the malleability of the power relationship in differing contexts. Power can be expressed in a top-down manner, but it is not limited to that. Power can be expressed through command, force and coercion, but it can also follow softer channels. As Richard Neustadt noted long ago, the power of the presidency, despite all of the resources found in the oval office, is the power to persuade, not to command (Neustadt, 1960). The tool of persuasion, it would seem, is not just a necessity for those who lack "formal" power but also for those who possess it in abundance.

If power is approached from the angle of "participation in decisions", then it can certainly encompass a wide range of actors and can take a variety of forms (Lasswell and Kaplan, 1968: 75). Joseph Nye, who popularized the term "soft power", illustrates this point when he writes, "In practice, effective leadership requires a mix of soft and hard power skills that I call *smart power*" (Nye, 2008: x). From this perspective, the error is to think of one form as always being better than the other. That's not smart, but combining "hard and soft power into an effective strategy" is (Nye, 2008: 43). Little wonder then that Nye calls his book on leadership *The Powers to Lead*.

If "power is the ability to affect the behavior of others to get the outcomes you want", then, according to Nye, leadership "is a relationship of power" (Nye, 2008: 27 and 25). And it is a relationship where "followers also have power both to resist and to lead" (Nye, 2008: 34). In short, when it comes to power and leadership, there are no one-way only streets.

THE QUESTION OF PURPOSE

In this relationship, leaders are, to use Nye's words that reflect the influence of Burns, "those who help a group create and achieve shared goals" and who "mobilize people to reach those goals" since leadership itself "means mobilizing people for a purpose" (Nye, 2008: 34 and 18). This brings us back to Burns who, despite his *mea culpa* concerning the discipline of political science and its emphasis on power, recognized that any effort to comprehend leadership still required an "understanding of the essence of power, for leadership is a special form of power". And the essence of power is found in "the role of purpose" (Burns, 1978: 12 and 13).

For Burns, the power approach errs in concentrating on the wants, needs and goals (that is, the purposes) of those who wield power, and that is very different from the leadership approach which is "exercised when persons with certain motives and purposes mobilize, in competition or conflict with others, institutional, political, psychological, and other resources so as to arouse, engage, and satisfy the motives of followers… in order to realize goals mutually held by *both* leaders and followers" (Burns, 1978: 18).

This road is also followed by Robert Tucker in his book *Politics as Leadership* originally published in 1981. Tucker begins by noting there exists a classic answer and a classic dissent to the question of what is politics, both of which can be found in the Platonic dialogues. The classic answer is that politics "is in essence the pursuit and exercise of power – in the interest of those who pursue and exercise it". The dissent, with which he agrees and labels the leadership approach, takes a different tact, highlighting, as it does, the positive function politics performs not for the ruler but "for the community of citizens" (Tucker, 1995: 1 and 2). At its core, power is one thing, leadership another.

Though Tucker makes a number of thoughtful points, he, like Burns, creates a distinction that need not be drawn at all. "A few decades ago," Nye writes, "some theorists contrasted a power approach with a leadership approach. But if one thinks of power as including both the hard power of coercion and the soft power of attraction, leadership and power are inextricably intertwined" (Nye, 2008: x).

Consider, for a moment, the question of purpose. "Power wielders", for Burns, "respond to their subjects' needs and motivations only to the extent that they have to in order to fulfill their own power objectives. True leaders, on the other hand, emerge from, and always return to, the wants and needs of their followers." Their purpose, if you will, is "the recognition and mobilization of their followers' needs". Beyond that, according to Burns, "The *truly* great or creative leaders do something more – they induce new, more activist tendencies in their followers; they arouse in them hopes, aspirations, and expectations" (Goodwin, 1987: 215).

Despite the obvious surface attraction of this perspective, it is not without equally obvious problems. In a highly differentiated, large-scale society, after all, undifferentiated wants and needs simply do not exist. Instead, there is substantive competition and frequently conflict among constituents (to use a term that Ronald Heifetz favors over followers) in this realm that cannot simply be resolved by referencing Abraham Maslow's hierarchy of needs.

Where the rubber of the leadership process meets the road of society, the issue is less that of addressing the wants, needs and aspirations of people than the concrete determination of whose wants, needs and aspirations should be satisfied and why. That's when politics – the activity which establishes ordered priorities among competing claims regarding the allocation of values and limited resources in a defined community – enters the picture.

Additionally, whether it is Burns or the advocates of "social identity" theory, in which leaders who best represent a group's identity have the greatest influence within the group, approaches to leadership that highlight the importance of leaders as reflectors of constituent values and views contain a significant caveat. For Burns, the caveat is the transforming leader's role in elevating the aspirations of constituents and satisfying their higher needs in a mutually reinforcing manner (Burns, 1978: 4). For the social identity proponents, the caveat comes in the form of the leader's need not only to conform to a group's norms, but to shape those norms as well (Reicher et al., 2007: 24 and 28). In either case, the issue of choice (rational or otherwise), and thus politics, is paramount (Lalman et al., 1993).

Though Burns understands the crucial nature of the conscious choices made by leaders from the roster of real alternatives, his insistence on equating power in political science with "brute power" underscores a blind spot, which is neither necessary nor particularly useful (Burns, 1978: 36). When politics is viewed as choice (in Aristotle's sense of politics as the master science), its overlapping dimensions of power, principle and purpose offer a framework that aids rather than retards our efforts at understanding leadership.

CAUSALITY AND THE EVALUATION OF LEADERS

In his 1975 essay in *Comparative Politics*, Lewis Edinger notes that the criteria for evaluating leadership can be either intrinsic or extrinsic. At the intrinsic level, the evaluation focuses on objective judgments concerning leadership performance relative to stated goals. Here the questions are: how close do leaders come to attaining their objectives and at what cost/benefit ratio? In contrast, the application of extrinsic criteria revolves around a more qualitative judgment regarding how closely leadership objectives and activities reflect the beliefs and values of the observer (Edinger, 1978: 403–5). Or, as Machiavelli well understood, people are "judged by qualities that attract praise or blame" (Machiavelli, 2007: 59).

Such a distinction represents, as Edinger readily admits, "an oversimplified dichotomy for heuristic purposes… intended to orient the reader of leadership studies toward the different sorts of biases on the part of their authors, as well as to help him identify those he brings to them himself" (Edinger, 1978: 405).

While Edinger's dichotomy contains a number of attractive elements, the duality that has taken hold in leadership studies is one that judges leaders along the separate, if interrelated, lines of being effective and being ethical, though, as Joanne Ciulla reminds us, the distinction between the two "is not always a crisp one" (Ciulla, 2004: 310). Crisp or not, the idea that the evaluative terms "good and bad" each contain two interconnected appraisals, one dealing with effectiveness and the other with ethics, has clear merit.

In his examination of this effectiveness–ethical distinction, Nye adds that each side of the leadership coin can be judged along three dimensions, goals, means and consequences (Nye, 2008: 111–12). Earlier, Nye offered a slightly different formulation of his three-dimensional analysis that referred to motives, means and consequences (Nye, 1986: 20–26). And whether one agrees with his substitution of goals for motives or believes that a four-dimensional, motives/means/goals/consequences model is even more useful, the point remains that the evaluation of leaders is a critical component in leadership studies. After all, as Ciulla notes, "History defines successful leaders largely in terms of their ability to bring about change for better or worse" (Ciulla, 2004: 310). And that brings us to the question of causality.

In Andrew McFarland's words, "Although the concept of 'power' is used in a variety of ways, there is considerable agreement among empirical political theorists that the power relation is a type of causality relation" (McFarland, 1969: 3). "Thus," he writes, "if a leader is defined as a person who exercises considerable power, then the theory of leadership is a theory of power, causation, and issue salience" (McFarland, 1969: 153). "In other words," McFarland continues, "the leader is one who makes things happen that would not happen otherwise" (McFarland, 1969: 155).

At first glance, this approach might appear to contradict the valuable idea that "Leadership is infinitely more complex than the efforts of any one individual" (Hickman and Couto, 2006: 161). But remember, McFarland is writing about leadership in the context of pluralist systems, and in that context there are numerous actors who have power, who have causal impact (McFarland, 1969: 31). Because a pluralist system is a system of complex causation, power is not expressed in terms of a simple hierarchy. Rather, causal impact can emerge from a web of leaders at different levels as well as those labeled followers.

Deciphering causality is certainly a complex undertaking and there is something to Burns's argument that, "No single discipline… alone can deal adequately with the phenomenon of causation because the subject lies outside as well as inside every discipline". For him, the solution resides instead in the "multidiscipline" of leadership, "the X factor in historic causation" (Burns, 2003: 21–2). That may be true, but it is equally true, in terms of causality, that the complex-causation model of pluralist political systems has merit for understanding leadership itself and deserves more than indifference.

THE RETURN OF *HOMO POLITICUS*

There is certainly more to the study of leadership than political science. But there is also more of a contribution that political science can make to the study of leadership than is often recognized, especially when emphasis is placed on the concept of choice and the idea of power as multilayered participation in the making of decisions.

In a 1949 essay on political leadership, Joseph Shannon noted that, "The essence of government is the relationship between the leaders and the led. Oddly enough, no aspect of political science has received less objective investigation" (Paige, 1977: 42). The following year, Lester Seligman suggested a "politics by leadership" orientation to the discipline based on "a conception of politics that finds power factors in society best approachable through the understanding of leader-led and leader–leader relations" (Paige, 1977: 43).

Over time, the discipline's interest in leadership has grown; and today, misgivings over power cannot justify locking *homo politicus* (political man) out of the arena of leadership studies. "Those who believe", Elaine Dunn writes, that "good leaders don't need to use power" might think again (Dunn, 2008: 132). And it is power that remains the common currency of *homo politicus*, defined by Lasswell and Kaplan as "the one who demands the maximization of his power in relation to all his values, who expects power to determine power, and who identifies with others as a means of enhancing power position and potential". At the same time, even this abstraction does not postulate "that those who demand power pursue power in preference to any other value" (Lasswell and Kaplan, 1968: 78).

In political psychology fashion, Lasswell defined *homo politicus* (P) with the equation $p\}d\}r\}=P$, meaning that p displaces personal needs (d) into public objects and rationalizes that displacement (r) as being in the public good (Post, 2004: 17). Whether or not one concurs with that particular perspective, it reminds us that the meaningful pursuit of leadership studies comes not from abandoning the idea of power but rather from exploring its wise use in making the good life possible – not from exiling *homo politicus* but instead embracing what that abstract figure tells us about ourselves. We are at our core, after all, to use Aristotle's phrase, a *zoon politikon*, a political being (Spiro, 1970: 7). From this perspective, in the words of James David Barber, politics is above all "a response to human needs" (Barber, 1988: 150). And, ultimately, so too is leadership.

REFERENCES

Anderson, Charles (1971), "Comparative policy analysis", *Comparative Politics*, **4**(1), 117–31.

Aristotle (1954), *Nicomachean Ethics*, translated by David Ross, London: Oxford University Press.

Barber, James David (1988), *Politics by Humans*, Durham, NC: Duke University Press.

Burns, James MacGregor (1978), *Leadership*, New York: Harper and Row.

Burns, James MacGregor (2003), *Transforming Leadership*, New York: Atlantic Monthly Press.

Ciulla, Joanne (2004), "Ethics and leadership effectiveness", in John Antonakis, Anna Ciancioli and Robert Sternberg (eds), *The Nature of Leadership*, Thousand Oaks, CA: Sage Publications.

Dunn, Elaine (2008), "Power", in Antonio Marturano and Jonathan Gosling (eds), *Leadership: Key Concepts*, New York: Routledge.

Easton, David (1953), *The Political System*, New York: Alfred Knopf.

Edinger, Lewis (1978), "The comparative analysis of political leadership", in Norman Provizer (ed.), *Analyzing the Third World*, Cambridge, MA: Schenkman Publishing.

Friedman, Thomas (2005), *The World is Flat*, New York: Farrar, Straus and Giroux.

Goodwin, Doris Kearns (1987), "True leadership", in William Pederson and Ann McLaurin (eds), *The Rating Game in American Politics*, New York: Irvington Publishers. This interview with James MacGregor Burns originally appeared in *Psychology Today*, **12**(5) (October 1980).

Harvey, Michael (2006), "Power", in George Goethals and Georgia Sorenson (eds), *The Quest for a General Theory of Leadership*, Cheltenham, UK and Northampton, MA, USA: Edward Elgar.

Heifetz, Ronald (1994), *Leadership Without Easy Answers*, Cambridge, MA: Belknap Press of Harvard University Press.

Hickman, Gill Robinson and Richard Couto (2006), "Causality, change and leadership", in George Goethals and Georgia Sorenson (eds), *The Quest for a General Theory of Leadership*, Cheltenham, UK and Northampton, MA, USA: Edward Elgar.

Kellerman, Barbara (2008), *Followership*, Boston, MA: Harvard Business Press.

Lalman, David, Joe Oppenheimer and Piotr Swistak (1993), "Formal rational choice theory: a cumulative science of politics", in Ada Finifter (ed.), *Political Science: The State of the Discipline II*, Washington: The American Political Science Association.

Lasswell, Harold (1936), *Politics: Who Gets What, When, How*, New York: McGraw-Hill.

Lasswell, Harold and Abraham Kaplan (1968), *Power and Society*, New Haven, CT: Yale University Press.

Lincoln, Abraham (1862), Annual address to the United States Senate and House of Representatives, 1 December, accessed at www.infoplease.com/t/hist/state-of-the-union/74/html.

Lord, Carnes (2003), *The Modern Prince*, New Haven, CT: Yale University Press.

Machiavelli, Niccolò (2007), *The Essential Writings of Machiavelli*, edited and translated by Peter Constantine, New York: The Modern Library.

Morgenthau, Hans (1971), "Power as a political concept", in John Champlin (ed.), *Power*, New York: Atherton Press.

McFarland, Andrew (1969), *Power and Leadership in Pluralist Systems*, Stanford, CA: Stanford University Press.

Neustadt, Richard (1960), *Presidential Power: The Politics of Leadership*. New York: Wiley.

Nye Jr, Joseph (1986), *Nuclear Ethics*, New York: The Free Press.

Nye Jr, Joseph (2008), *The Powers to Lead*, New York: Oxford University Press.

Paige, Glenn (1972), "Part one overview", in Glenn Paige (ed.), *Political Leadership*, New York: The Free Press.

Paige, Glenn (1977), *The Scientific Study of Political Leadership*, New York: The Free Press.

Post, Jerrold (2004), *Leaders and Their Followers in a Dangerous World*, Ithaca, NY: Cornell University Press.

Provizer, Norman (1978), "Leadership and public policy", in Norman Provizer (ed.), *Analyzing the Third World*, Cambridge, MA: Schenkman Publishing.

Reicher, Stephen, S. Alexander Haslan and Michael Platow (2007), "The new psychology of leadership", *Scientific American Mind*, **18**(4), July/August.

Rustow, Dankwart (1967), *A World of Nations*, Washington, DC: The Brookings Institution.

Shively, Phillip (2008), *Power and Choice*, New York: McGraw-Hill.

Sorenson, Georgia (2002), "An intellectual history of leadership studies: The role of James MacGregor Burns, College Park, MD: The James MacGregor Burns Academy of Leadership", paper originally presented at the 2000 meeting of the American Political Science Association.

Spiro, Herbert (1970), *Politics as the Master Science*, New York: Harper and Row.

Tucker, Robert (1995), *Politics as Leadership*, Columbia, MO: University of Missouri Press.

Wiseman, Victor (1969), *Politics: The Master Science*, New York: Pegasus.

13. Leadership and education: leadership stories

Robert J. Sternberg

John Kerry's campaign in the 2004 Presidential election was ruined by a story. Leaders have a story to tell. John Kerry's story was of a brave and successful military veteran who would bring to the presidency the skills he had learned in the military, seasoned by his years in the Senate. Kerry had been a warrior chieftain. "Swift Boat Veterans for Truth" was an organization devoted to wrecking that story. They presented a counter-story of Kerry as, basically, a liar and a coward. They cast enough doubt upon Kerry's story that his campaign largely imploded.

Stories are at the heart of leadership. In the 2008 US Presidential election, John McCain ran on the story of a heroic veteran of the Vietnam War, like Kerry, a warrior chieftain, but one who served time in the "Hanoi Hilton". Barack Obama campaigned on a story of a turn-around specialist who would bring positive change to the country, and Hillary Clinton on a story of being a consummate organizer who would bring order from chaos and who will be ready to go her first day in office. Clinton later changed her campaign manager: the story was not working as planned. Such stories are usually oversimplifications of what a candidate stands for. But they are messages that candidates and other leaders can convey that people understand. It is no coincidence, for example, that Obama supporters kept reminding the electorate of the Camelot that existed under President John F. Kennedy. No matter that it never was quite Camelot. It is a story people can understand and relate to. Ronald Reagan was the Great Communicator at a time people felt they needed – a great communicator.

These examples point out the important role that stories play in leadership. Of course, there are many other aspects to leadership. One can study traits, behaviors, situations, person × situation interactions, and the like. But the view of this chapter is that stories are at the very heart of leadership. Leaders succeed or fail in large part by virtue of the stories they have to tell. Stories are simultaneously organizing concepts, rallying cries and marketing tools. The role of stories in leadership has been recognized in various theories of leadership. Consider two such theories and what they can tell us about the role of stories in leadership.

GARDNER'S VIEW OF LEADERSHIP STORIES

Howard Gardner (1995) proposed a view of leadership according to which successful leaders have a story to tell and a message to convey. The story tends to be more effective to the extent that it appeals to what Gardner (1991) refers to as the "unschooled mind", that is, a mind that, in terms of modern cognitive theory, is more experiential than rational in its thinking (Epstein, 1993; Sloman, 1996). In elections, one might argue, such stories are almost a necessity. Complicated, nuanced stories tend not to be valued. Stories need to address both individuals' own identities and those of the group or groups to which they belong. A story is more likely to succeed if it is central to what the leader actually does in his or her action, if the story can be unfolded over a long period of time, and if it can be stated in a time of relative calm. In times of crisis, according to Gardner, stories need to be simplified.

Stories may be inclusionary or exclusionary. Inclusionary leaders try to ensure that all of the followers for whom they are responsible somehow are made to feel inside the fold. Exclusionary leaders do not include everyone and, in extreme cases, such as Hitler or Stalin, turn on segments of the population whom they are entrusted to lead. The 2004 US Presidential election appears to have been characterized by exclusionary stories, resulting in one of the most polarized electorates in memory.

The story must reach and connect with an audience. Gardner (1995) points out that no matter what the story, if there is no audience for it, it is dead. So a leader needs a story to which his or her audience will respond. The leader needs to take into account the experiential mode of thinking of the audience, and the kinds of changes in points of view to which the audience is likely to be responsive. The leader must also have an organizational structure to implement the structure. Part of the failure of the US military adventure in Iraq was that such an organizational structure was weak and practically invisible. Further, leaders need in some way to embody the story they have to tell. If the leader fails to do so, then that leader's leadership may come to be seen as bankrupt. Many people lost faith in certain church leaders, such as Ted Haggard or, earlier, Jim Bakker and Jimmy Swaggart, who held their flocks to a standard of morality that they themselves flagrantly violated by abusing children or covering up such abuse. One cannot lead effectively if one talks the talk, but does not walk the walk.

Gardner (2004) further suggested that a good story overcomes resistances. Leaders must expect groups of followers to resist some of the leaders' ideas. It is the leaders' responsibility to devise ways to overcome these resistances. Part of Mitt Romney's failure in the 2008 Republican primary campaign was that his story was unclear, had changed many times, and encountered resistance because it seemed to many people to be less than genuine. Romney's campaign organization failed to overcome the perception that Romney was a fake. In the end, his "perfect" family and "perfect" hair-do contributed to that perception – that he was an illusion.

Good stories also involve representational redescription. Ideas can be expressed in many ways. The more different ways in which a leader's ideas can be expressed, and the more compelling these ways are, the more likely the leader is to persuade followers to come along. Ronald Reagan was successful in his campaign and is still revered by many Republicans because he was so many different things to so many different people.

A good story also embodies resonance. At a given time and in a given place, certain ideas will resonate with followers; others will not. Establishing resonance can go a long way toward persuading people to listen. In the 2008 Republican primary, Candidate Fred Thompson failed because, although he had a straight-line conservative story to tell, he failed to establish resonance for his story and thus to connect with the voters.

Finally, the story will be more effective to the extent that it incorporates real-world events. Followers need to see how the leader's ideas relate to the lives the followers live from day to day.

STERNBERG'S VIEW OF LEADERSHIP STORIES

Characterization of Stable Story Elements

Stories have certain stable elements (Sternberg, 1995, 1998, 2008; Sternberg et al., 2001). First, they have beginnings, middles and ends. In this way, they are like scripts (Schank and Abelson, 1977). Sometimes, leaders start with a story that works well in the beginning and discover that the end does not work. They either change stories, or they lose the support of their followers. Donald Rumsfeld, despite the events of 9/11 and his capitalization upon them, was unable successfully to change his story during his tenure as Secretary of Defense, and thus lost most of his support both from politicians and from the general public. Indeed, stories need constantly to be rewritten in order to suit the needs of the leader–follower unit. For example, the story of the war in Iraq changed multiple times in 2004 in order to accommodate emerging facts and the perceived needs of followers, but the changes in the story failed to gain resonance among listeners. Some individuals found it distressing that certain politicians seemed to care little about the changes in the stories. The politicians cared more about having a story with resonance than one that was necessarily "true" in any meaningful sense. In the end, they got neither resonance nor truth.

Stories also have plots, themes and characters. For example, a common story now for political leaders is the warrior chieftain who will fight terrorists. The plot is the battle against terrorists. The limitations of particular stories are shown by the implosion of Rudy Giuliani's 2008 presidential campaign. Giuliani very much emphasized one story: 9/11. In his speeches, he seemed unable to get away from 9/11. Had he been running in 2004, the story might have stuck. By 2008, it seemed old and tired, and so did he. In the end, the story was not one that grabbed people's attention, and so his candidacy as well failed to grab their attention.

Themes give stories meaning. They help people understand why the story is important and what script it will follow. One theme is that the leader must constantly prepare his followers to combat the terrorists; another is that followers must give up some of their liberty to enable the leader to fight the terrorists in an effective way. Vladimir Putin, for example, announced in September, 2004, a major reorganization of the Russian government to enable effective mobilization against terrorists. The reorganization concentrated more power in his hands. The characters in the battle are the terrorists, the victims, the warriors who oppose the terrorists, and the (often passive) observers who watch what is happening. By 2008, Putin had become highly aggressive, a story of the resurgence of an imperial power that had, for some years, been waylaid and forced to watch events from the sidelines.

Sometimes themes fail to connect. Mitt Romney took as his theme in the 2008 Presidential primaries true conservatism in the mantel of Ronald Reagan. It failed to connect, not because Republicans did not like the story, but because they did not believe in the storyteller. Because Romney had rather recently, as Governor of Massachusetts, told a very different story – that of a Republican moderate – the story seemed to be a convenient fiction aimed at getting elected, and it failed. Romney's stories failed until the very end. When he dropped out, he claimed it was because he did not want to give comfort to terrorists: Hillary Clinton and Barack Obama, he argued, would be soft on terrorism, and he could not risk their winning because he stayed in the race.

Failed stories are not limited to Republicans. Bill Clinton's story – that he did not have a sexual relationship with "that Lewinsky woman", failed when the evidence proved the assertion, later made under oath, to be false. It might have been a good story, had Lewinsky not saved a dress with Clinton's DNA embedded in a semen stain.

Perceptions of leaders, then, are filtered through stories. The reality may be quite different from the stories. For example, Mao Tse-tung was responsible for the deaths of many millions of Chinese citizens. Yet when he died, there was a great deal of sadness among many citizens of China, and Mao is still revered there. Some people still idolize Hitler. People see the leaders only through their stories, not through any objective reality. The stories may be based in part on objective reality, but the part may be fairly small.

Stories are social constructions. Different people and different groups may interpret the same events in different ways. Leadership is the attempt to capture the minds of the people to accept one's version of events. In Presidential campaigns, such as that of 2004 between Bush and Kerry, much of the campaign is devoted to the fight for the storyline that people will accept. In 2008, the Democratic primary debate was about change (Obama) versus experience (Clinton), although it was not clear exactly what change Obama would bring or how much experience Clinton really had. As another example, was the war in Iraq a war against international terrorists or against a bad regime unconnected with international terrorists? The 2004 Presidential candidates took opposite positions, each trying to persuade listeners to believe his story. Of course, there is a truth underlying the battle: the regime either was or was not connected to international terrorists. For better or worse, truth plays at best a minor role in persuading people one way or another. Strong emotions, such as fear, rage, joy and sorrow, probably play much more powerful roles.

Stories are hierarchically arranged so that people have multiple stories they can accept at a given time. The challenge of the leader is to create a story that is higher in people's hierarchies rather than lower. Moreover, the leader in a competition may try to undermine the story or stories of his or her competitors, trying to show that the story he or she proposes is the one that followers should accept. Again, truth may play a relatively small role in what stories people accept. Rather, their emotional needs are likely to be key. Effective leaders know this, and pitch their stories to resonate with people's emotions.

Stories can become self-fulfilling prophecies. For example, the governments of both the United States and Russia have a history of acting aggressively toward nations or interest groups that displease them. In Chechnya, the Russian government has acted in very harsh ways to suppress rebellions. The harshness of the actions creates resistance, which in turn creates more harshness, and so forth. Arguably, the same thing has happened as a result of the US intervention in Iraq. The same dynamic has played out in the Israeli–Palestinian conflict. When people have stories, they act in ways to make them come true, and often they do.

Stories always have two principal roles. One is for the leader, the other for followers. Some of the stories are more symmetrical, others less so. For example, a democratic leader expects a great deal of participation from followers in setting and determining policies. An autocratic leader expects little or no participation. Leaders and followers clearly differ in the level of symmetry with which they are comfortable. For example, Russia has a history of less symmetry, and when more symmetry was introduced, the system as implemented under Boris Yeltsin was not particularly successful. Today, Vladimir Putin is moving back toward a more asymmetrical system.

Success or Failure of Stories

Leaders succeed to the extent that they (a) have a story that fits their followers' needs; (b) communicate that story in a compelling way; (c) implement the story in a way that suggests it is succeeding (given that there may be a difference between the perception and the reality); and (d) persuade followers, in the end, that the story accomplished what it was supposed to have accomplished. Leaders fail to the extent that they (a) have a story that fails to fit their followers' needs; (b) fail in communicating their story; (c) fail in implementing the story; (d) fail in persuading followers that they have accomplished what they promised; (e) fail to have any coherent story at all; (f) seem to move from story to story without convincing followers that there is a need to change stories; or (g) allow a story of successful leadership to be replaced with a story of personal failings. For example, the leader may come to be viewed as in power not to lead, but to maintain power at all costs, to enrich him or herself personally, to increase his or her power to the maximum extent possible, or to harm groups not obeying him or her. In these cases, stories of leadership come to be replaced with stories of personal failings.

Leaders need to be creative in inventing their stories, analytically intelligent in addressing the strengths and weaknesses of their stories, practically intelligent in implementing the stories and persuading followers to listen to them, and wise in generating and instantiating stories that are for the common good (Sternberg, 2005, 2007). They may fail if they lack creativity, intelligence or wisdom, and especially if they foolishly succumb to the fallacies described earlier (such as egocentrism), which can divert them from a successful leadership story to a story of failed leadership.

Stories fit into a contingency-based notion of leadership. There is no one story that works for all organizations in all times or all places. Rather, success of a story fits into the situation at a given time and place. When Tolstoy speculated, in *Anna Karenina*, that if it had not been Napoleon, it would have been someone else fitting that particular situation, he was partially right. The situation demanded a certain kind of story. But it was not certain that anyone would come along who could tell that story in a compelling way and convince people to listen to him or her.

Classification of Stories

Christopher Rate, formerly a graduate student at Yale, and I have created a partial taxonomy of stories. Our main hypothesis has been that that leaders will succeed differentially well, depending in large part on the extent of match between the stories of the leaders and the followers. Some tentative examples of stories are

- The carpenter: the leader who can build a new organization or society
- The CEO: the leader who can "get things done"
- The communicator: the leader who can communicate with diverse followers
- The conqueror: the leader who is going to conquer all enemies
- The conserver: the leader who will make sure things stay the wonderful way they are
- The cook: the leader who has the recipe to improve the life of his or her followers
- The deep thinker : the leader who will make sense out of what is going on
- The defender: the leader who will save all followers from harm
- The deity: the leader who presents him or herself as savior
- The diplomat: the leader who can get everyone to work together
- The doctor: the leader who can cure what is wrong with the organization
- The ethicist: the leader who pledges to clean up the place
- The lifesaver: the leader who will rescue followers from otherwise certain death
- The organizer: the leader who can create order out of chaos
- The plumber: the leader who can fix all the leaks
- The politician: the leader who understands how "the system" works
- The replicator: the leader who is going to be like some past individual
- The scout: the leader who can lead followers to new and uncharted territory
- The ship captain: the captain of a ship navigating through turbulent times
- The turn-around specialist: the leader who can turn around a failing organization
- The warrior chieftain: the leader who will lead followers to fight, defensively or offensively, enemies, seen or unseen

These stories differ in the kinds of leadership they show, as well as in the motivating forces behind the leadership.

Forms of Leadership

The creativity inherent in leadership can take different forms. (Sternberg, 1999; Sternberg et al., 2003). Some of these forms accept current ways of doing things, others do not; and still another attempts to integrate different current practices. What are these forms of leadership?

Replication

This type of leadership is an attempt to show that a field or organization is in the right place at the right time. The leader therefore attempts to maintain it in that place. The leader keeps the organization where it is rather than moving it. The view of the leader is that the organization is where it needs to be. The leader's role is to keep it there. This is a limiting case of creative leadership, requiring the leader only to apply in new circumstances techniques that have been used before.

Redefinition

This type of leadership is an attempt to show that a field or organization is in the right place, but not for the reason(s) that others, including previous leaders, think it is. The current status of the organization thus is seen from a different point of view. Redefiners often end up taking credit for ideas of others because they find a better reason to implement the others' ideas, or say they do.

Forward incrementation

This type of leadership is an attempt to lead a field or an organization forward in the direction it is already going. Most leadership is probably forward incrementation. In such leadership, one takes on the helm with the idea of advancing the leadership program of whomever one has succeeded. The promise is of progress through continuity. Creativity through forward incrementation is probably the kind that is most easily recognized and appreciated as creativity. Because it extends existing notions, it is seen as creative. Because it does not threaten the assumptions of such notions, it is not rejected as useless or even harmful.

Advance forward incrementation

This type of leadership is an attempt to move an organization forward in the direction it is already going, but by moving beyond where others are ready for it to go. The leader moves followers in an accelerated way beyond the expected rate of forward progression. Advance forward incrementations often are not successful at the time they are attempted. Followers in fields and organizations are not ready to go where the leader wants to lead, or significant portions of them may not wish to go to that point. In that case, they form an organized and sometimes successful source of resistance.

Redirection

This type of leadership is an attempt to redirect an organization, field or product line from where it is headed toward a different direction. Redirective leaders need to match to environmental circumstances to succeed (Sternberg and

Vroom, 2002). If they do not have the luck to have matching environmental circumstances, their best intentions may go awry.

Reconstruction/redirection
This type of creative leadership is an attempt to move a field or an organization or a product line back to where it once was (a reconstruction of the past) so that it may move onward from that point, but in a direction different from the one it took from that point onward.

Reinitiation
This type of leadership is an attempt to move a field, organization or product line to a different, as yet unreached, starting point and then to move from that point. The leaders takes followers from a new starting point in a direction that is different from the one that the field, organization or product line has pursued previously.

Synthesis
In this type of creative leadership, the creator integrates two ideas that previously were seen as unrelated or even as opposed. What formerly were viewed as distinct ideas now are viewed as related and capable of being unified. Integration is a key means by which progress is attained in the sciences. It represents neither an acceptance nor a rejection of existing paradigms. Rather, it represents a merger of them.

In terms of the model of types of creativity described above, the kinds of leaders vary widely. For example, replicators and conservers pretty much leave existing paradigms as they are. Doctors change things that are wrong. Turnaround specialists make major changes in the organization they lead. They are redirectors or reinitiators.

CONCLUSION

Leadership involves many aspects. One aspect is the story that underlies the leadership effort. In this chapter, I have discussed some aspects of stories and how they function in leadership situations. I have discussed properties of stories as well as some of the various types of stories leaders may choose. Stories are not, in and of themselves, good or bad. Rather, they work differentially well in particular contexts. A successful leader, then, is one who can match her or his story to the needs of her or his followers in a given time or place. A good leader additionally has a story that will take followers in the direction they need to go. When the needs of the followers change, the leader's story must change as well, or else a leader who has been successful may find him or herself starting to fail.

Stories are not, of course, all that underlie leadership (see Antonakis et al., 2004; Goethals and Sorenson, 2007, for reviews). But they are a critical factor in the success or failure of a given leader's leadership.

REFERENCES

Antonakis, John, Anna T. Cianciolo and Robert J. Sternberg (eds), (2004), *The Nature of Leadership*, Thousand Oaks, CA: Sage Publications.

Epstein, Seymour (1993), *You're Smarter than You Think: How to Develop Your Practical Intelligence for Success in Living,* New York: Simon and Schuster.

Gardner, Howard (1991), *The Unschooled Mind*, New York: Basic Books.

Gardner, Howard (1995), *Leading Minds*, New York: Basic Books.

Gardner, Howard (2004), *Changing Minds: The Art and Science of Changing our Own and Other People's Minds*, Boston, MA: Harvard Business School Press.

Goethals, George R. and Georgia J. Sorenson (eds) (2007), *The Quest for a General Theory of Leadership,* Cheltenham, UK and Northampton, MA, USA: Edward Elgar.

Schank, Roger C. and Robert P. Abelson (1977), *Scripts, Plans, Goals, and Understanding,* Hillsdale. NJ: Erlbaum.

Sloman, Steven A. (1996), "The empirical case for two systems of reasoning", *Psychological Bulletin*, **119**, 3–22.

Sternberg, Robert J. (1995), "Love as a story", *Journal of Social and Personal Relationships*, **12** (4), 541–6.

Sternberg, Robert J. (1998), *Love is a Story,* New York: Oxford University Press.

Sternberg, Robert J. (1999), "A propulsion model of types of creative contributions", *Review of General Psychology*, **3**, 83–100.

Sternberg, R.J. (2005), "WICS: a model of leadership", *The Psychologist-Manager Journal*, **8**(1), 29–43.

Sternberg, R.J. (2007), "A systems model of leadership: WICS", *American Psychologist*, **62**(1), 34–42.

Sternberg, Robert J. (2008), "The WICS approach to leadership: stories of leadership and the structures and processes that support them", *The Leadership Quarterly*, **19**(3), 360–71.

Sternberg, Robert J. and Victor H. Vroom (2002), "The person versus the situation in leadership", *Leadership Quarterly*, **13**, 301–23.

Sternberg, Robert J., Mahzad Hojjat and Michael L. Barnes (2001), "Empirical aspects of a theory of love as a story", *European Journal of Personality*, **15**, 1–20.

Sternberg, Robert J., James C. Kaufman and Jean E. Pretz (2003), "A propulsion model of creative leadership", *Leadership Quarterly*, **14**, 455–473.

14. Leadership in literary perspective

Nicholas O. Warner

Literature abounds with depictions of leadership in virtually every area of life – political, religious, military, commercial, familial, educational, athletic – yet the topic of leadership in literature, as in other arts, has yet to receive the attention it deserves. Citations of imaginative literature in leadership studies tend to be fleeting and illustrative rather than analytical, while more extended discussions often approach literature as a resource for "tips" on successful leadership practices, especially in business.[1] For their part, literary scholars have produced surprisingly few studies of leadership; the full-scale, professional analysis of leadership in literature is rare, though the number of instances of such an approach is gradually increasing. Unlike the situation in, say, organizational psychology or political science, it is still too early to identify key contributions made by literary criticism (or art history or film studies) to the study of leadership. Nor has the analysis of leadership in literature achieved sufficient critical mass to constitute a literary subfield along the lines of, say, eco-criticism or women's studies. Consequently, this chapter will focus not on literary criticism's contributions to leadership studies, but on the potential benefits of approaching leadership through literature. Such a discussion will, I hope, stimulate leadership scholars to look more closely at literature, and literary scholars to look more closely at leadership.[2]

Although leadership seems a natural fit with the study of politics and other social sciences, the political scientist Bryan D. Jones has pointed out that "Leadership in politics is one of the least tractable topics that political scientists deal with. To most people, leadership implies creativity, and creativity is not very amenable to the standard tools of analysis prevalent in political and other social sciences." This does not mean, Jones goes on to say, "that leadership is resistant to systematic inquiry" – the kind of systematic inquiry found in his own and the work of many other social scientists who study leadership (Jones, 1989: vii). But Jones's comments do suggest that some important aspects of leadership, such as creativity, would benefit from approaches other than those of quantifiable research. Certainly literature, which itself is a manifestation of human creativity, and which often deals with people engaged in various forms of creative endeavor, is one promising avenue for studying leadership. In fact, the main argument of this chapter is that literature's great relevance to leadership lies in its capacity for vividly representing, and asking probing questions about, the interpersonal dynamics and social, emotional, and ethical dimensions of leader–follower relations.

Literature's most fundamental link to leadership is identical with its most fundamental link to society in general – language whether literal or metaphorical. After all, "literature is a social institution, using as its medium language, a social creation" (Wellek and Warren, 1970: 94). And among the most universal and potent uses of language is storytelling, which can take a plethora of forms, from prose fictions (short stories, novels) to oral epics, plays, films, musicals, lyric poems (which can be seen as stories about feeling), and of course the various narratives or "stories" that people tell about themselves – and about others. In addressing the power of the stories that we generally label as "literature", the Italian novelist and critic Italo Calvino has observed that "Literature is one of a society's instruments of self-awareness – certainly not the only one, but nonetheless an essential instrument, because its origins are connected with the origins of various types of knowledge, various codes, various forms of critical thought" (Calvino, 1986: 97). But self-awareness can also grow, paradoxically, through awareness of the other, of other experiences, perspectives and modes of being – we might also say other modes of leading and following than the ones we may know or prefer. This notion of coming not only to understand ourselves through literature, but also to understand the other, is key to Martha Nussbaum's argument for the illuminative power of literary works: "the ability to imagine the concrete ways in which people different from oneself grapple with disadvantage" has, writes Nussbaum, "great practical and public value" (Nussbaum, 1995: xvi). Building on Aristotle's famous observation in *The Poetics*, that poetry is a more philosophical thing than history, because while history deals with what happened, literature deals with what *may* happen, Nussbaum observes that "literary works typically invite their readers to put themselves in the place of people of many different kinds and to take on their experiences" (Nussbaum 1995: 5); through literature, readers attain vicarious "knowledge of what it will be like to 'live through' the situation portrayed" (Zamir, 2007: 6). In a sense, the literary work creates a kind of laboratory of the imagination, within which we can observe human beings engaging in activities and interactions that we observe and mentally share as we place ourselves in the characters' situations. Literature allows us to see, via the windows of imagination opened by the words we read, into the inner world of others. In this way our reading consciousness begins to overlap with that of the author and of the characters we encounter; as a result, we may perceive the ways that leaders perceive and in turn are perceived by followers, and we can experience, on the level of the reading consciousness, what it is like to lead, and to follow, in a wide range of contexts.

As private individuals, of course, readers attuned to literature will experience it in just these ways. As professionals, however, social scientists who use literature or other art forms in their research tend to view the work of art not in its particularity or artistic excellence, but mainly in one of two ways: first, as a piece of social or cultural data that may be correlated, often statistically, with other, similar pieces of data from which one may draw conclusions about a certain group's attitudes, values, tastes, and the like. Second, the work of art serves as an illustrative detail, an interesting but singular piece of anecdotal evidence used to support or enhance a larger argument within the disciplinary framework of the social sciences, not the humanities. Such approaches to literature for the purposes of social science can be valuable. But they are not how professional literary scholars approach literature. Let me clarify with some particulars. One example of literature used as data for the social scientist is a highly regarded study produced some two decades ago by the sociologist Elizabeth Long. Her book *The American Dream and the Popular Novel* (1985) is an ambitious sociological analysis of how American bestsellers reflected middle-class notions of the American Dream between 1945 and 1975. But Long's work, although it includes intelligent readings of various novels, was not concerned with the individual artistic integrity of the texts covered in her book; her choice of titles on the basis of sales made economic success the first principle of selection – a valid principle, but not an artistic one. Long's study made a contribution to the sociology of literature, and even to the study of the reception of popular fiction in relation to the concept of the American Dream. But her book approached literature from the professional standpoint of the social sciences – not of the humanities.

To clarify the second social science approach to the arts mentioned earlier – that of citing a particular work in order to illustrate a larger point – I turn to a recent discussion of leadership by the political scholar, Aaron Wildavsky. Analyzing the topic of hierarchy in cultural theories of leadership, Wildavsky includes a reference, not to literature, but to the related narrative medium of film:

> As the classical scholars who studied traditional societies from Sir Henry Maine to Max Weber have maintained, obligations were reciprocal: the rules and statutes that enabled the top to give orders down the line also, by virtue of their binding character, limited what leaders could do to followers. "I must obey here, but you have no right to give orders there". The numerous motion pictures on military life – I think of John Ford's *She Wore a Yellow Ribbon* – which show sergeants being deferential to officers on the battlefield but using customary practice to avoid encroachment on their family life – the colonel cannot give orders to the sergeant's children or invade his home – fit the picture (Wildavsky, 1989: 103).

Wildavsky's observation is useful to anyone interested in hierarchies of leadership, and his example from Ford's work is apt, although the film he has in mind is actually not *She Wore a Yellow Ribbon* but *Fort Apache*, another John Ford film in a trilogy about the US cavalry: it is in *Fort Apache*, not *She Wore a Yellow Ribbon*, that the incident with the sergeant occurs. But for Wildavsky's purposes, the John Ford film is incidental and merely supplementary to the analysis of political leadership. For a literary or film critic, however, Ford's motion picture would be far closer to the center, if not at the very center, of scholarly attention. In contrast to Wildavsky's passing reference, the incident between colonel and sergeant would be part of a much fuller exploration of their relations, and indeed of the other dimensions of leadership that emerge through the cinematic art of *Fort Apache*. The approach to this film from the humanities might be traditional, emphasizing imagery or storyline and close attention to details so as accurately to convey the film's meaning; or the approach might be deconstructive, seeking out ways that the film subverts its own putative messages or ideological stance; or post-colonialist, examining the depiction of Native Americans within the film, including contrasts in the leadership styles of the film's three main leaders: Colonel Thursday, his second-in-command, Captain Kirby, and the Apache chief, Cochise; or psychoanalytic, reading both male and female characters in positions of authority or subordination in terms of, say, sexual frustration, projection and sublimation; or feminist, examining the ways that gender stereotypes tie in with the presentation of male and female characters as followers and leaders throughout the film. But regardless of methodology, literary or film scholars discussing leadership in *Fort Apache* would tend to analyze the ways that devices of the cinematic medium (for example, dialogue, camera work, editing, sound effects), and details of film history (for example, production guidelines, studio memos, screenplay drafts, other motion pictures directed by Ford) affect our understanding of leadership in this particular film. More broadly, such a discussion could deepen our sense of how artistic representations of leadership both reflect and shape attitudes toward leadership, and how our own leadership experiences might have analogues to the situations presented in *Fort Apache* and other works.

This is not the place to launch into the sort of extended analysis described above; examples of such analysis may be found in the studies cited in note 2, and in the bibliographies of those studies. Rather, I turn to several salient aspects of literature that have particular relevance to the study of leadership: literature's use of characterization to present human personality; its ability to render emotions; its vivid representation of concrete events and situations; and the pervasiveness of ethical issues in literary works. These are not the only factors to consider in literature, of course – such a list could easily exceed the length of this entire chapter – but they are important enough and inclusive enough to indicate what a literary approach can contribute to the study of leadership.

In its very essence, leadership is a human relationship between leaders and followers, with all of the complexity that human relationships entail. Given its attention to human beings' thoughts, feelings, experiences, and its presentations of people speaking to each other, working together or fighting, helping and hindering one another, loving and hating one another, literature provides an inexhaustible supply of examples for the study of human interaction, including the interaction that occurs between leaders and followers in all areas of life. To convey such interactions persuasively requires the detailed, individualized delineation of personality found in successful literary characterization.

Connected to such individuation of character is emotion, which is also key to much leadership: "Whatever else an effective leader does, whether he or she makes people think or remember or act, he or she makes others *feel*, whether pride or hatred or imagination of love or fear" (Solomon, 2005: 28). Recent scholarship has increasingly examined emotion in leadership, including such things as emotional intelligence, the role of emotion in followers as well as in leaders, and the correlation of emotion with certain kinds of leadership, especially transformational leadership (Goleman, 1995; Bass and Riggio, 2006; Caruso et al., 2002; Riggio and Reichard, 2008). In addition to the more quantitative assessments found in many social science approaches to leadership, it should not be surprising that literature, with its extensive depictions of human emotion, can show much about the emotional factors of leadership.

Literature's vivid descriptive power, including the placement of human beings in specific environments, produces a concreteness of context – or, in Shakespeare's words from *A Midsummer Night's Dream*, "gives to airy nothing/A local habitation and a name" (Shakespeare, 1969: 169). As a result of this concreteness, readers can engage their imaginations more fully with people in "local habitations" different from their own, and consider disjunctions and sometimes surprising connections between themselves and that which seems to be "other". This aspect of literary works is particularly apt for leadership studies in light of the contemporary influence of situational-contingency approaches to leadership, with their emphasis on matching particular leadership styles to different situations and follower populations. (On the emergence of situational and contingency leadership paradigms in the 1960s and later, see Chemers, 1997: 28–60.)

Ethics, as Joanne Ciulla points out, is "central to the special role that [leaders] play" (Ciulla, 2005: 1). While a poem, play, or novel may or may not address ethics, the centrality of ethics to many literary works makes literature an extraordinarily useful site of moral reflection about leadership. Whether in Achilles' argument with Agamemnon at the beginning of *The Iliad* about what ethically is owed to the rank and file in the division of spoils, or King Henry's rationalizations for invading France in Shakespeare's *Henry V*, or the dilemmas between family feeling and sound business judgment confronting

Alexandra Bergson in Willa Cather's novel, *O Pioneers!*, literature invites consideration of ethical choices, moral ambiguities, and questions of balancing leadership effectiveness and ethics. But questions of ethics in a work of art entail aesthetic questions as well. In Dickens' *Hard Times*, for instance, the novel's "moral operations are not independent of its aesthetic excellence. A tedious novel would not have had the same moral power" (Nussbaum, 1995: 5). This integration of ethics with esthetics is what Wayne Booth addresses when he writes of "the ethical appraisal that is inseparable from what looks like judgment of sheer craft" (Booth, 1988: 107); as Booth further explains, this does not mean that a reader cannot come to conclusions or moral evaluations different from those expressed in a text (Booth, 1988: 107–9). But it does mean that the ethical import of a text intersects with our understanding of the aesthetic elements in which that import is embedded and through which it is expressed. Because of this, an ethical evaluation of a work of art must not only acknowledge the interplay of Nussbaum's "moral operations" and "aesthetic excellence", but must also confront the problem of "aesthetically compelling representations of morally reprehensible acts" (Zamir, 2007: 36). Negotiating such matters is an important part of ethically oriented literary criticism, a criticism that has particular relevance to texts where questions of leadership and moral choice are prominent – which is to say the vast majority of texts that examine leadership at all.

The opening of one of Western literature's foundational works, *The Iliad*, dramatically illustrates the convergence of all of the above qualities in relation to leadership: character, emotion, setting and ethics. The famous central theme of Homer's epic, the rage of Achilles, originates from a dispute between two leaders – Achilles and Agamemnon – precisely over matters of a leader's prestige, ethical obligations between leaders and followers, rights of command, and duties of obedience. The personalities of both leaders are central to this incident, as we watch the arrogant, grasping Agamemnon clash with the hot-tempered, touchily honorable Achilles. Through a few quick strokes of dialogue, Homer has Agamemnon, King of Mycenae and commander of the Argive (Greek) confederation attacking Troy, unwittingly unveil his own character as a rapacious bully who takes the slogan "greed is good" to depths that *Wall Street*'s Gordon Gecko never dreamed of. Furious at having to give up Chryseis, the daughter of Apollo's priest, from his supply of war spoils, Agamemnon demands compensatory war booty from others. Achilles, another high-ranking Argive leader but still subordinate to Agamemnon (who is both a king and the supreme commander of the Argive forces), becomes infuriated in his turn as the two men debate the question of what spoils are owed to leaders, and from whom they should be taken. Glory in battle is as important to Achilles as it is to Agamemnon – even more so since, having exchanged longevity for a short but glorious life, Achilles' need for the trappings of glory is the more urgent. But unlike Agamemnon, Achilles balks at taking spoils from the common soldiers – although he cannot countermand Agamemnon's orders, he can argue with him, pithily expressing his own contempt for Agamemnon's readiness to extort goods from their followers:

> Whatever we dragged from towns we plundered,
> all's been portioned out. But collect it, call it back
> from the rank and file? *That* would be the disgrace.
> So return the girl to the god, at least for now. (Homer, 1990: 81)

The leaders' conflict intensifies until Achilles, cooled by the rational counsel of the goddess of wisdom, Athena, agrees to give up his own female prize, Briseis, to Agamemnon – upon which Achilles sulkily withdraws from the war, waiting in his own ship for Argive war losses to mount up until the Argives come begging for him to return his supreme fighting powers to the battle.

Both through dialogue and narration, *The Iliad* continuously reveals the role of personality in the dispute between these two leaders, and the escalation of emotion as they argue. Moreover, the importance of their specific roles as besiegers of Troy and military leaders, and of their own personal circumstances, contribute to our understanding and judgment of these characters. Agamemnon, heading an army of Argive leaders to regain his brother Menelaus' wife, Helen, has been commanding the Greek forces for a decade of thus far futile war. He fears that the Greek warrior chieftains and lesser soldiers may slip away from his control, which in part explains his obsession with booty – this is one way of maintaining the prestige he needs in order to retain not simply nominal but actual control over a war-weary and only loosely unified group of Argives. As Richmond Lattimore reminds us, at the same time that Agamemnon is a "brave and effective… personal fighter", he is also "a worried, uncertain man" because of his tenuous hold on his followers. His "irresolution and consequent anger combine with the anger of [Achilles] to motivate tragedy" (Lattimore, 1951: 49). Meanwhile Achilles, superstar of the Argive army, has his own subgroup of forces to lead, the Myrmidons, whose ultimate allegiance is to him, not to the Argive force as a whole. Although in confederacy with Agamemnon and Menelaus, Achilles sees their cause – regaining Helen – as a private quarrel in which he has no personal interest: "The Trojans never did *me* damage, not in the least" declares Achilles, as he rationalizes his abandonment of the war against Troy (Homer, 1990: 82). This war mainly offers Achilles a chance for the military glory he constantly seeks, and for the spoils whose main value is their testimony to that glory. Also underlying the relationship between these two men is the tension between Agamemnon as the commander-in-chief and Achilles as the undisputed supreme fighter – a tension between official leadership position and skill that can appear in a sports team, a corporation, or virtually any organization.

Entwined with all of these issues is, of course, ethics – or the lack of it. For Agamemnon, questions of ethics are largely irrelevant, as seen in his gratuitous cruelty toward Chryseis' father, whom he tortures with descriptions of how Chryseis will languish, exploited sexually and by hard labor, far from her father's home when Agamemnon takes her with him after the war. Although Achilles is no less brutal in his own way, he does approach the division of spoils with more ethical concerns, as a just sign of service rendered, not of pure rank. This is why, violent hot-head though he is, Achilles reveals a moral reasoning of sorts, which includes consideration of doing the right thing by the rank and file as well as by the leaders. But the moral and leadership issues here are far from simple. For all of his expressed concern for the troops, Achilles is perfectly willing to allow hundreds of Greeks to be killed by Trojans because, in pique at Agamemnon's seizure of his own slave-girl Briseis, Achilles will refuse to fight the Trojans until further notice.

The emotional volatility of Achilles and Agamemnon, their hypersensitivity, their conflicting attitudes toward the rights of followers, and the ethical ramifications of their decisions as leaders – Agamemnon's to insist on seizing Achilles' rightful prize to replace his own, Achilles' to abandon his erstwhile allies because of a personal tiff with Agamemnon – all of these details from the opening book of *The Iliad* speak powerfully to still pertinent questions of leadership, such as organizational purpose; compensation for services rendered and for position occupied; the appropriate roles of leaders and followers; the ethical bases of allegiance and of disaffiliation. Nor do such questions end with Book One, but continue, with enormous variation and complexity, throughout all the remaining 23 books of this turbulent epic.

Besides *The Iliad*, classical literature overflows with instances of leadership related to powerful personalities, intense emotions, complex circumstances and ethical dilemmas, as in *The Odyssey*, *Antigone*, *The Aeneid*, and a nearly endless list of other texts. But many later works also demonstrate thought-provoking perspectives on leadership. Sometimes the topics of these works makes them likely candidates for examining leadership: Tolstoy's *War and Peace*, with its portrayal of historical figures, such as Napoleon and the Russian generals marshaling their followers against him; Henrik Ibsen's *An Enemy of the People*, a play that presents several characters from different walks of life jockeying for power and influence over a single community; Robert Penn Warren's political novel, *All the King's Men*, centering on the leadership and mis-leadership of its protagonist, Governor Willie Stark; or Sembene Ousmane's *God's Bits of Wood*, a fictional account of the 1948 Dakar–Niger railway strike by Senegalese laborers against their French colonial bosses, which explores the varieties and vagaries of leadership (and demagoguery) in relation to union organization, gender roles, racial identity, politics and religion – all matters that overlapped during the strike. A less predictable text, however, would be something like Cather's *O Pioneers!*, whose protagonist, Alexandra Bergson, lives in relative isolation on the Nebraska plains. But this limpidly written, subtle novel exemplifies how even a work not putatively "about" leadership can still have much to say on this subject. The novel briefly but unforgettably demonstrates the painful gender biases that Alexandra encounters from her own stolid brothers who resent her control of the family farm, bestowed upon her by their dying father. The book is also unusual among works of art in that the heroine embodies emphatically non-charismatic leadership. Yes, Alexandra has vision and determination, and like many successful leaders examined in leadership research, she is willing to take risks: countering her family's wish to move to a lower, more secure part of the land, Alexandra prefers to take "a big chance" over "a little certainty" (Cather, 1988: 37). Yet she is not an inspiring leader. As the novel makes clear, while she is wise, ethical and persistent, Alexandra also is "slow, truthful, steadfast" (Cather, 1988: 35) – not in any sense charismatic. From my own teaching of this work, I know how engaged readers can become defending Alexandra's rational, methodical style of leading or, conversely, ascribing some of the problems she encounters to her lack of charisma, eloquence and spontaneity.

The novel also movingly portrays some of the personal, emotional costs of leadership. In her middle years, Alexandra – now rich, prominent, and independent – confesses that she has had "a pretty lonely life" (Cather, 1988: 103), and would gladly trade her land for the freedom enjoyed by others. Most severe of all these costs is her emotional blindness to the romance brewing between her beloved nephew and a married woman neighbor. Alexandra is preoccupied with, and exhausted by, building her fortune, leading recalcitrant followers, and simultaneously running the family household and the family business. As a result, she completely misses the emotional signals which, if detected and acted upon, might have prevented the grisly tragedy that occurs toward the end of the book.

Working with this novel, a reader could explore not just successful leadership strategies, but also the nuances of leadership style, the complexities that arise when familial and business enterprises overlap, and the sympathetic but clear-eyed way that Cather shows the price exacted for the leadership success achieved by Alexandra. Although it is far removed from conventional notions of leadership in the military, political or corporate worlds, and indeed, partly because of this, *O Pioneers!* has much to offer to students of leadership.

The narrative organization of many novels and plays ties in easily with leadership, what with the tendency of these genres toward multiple characters, extensive dialogue, strong plot line, and detailed presentation of human action. Such leadership-related issues as motivation, persuasion, loyalty, betrayal, teamwork, ambition, cooperation and rivalry seem naturally to accord with the fictional and dramatic modes of literature. But poetry too can be as relevant to leadership as any other medium. This is most obviously true with epic poems like *The Iliad* and, much later, Milton's *Paradise Lost*, with its profound excavations of authority, obedience, rebellion, charisma (especially in the figure of Satan, one of literature's most charismatic characters), and the choices we make about which principles and leaders to follow. In more oblique but also significant ways, lyric poems have long dealt with issues related to leadership; the few examples cited here represent part of a much vaster body of poetry articulating various perspectives on leaders, followers, the nature of leadership, and the interpenetration of politics or ideology with personal attachments, attitudes and values. Among many other instances are: Milton's attack on religious persecution and abuse of power in the sonnet, "On the Late Massacre in Piedmont"; Wordsworth's celebration of the Haitian revolutionary leader named in the title of "To Toussaint L'Ouverture" (another contribution in the sonnet form); Yeats' numerous poetic meditations on the political turmoil and violence of his time, as in his famous treatment of the Irish rebellion's "terrible beauty" in "Easter, 1916"; the Russian poet Osip Mandelstam's unbelievably courageous, originally untitled poem about Stalin, now often referred to as the "Stalin Epigram", which satirized both the Soviet dictator and his fawning followers, and which eventually resulted in Mandelstam's imprisonment and death in the gulag.

But a poem dealing with leadership need not be as topical as the above examples – far from it. One such text is the dramatic monologue "Elegy of Fortinbras", by the twentieth-century Polish poet Zbigniew Herbert (Herbert, 1986: 301–2). Based, as its title implies, on Shakespeare's *Hamlet*, this poem offers no definitive position on leadership, or followers, or charisma, or ethics; rather, it invites readers to meditate on such important issues as the kinds of characteristics that leadership calls forth, and to ask ourselves such questions as what we expect from our rulers, and whether what we want in a political leader applies to leadership in other spheres. Both somber and playful, the poem presents, without either affirming or rejecting, the imagined perspective of Fortinbras, the blunt, aggressive leader who readily fills the power vacuum he finds at the death-strewn royal court of Elsinore. Readers or viewers of *Hamlet* may recall that it is Fortinbras who re-establishes order at the end: uttering a few words of tribute to the dead Hamlet, Fortinbras commands that the funeral rites begin, and concludes the play with the command, "Go, bid the soldiers shoot" (as a salute to the dead, and also as a possible reminder of his freshly asserted authority).

In the Herbert poem, Fortinbras scorns Hamlet's "crystal notions"; his own leadership style, like his personality, is tough, pragmatic, efficient, assured: "one has to take the city by the neck and shake it a bit", he says with grim humor. Concerns about relationship-oriented leadership or "least preferred coworkers", which are so common in contemporary leadership theory

(Chemers, 2002), could not even flicker on this man's horizon of thought, but when it comes to the task, Fortinbras will achieve it, come what may. Subverting one of English literature's most famous phrases (Hamlet's dying words, "the rest is silence"), Herbert's Fortinbras declares,

> Now you have peace Hamlet you accomplished what you had to
> and you have peace   The rest is not silence but belongs to me
> you chose the easier part an elegant thrust
> but what is heroic death compared with eternal watching
> with a cold apple in one's hand on a narrow chair
> with a view of the ant-hill and the clock's dial.

In phrasing that vividly encapsulates the prosaic nature of his concerns, and of the task-centered, managerial style of his authority, Fortinbras continues:

> Adieu prince   I have tasks – a sewer project
> and a decree on prostitutes and beggars.

At the same time, though chillingly reminiscent of the "strong-arm" (*Fort-in-bras*) tactics of rulers that would have been all too familiar to Herbert, who grew up in Communist-dominated Poland, his Fortinbras is capable of honest, intelligent and oddly touching insights into the differences between himself and the volatile, gloriously imaginative prince. "This night is born/a star named Hamlet", Fortinbras says, acknowledging that "what I shall leave will not be worth a tragedy" – which may, in fact, be a good thing. And the poem concludes with a vivid image of the gulf between the ever-doubting Hamlet and the never-doubting Fortinbras, between, perhaps, those who question power and those who wield it:

> It is not for us to greet each other or bid farewell we live on archipelagos
> and that water, these words what can they do what can they do prince.

At times, a work of literature is compelling by being explicit, at times by being elliptical and suggestive. It is the latter quality that emerges in these lines, which all the more deeply draw us to reflect upon power, personality, dreams, social realities – and leadership.

Precisely because literature explores all areas of human experience, the study of literature often draws on a wide array of disciplines; thus, while literary criticism is a distinct discipline in its own right, it is also perhaps the most naturally multidisciplinary of fields. In a work of literature, things like economic reality, religious ideals, personality, desire and duty, selfishness and altruism do not stay in neatly arranged, separate categories, but have the messy, mutual permeability that they do in life itself. This in turn makes literature an excellent tool for studying so multifaceted a subject as leadership.

Literature can, in effect, serve as a crossroads where different perspectives meet, mingle, and produce new directions for exploring and understanding leaders, followers, and the ways that they interact. This is why in leadership, as in so many other areas, Picasso's famous statement once again rings true: "We all know that art is not truth. Art is a lie that makes us realize truth" (Ashton, 1988: 3).[3]

NOTES

1. Some recent books on leadership in literature illustrate this pattern, for example, Brawer (1998), Whitney and Packer (2002) and Badaracco (2006), each of which emphasizes business applications of literary texts. While broader in approach, the Hartwick Leadership case studies, published by Hartwick Management in Humanities Institute, are prepared mainly as guidelines for teachers using literary works and films in classes on leadership.
2. Among literary discussions of leadership see Patterson (1984) and Warner (2008), which specifically address leadership in Melville's *Moby-Dick*; Jordan (1999), which focuses not on leadership per se, but on the related theme of Renaissance notions of rulers and their subjects and their relationship to Shakespeare's romances; Warner (2007), on film versions of Shakespeare's *Henry V*; and McCann (2008), on parallels between executive power in the American presidency and narrative power in American fiction.
3. I wish to thank my colleague, Professor John Farrell, for valuable comments on an earlier draft of this chapter.

REFERENCES

Ashton, D. (ed.) (1988), *Picasso on Art: A Selection of Views,* New York: Da Capo Books.

Badaracco, J. (2006), *Questions of Character: Illuminating the Heart of Leadership through Literature,* Cambridge, MA: Harvard Business School Press.

Bass, B.M. and R.E. Riggio (2006), *Transformational Leadership*, 2nd edn, Mahwah, NJ: Lawrence Erlbaum Associates.

Booth, W. (1988), *The Company We Keep: An Ethics of Fiction*, Chicago, IL: University of Chicago Press.

Brawer, R.A. (1998), *Fictions of Business: Insights on Management from Great Literature*, New York: John Wiley and Sons.

Calvino, I. (1986), *The Uses of Literature*, translated by P. Creagh, New York: Harcourt, Brace.

Caruso, D., J.D. Mayer, P. Salovey (2002), "Emotional intelligence and emotional leadership", in R.E. Riggio, S.E. Murphy and F.J. Pirozzolo (eds), *Multiple Intelligences and Leadership*, Mahwah, NJ: Lawrence Erlbaum Associates, pp. 55–74.

Cather, W. (1988), *O Pioneers!*, Boston, MA: Houghton Mifflin.

Chemers, M.M. (1997), *An Integrative Theory of Leadership*, Mahwah, NJ: Lawrence Erlbaum Associates.

Chemers, M.M. (2002), "Integrating models of leadership and intelligence: efficacy and effectiveness", in R.E. Riggio, S.E. Murphy and F.J. Pirozzolo (eds), *Multiple Intelligences and Leadership*, Mahwah, NJ: Lawrence Erlbaum Associates, pp. 1139–60.

Ciulla, J.B. (2005), "Introduction", in J.B. Ciulla, T.L. Price and S.E. Murphy (eds), *The Quest for Moral Leaders: Essays on Leadership Ethics,* Cheltenham, UK and Northampton, MA, USA: Edward Elgar, pp. 1–9.

Goleman, D. (1995), *Emotional Intelligence: Why it Can Matter More than IQ*, New York: Bantam Books.

Herbert, Z. (1986), "Elegy of Fortinbras", translated by C. Milosz and P.D. Scott, in C. Milosz (ed.), *A Book of Luminous Things: An International Anthology of Poetry*, San Diego, CA: Harcourt, Brace, pp. 301–2.

Homer (1990), *The Iliad*, translated by R. Fagles, New York: Penguin.

Jones, B.D. (1989), "Preface", in B.D. Jones (ed.), *Leadership and Politics: New Perspectives in Political Science*, Lawrence, KS: University Press of Kansas, pp. vii–viii.

Jordan, C. (1999), *Shakespeare's Monarchies: Ruler and Subject in the Romances*, Ithaca, NY: Cornell University Press.

Lattimore, R. (1951), "Introduction", in R. Lattimore (ed. and translator), *Homer, The Iliad,* Chicago, IL: University of Chicago Press, pp. 11–55.

Long, E. (1985), *The American Dream and the Popular Novel*, London: Routledge and Kegan Paul.

McCann, S. (2008). *A Pinnacle of Feeling: American Literature and Presidential Government*, Princeton, MA: Princeton University Press.

Nussbaum, M. (1995). *Poetic Justice*: *The Literary Imagination and Public Life*, Boston: Beacon Press.

Patterson, M.R. (1984), "Democratic leadership and narrative authority in *Moby-Dick*", *Studies in the Novel*, **16**, 288–303.

Riggio, R.E. and R.J. Reichard (2008), "The emotional and social intelligences of effective leadership: an emotional and social skill approach", *Journal of Managerial Psychology*, **23**, 169–85.

Shakespeare, W. (1969), *A Midsummer Night's Dream*, in A. Harbage (ed.), *William Shakespeare, The Complete Works*, Baltimore: Penguin Books, p. 169.

Solomon, R.C. (2005), "Emotional leadership, emotional entegrity", in J.B. Ciulla, T.L. Price, and S.E. Murphy (eds), *The Quest for Moral Leaders: Essays on Leadership Ethics*, Cheltenham, UK and Northampton, MA, USA: Edward Elgar, pp. 28–44.

Warner, N. (2007), "Screening leadership through Shakespeare: paradoxes of leader–follower relations in *Henry V* on film", *The Leadership Quarterly*, **18**, 1–15.

Warner, N. (2008), "Of gods and commodores: leadership in Melville's *Moby-Dick*", in J.B. Ciulla (ed.), *Leadership and the Humanities*, Westport, CT: Praeger.

Wellek, R. and A. Warren (1970), *Theory of Literature*, New York: Harcourt, Brace.

Whitney, J.O. and T. Packer (2002), *Power Plays: Shakespeare's Lessons in Leadership and Management*, New York: John Wiley and Sons.

Wildavsky, A. (1969), "A cultural theory of leadership", in B.D. Jones (ed.), *Leadership and Politics: New Perspectives in Political Science*, Lawrence, KS: University Press of Kansas, pp. 87–113.

Zamir, T. (2007), *Double Vision: Moral Philosophy and Shakespearean Drama*, Princeton, NJ: Princeton University Press.

15. Learning how to look: the art of observation and leadership development

Anu M. Mitra

From ancient times, prophets and seers have exhorted us to look deeper into our surroundings. Perhaps a seer or dreamer stood within the caves at Lascaux or Altamira and bid her audience to gaze deep into the images painted on the walls – or perhaps this special seeing was reserved for a chosen few. As we learn to see, the prophets have said, as we begin to look, to observe, to reflect and to wrest meaning and patterns out of the world around us, we gain surer knowledge of that world, and of ourselves. Josè Saramago, the Portuguese writer and Nobel laureate, gives his novel *Blindness* an epigraph from the Book of Exhortations:

> If you can see, learn how to look
> If you can look, learn how to observe.

"To see", "to look", "to observe" – acknowledging the differences among these acts is at the heart of every successful viewer of the visual field. In the fifteenth century, in his copious journals extending beyond 13 000 pages, Leonardo da Vinci harnessed the energy of his imagination by teaching himself how to see things as if for the first time. Thus, an ordinary coin merits multiple pages of description as well as a detailed, x-ray-like drawing that cuts through the object and seems to give it a life of its own. In these pages as well as in his art, da Vinci teaches himself to look and observe with utter clarity, so as to know the object, and, by extension, his surroundings, without the prop of presumed answers. Reflecting on his cross-section anatomical drawing of a human body, the first such effort to see "scientifically", da Vinci comments:

> This depiction of mine of the human body will be as clear to you as if you had the natural man before you; and the reason is that if you wish thoroughly to know the parts of the man, anatomically, you, or your eye, require to see it from different aspects, considering it from below and from above and from its sides, turning it about and seeking the origin of each member. … Therefore by my drawings every part will be known to you, and by all means of demonstrations from three different points of view of each part. (Gelb, 1998: 53)

The point of looking and observing with clarity, and assessing evidence from multiple points of view, lies at the root of knowledge, of what each one of us can know and chooses to know. "[P]erception structures thought", the contemporary American sculptor Richard Serra observes; "to see is to think and conversely to think is to see. … No one perceives anything alike; we only perceive as we are and it is our individual reality that counts" (Serra, 2008).

Thus, the ways of *seeing* teach us to discover, recognize, visualize and understand our world. The ways of *observing* (or *looking* with intentionality) require us to go another step (or two) and to use our judgment and inference-making abilities to arrive at something resembling knowledge. Dictionaries hedge "observe" with caveats: "guard", "watch", "inspect", "remark" and "comment". As Sturken and Cartwright point out in the *Practices of Looking*, "Seeing is something that we do somewhat arbitrarily as we go about our daily lives. Looking is an activity that involves a greater sense of purpose and direction. … Looking involves learning to interpret and like other practices, looking involves relationships of power" (Sturken and Cartwright, 2000: 10). The ways of observing naturally lead to *reflection*, from the Latin *reflectere*, which literally means to bend back. Alternative meanings of the word include "to turn into or away from a course" and "to cause to change direction". Reflection on what we see allows us to come up with new, refreshing, relevant and unique perspectives, with new solutions to sometimes too-familiar problems. Ultimately, the acts of observation and reflection compel us to become more alive to how we solve problems in our own lives.

The Learning How to Look program of the Union Institute and University, held at the Cincinnati Art Museum, enables participants to do just that. Originally introduced to medical students at the University of Cincinnati Medical School in 2003, the program teaches differential diagnosis – or how we weigh the evidence of differing options to arrive at our own unique diagnosis, interpretation or solution. Students at the Union Institute are non-traditional learners who have had a broad swath of experiences in the world, from police officers and superintendents of school systems, to journalists and pastors. Such students tend to bring a strong interest in the practical aspect of education. They have typically had limited exposure to art and the museum experience, and often begin the program with a sense of ambiguity and ambivalence about its value and usefulness. Quickly, they learn to make sense of the chaos that is presented before them. In the museum setting, they are placed in a situation where they must "read" an art piece. The act of looking – Da Vinci-like, as if for the first time – urges participants to see comprehensively, accurately and contextually. It provides an opportunity to think creatively on how the art of looking is related to how each one of us is able to empower ourselves to express our full potential as leaders in our field of inquiry.

LOOKING AND LEADERSHIP

Understanding and communication are complex processes that depend on both verbal and non-verbal skills. On the verbal side of the ledger, the modern educational system aims to provide relatively intensive preparation in developing the verbal skills of asking questions, framing arguments and counter-arguments, and manipulating words. But in the modern educational system, the non-verbal or extra-verbal skills of seeing, looking and observing tend to be overlooked. Bluntly, while we aim to teach students to read and write, we are content to produce graduates who are visually illiterate. If how we see, and how we look, shape how we think, this is a massive squandered opportunity in the proper education of citizens and leaders. Leaders excel in reading their environments with accuracy. "We become leaders", as G.T. Fairhurst and R.A. Sarr write, "through our ability to decipher and communicate meaning out of complex and confusing situations" (Fairhurst and Sarr, 1996). In a world of complexity, difficult-to-discern patterns, and the onrush of oceans of data, the ability to see clearly is critical for effective leadership. Reading our environment with clarity, and then discerning the solutions to the issues that lie before us, are at the heart of creating and sustaining leaders today.

The Learning How to Look program began as a way of instilling the practice of intentional observation. How could students engage in the practice of seeing, and thus offering, a pure description of what lay before them? How could initiates in the field of art be trained to look without bias or judgment in order to offer a sustained analysis of the problem that was literally within their field of vision? How could they learn to synthesize what they were seeing with general, universal principles, which then offered them clues on multiple resolutions? How could strategies widely successful in the visual arts be used to tackle leadership dilemmas in the education and business fields? How could the "simple" act of seeing and looking enhance leadership potential in our present and future leaders? To foster this skill, especially among students with little training in art, the program teaches three primary modes of looking and reasoning.

The first set of practices is called *inductive looking*, where the student becomes introduced or initiated into a particular way of seeing; she or he looks in order to make sense of the world. Primarily, the student describes what he or she sees by offering pure description; judgment and commentary are discouraged in favor of accuracy and integrity. The student is taught to provide an answer to the most basic of questions: "what?" This inductive mode is unexpectedly challenging for students, for most of us are unaware of how much we rely on mental blinders or shortcuts to "guide" or constrain how we see the world around us.

The second set of practices that the Learning How to Look program instills in the student is called *deductive looking.* In this practice, inferences are made in which the conclusion evolves necessarily from general or universal principles. In this interpretative section, the student attempts to generally provide the answers to the question: "now what?" With the raw data now on hand, the student uses judgment, discernment, cultural context and presuppositions to derive some general conclusions about what could be happening in the range of vision.

The last set of practices is best described as *abductive thinking.* In this scenario, the student literally "takes off" or "seizes away" (as in abducting) from normative action. The student spreads away from the usual course of events and practices possibilities thinking. How best can one think of solutions to the issue on hand and come away with a range of possibilities that defy tradition/convention? What are the options that are on hand which allow the viewer to come up with a differential diagnosis? The student attempts to answer the question: "so what?"

The three practices are further explored in the context of two exercises that are conducted in the program at the Cincinnati Art Museum:

1. *Emotional exercises*: Inductive, deductive and abductive reasoning is unleashed in the context of art that is non-representative, abstract and abstruse. How does one make sense of such a reality? How does one deal with the highest levels of ambiguity? How high is one's level of confusion endurance?[1]
2. *Intellectual exercises*: Inductive, deductive, and abductive reasoning[2] is used in the context of art that has a narrative structure that opens itself up to interpretation. When the rational structure is mined for detail, what does it reveal about the overall conclusions at which one arrives?

EMOTIONAL EXERCISE: A CASE STUDY 1

Inductive Thinking

Painted in 1963, Hans Hofmann's *Toward Crepuscule* shows intense colors pitted against each other (see Figure 15.1). The composition also has two rectangles and a square sitting alongside each other waiting to reveal the contents of the boxes for those who are willing to go deeper. The cool colors of blue and white seem to line one side of the large canvas. Streaks of white, meteor-like, also flash through this blueness. On the polar opposite, the warm colors of fiery yellow, orange, and red provides symmetrical balance. The green box in the middle of the composition grabs one's attention.

Note: The Hans Hofmann image, *Toward Crepuscule*, is reprinted permission of the Cincinnati Art Museum, the Edwina and Virginia Irwin Memorial Fund. The image is copyrighted by the Renate, Hans and Maria Hofmann Trust/Artists Rights Society (ARS), New York, 2008, and is reprinted with their permission.

Figure 15.1 Case history 1: emotional exercise: Hans Hofmann, Toward Crepuscule, *1963*

Deductive Thinking

Hofmann claimed that paintings such as *Toward Crepuscule* were derived from nature, even though no representational imagery can be found. This is at the same time a vocabulary of flat forms as well as pulsating color linked by geometry, faceted planes and rhythmic syncopations. The use of color rectangles is used as a major expressive device. Hofmann knew very well that the cool blues and greens would normally recede and the warm oranges and reds would emerge; but the sharp edges and the interposition of the square and rectangles press the green area forward, creating tension between the planes and flattening the canvas. Hofmann saw this tension as symbolic of the push and pull of nature, as if a struggle is going on with greenness emerging as a possible victor. The mood of this painting, however, is mostly joyous and inspiring. *Toward Crepuscule* (or toward dawn) might be considered a culmination of how the artist had been thinking of his life till that point.

Abductive Thinking

Hans Hofmann's painting was completed in the last few years of his life. In this painting, he is perhaps ruminating on those aspects of our lives that can only be intuited and perhaps not spelled out in so many words, when all sorts of secrets are dredged loose from the unconscious. At once, there is intense activity in the life of the world and in the life of the mind. This inherent struggle is implicit in all things in nature, and is perhaps represented best in the full canvass of a man's life. Is youth pitted against old age; yin against yang; spontaneity against wisdom; life against death? What are the polar opposites that seem to be playing out their part? In this piece, Hofmann gives us hints, clues and suggestions and expects the viewer to piece things together. Working in connotative and alchemical language, he alludes to the cycle of life, to the seasons consummating themselves in the ashes of the next one, in the flash of exhilaration that comes upon us. This painting confirms for us the idea that pure knowledge is born of struggle as well as joy.

Biographical Information

Hans Hofmann was an American artist born in Germany in 1880. He studied in Paris and witnessed at close hand the Fauvists' use of high-keyed colors and the Cubists' resolution of shapes into abstract planes. He came to the US in 1930 and began teaching at UC/Berkeley. Settling in New York, Hofmann established a school of fine art in the city in 1933 and another school in Provincetown, Massachusetts, in 1934. He became one of America's most influential art teachers and helped establish what is now known as the New York School. He died in 1966.[3]

INTELLECTUAL EXERCISE: A CASE STUDY 2

Inductive Reasoning

The painting in Figure 15.2 is one in which the narrative content clearly unfolds before our eyes. Thus, it does not defy our sense of who we are in the same way in which the Hans Hofmann piece did for us. In this painting, Pieter Claesz (1597/98–1661) depicts an *ontbijt*, a light meal that might take place at

Note: The Pieter Claesz image, *Still Life*, is reprinted permission of the Cincinnati Art Museum, Mr and Mrs Harry S. Leyman Endowment and Bequest of Mr and Mrs Walter J. Wichgar.

Figure 5.2 Case history 2: intellectual exercise: Pieter Claesz, Still Life *(*Breakfast Piece with Berckemeyer*), 1641*

any time of the day. Represented on a white, cloth-draped table, apparently just vacated by the diners, is a plate with rolls and bread, a sliced and peeled lemon, a raisin or mince pie, some nuts, a small clock or watch, and two drinking glasses – one with wine, one upended on the pewter tankard's spout. These glasses are specific to Dutch and German glassmaking, and the type with flaring cup and applied prunts is called a *berckemeyer*. The artist's monogram appears on the knife blade. The knife projects precariously beyond the edge of the table, as do the smaller plates. The artist's virtuosity in the depiction of textures and finishes is obvious. The overall composition of objects placed close to the edge of the table, or ledge, and the reflections in the glass and silver demonstrate the use of optics. You can see reverse reflections in the bowl of the spoon and the belly of the flagon. You can also see a window reflected in these materials.

Deductive Reasoning

Signs of affluence in the painting are numerous: in the simple but elegant objects, the foreign carpet, the knife with the mother-of-pearl handle, the imported lemon and the glass. The painting may be dated by the fact that the fork was not invented till the last third of the seventeenth century, giving rise to the need for the knobs on the berckemeyer so that greasy fingers were able to grasp the stemware.

At the symbolic level, this is a classic example of a memento mori, with the watch ticking away, the unfinished food right before the beginning of decay, the objects in tenuous balance – all reminders of the transitory nature of existence.

Artistically, the limited range of color and tonality (gray, white, brown, yellow) in the palette needs mention, as it evokes the Picasso of a few centuries later. Also, the depth of the plane of the painting, the kinds of backgrounds, the tabletops with corners and sharp edges, the strong horizontal across the entire bottom of the painting ought not to be overlooked. Typically, this painting would hang in the room where meals were eaten, serving as decoration for the room as well as having functioned as philosophical objects since many Dutch still lifes contained symbolic moral messages apparent to the seventeenth-century viewer. Symbolic imagery is used to convey the vanity of all earthly things. They appear in paintings of the time and the artists use them to point out the virtue of hard work, frugality and temperance, and contemplate the swiftness of life and the inevitability of death. Thus, at the height of its fullness, this meal – which has been half-eaten – is already on its way to decay.

Abductive Reasoning

Netherlands in the late fifteenth to the late seventeenth centuries endured religious and social turmoil. The Reformation, Establishment of Protestantism, and the Counter Reformation followed in close succession, with the area being divided between the Protestants in the North and the Catholics in the South. There was continuous warfare triggered by the expansionist desires of Europe's powerful, noble houses. By the end of the seventeenth century, the country was divided into Northern and Southern Netherlands. Flanders or the Southern Netherlands belonged to Spain throughout the seventeenth century and remained Roman Catholic. Its art was influenced by the classicism of Italy, Spain and France, seen by classic design (use of triangular structures), interest in depth and perspective, and elements that convey elegance, dignity and nobility to the subject; precision in thinking; realism; and attention to detail. The Dutch – of the Northern

Netherlands – were much affected by the Protestant Reformation, with its disregard of ritual, and its emphasis on individualism. It was a middle-class culture that avoided aristocratic values and emphasized family and merchant values, including no flattery or exaggeration; love of the familiar; love of light and space; powerful emotional content; importance of character; and the dramatic use of light and dark. Paintings are now telling the story of the merchant class and showing their economic status in society – and small paintings are possessions that the middle class can now buy, enjoy and show off to the world. The prosperous life became the subject matter of still lifes, and *Still Life with Berckemeyer* is a wonderful example of the Northern Dutch school of painting.

Global exploration (such as in our times) and exhaustion from political/religious turmoil contributed to the focus on a scene from everyday life. Artists and patrons were less concerned with overtly religious or mythological themes, but rather with images that reflected the country's wealth and the world of the prosperous middle class. Thus, *Still Life* is an example of a genre painting. Eating and socializing habits, the economic conditions of this family, the social enjoyment that ordinary citizens derived from everyday life are all represented in this work.

This painting also includes Eucharistic symbols of bread and wine, which were frequently portrayed in the still lifes of this period. The piece also includes a lemon, which may signify original sin, since the Bible speaks of the fruit of a lemon tree. It has also been suggested that the lemon is symbolic of luxury: just as the lemon is outwardly inviting, the fruit inside the beautiful peel is sour; so too is excess, alluring on the surface but ultimately leading to alienation from God.

Biographical Information

Pieter Claesz was a Calvinist who was born in Westphalia in Germany. By 1617, he was working in Haarlem where he probably spent most of his life. Although little is known of his life, he became a leading artist of still life in the first half of the seventeenth century. Religious, political and social factors are revealed in the unique tradition of Claesz' art. In the democratic society of Holland, artists specialized in a single genre category. Claesz was one of the leading painters of the breakfast piece, which is a subcategory within the still life genre. By 1630, Claesz' mature period began, and in this period, his palette became monochromatic (painted in a uniform tone) utilizing grays, earth tones, pewter colors, and in this case, yellows and browns. His experiments with lighting effects, ranging from clear daylight to deep chiaroscuro (a dramatic use of light and shade), were revolutionary in their day.[3]

LEADERSHIP IMPLICATIONS

How does the Learning How to Look program have relevance to our lives as leaders in our chosen field? If we choose to play along with the exercises that sharpen our skill as a seer and reader of our environment, data has shown that we will become more intentional, inclusive and methodical in our approach to leadership. If we choose to consider the painting as a business challenge, and consider each set of reasoning tools as something that hones our skill as leader, then our range of possibilities in problem-solving will indeed take on a comprehensive, global range.

Inductive Reasoning

A pure description of the problem on hand is key to establishing our framework. What seems to be the issue? What is going on? How can each one of us on the team describe the "what" factor – to describe for the benefit of our own mind and other team members what is at stake. Thus, without resorting to autopilot as an immediate reaction, and going to the end without assessing the beginning, we start with the simple details first. We train ourselves to look at the first facts with an open mind, without interpretation or presupposition.

Deductive Reasoning

In this section, we work with ourselves or with our team members to arrive at an analysis of options. From the "what" factor, we have now progressed to the "now what" section in scenario-building. From the details that form our scenario, we attempt to make deductions and generalizations that are symbiotic in nature. Thus deductive analysis without the benefit of supporting evidence is not helpful or accurate, and as we prepare our differential diagnosis, we are mindful at all times of the complex, interweaving relationship between fact and interpretation. In any challenging circumstance, deductive reasoning helps us come up with potential scenarios and road map analysis of logically getting to decisions and possible outcomes at each step. The step-by-step methodology allows for the outcome to be more holistic and broad-based and to already anticipate a range of possibilities in the next set of reasoning.

Abductive Reasoning

We have by now seen the entire gamut from the trees to the forest. We have emerged from the minutiae of detail to a broader, holistic and comprehensive picture of the nature of our problem. Instead of dealing with issues in a myopic manner, we now have created a range of possibilities that allow for differing options/diagnosis/interpretation. This last set of practices can best be described as the "so what" factor. What is the implication of our decision – is it a speedier evaluation of options; more methodical way of solving problems; or the creation of a broad band of opportunities that help us travel the entire journey with greater inclusivity?

CONCLUSION

Detailed, evaluative analysis of the Learning How to Look program conducted among Union Institute doctoral students and the University of Cincinnati medical students has shown that its seems to work in bringing individuals into awareness of their own potential. This is as true in the twenty-first century as it was in the time of Gilgamesh, the third century BCE epic hero, who came into his own as a discoverer of his own worth. Writing on the hero's epic journey of self-discovery, the literary critic Michael Harvey (2008) writes

> When we read [*Gilgamesh*], we feel both very old and newly risen on the earth, seeing with fresh eyes our own world and our own lives: the everyday magic of life and death, friendship and loss, terrible grief and painfully gained knowledge – self-knowledge, but also knowledge of others, and of the fragile but vital threads that weave our lives together.

This is what Gilgamesh must do to return to his intuitive understanding of matters. Learning to see, as if for the first time, helps him separate his immediate reality from his delusional version of it. He sees in humility, with attention to detail, to gain meaning from the context rather than to impose his expectations on a set of variables.

In the beginning of the epic, we see Gilgamesh as a strong and formidable leader. He "knew the way things were before the Flood,/ the secret things, the mystery: who went/to the end of the earth and over". He is a discoverer, a purveyor of secret knowledge, a city builder – as we come to know in subsequent passages. He is also "the strongest one of all, the perfect, the terror" so much so that he is billed as "two-thirds a god, one-third a man, the king".

Harvey points out that all of this force must come at a steep price, and indeed it does. Gilgamesh is so taken with his own prowess that he fails to see the plight of his own people, and in this simple act of non-recognition lies the seed of his downfall. At once, the brightness of the hero's glory is diminished by the fatal flaws inherent in his narcissism, in Gilgamesh's refusal to see things from another point of view.

As a result, Gilgamesh must go through terrible grief and suffering. The gods answer the people's prayers and "create Enkidu, 'the stormy-hearted other'". They engage in violent conflict till Gilgamesh becomes aware that he might have met his match. They become friends, and as Harvey points out, "the poem suggests that understanding others must begin with an understanding of oneself". Gilgamesh and Enkidu, emboldened by the strength of their friendship, venture into the "terrible cedar forest" to confront Enkidu's demons. They prevail and Huwawa is felled. However, the combined forces of Gilgamesh and Enkidu and their arrogance irk the gods. They bring disease upon Enkidu and he dies, leaving Gilgamesh in the throes of isolation and loss. Gilgamesh ventures after immortality and after a series of adventures is able to perceive "a sense of the fragility of human things, and the recognition that all men and women, from the mightiest to the humblest, share a common human identity". It is the ultimate act of recognizing – through seeing, looking and observing – that Gilgamesh becomes aware of his own mortality. Individuals in all times are entrenched in their own world, and have set beliefs on how they think and what they believe in. This fixed methodology often transfers over to the world in which we operate; Gilgamesh has been guilty of this on all counts and he recognizes that change is a constant in our world.

The Learning How to Look program enables participants to deal with rapid, quickly-shifting scenarios and to navigate the shores of ambiguity. It helps participants deal with the fact of not knowing all the answers at a given point in time, and of moving forward in spite of confusion and chaos in our world.

Human suffering has also long remained a constant in our world. In the realm of art, artists from centuries ago have captured their joys and struggles for us, so that we may peek into their worlds and perhaps even learn how to cope from them. The Learning How to Look program's emphasis on art provides a way for us to learn more about our potential as human beings and leaders. It allows us to value the human condition (as presented in art) and to become more alive to and appreciative of our own humanity.

NOTES

1. The term "confusion endurance" is coined by Gelb (1998).
2. The term "abductive *reasoning*" is widely used in design thinking, referenced in *Business Week* (7 November 2007), "Mosh pits of creativity", and (28 July 2008), "P&G changes its game".
3. Information on Hans Hofmann and Pieter Claesz are obtained from curatorial and docent notes of the Cincinnati Art Museum.

REFERENCES

Fairhurst, G.T. and R.A. Sarr (1996), *The Art of Framing: Managing the Language of Leadership*, San Francisco, CA: Jossey-Bass.

Gelb, Michael (1998), *How to Think Like Leonardo da Vinci: Seven Steps to Genius Everyday*, New York: Dell Publishing.

Harvey, M. (2008), "Against the heroic: Gilgamesh and his city", in Joanne B. Ciulla (ed.), *Leadership and the Humanities*, vol. 3 of *Leadership at the Crossroads*, Westport, CT: Praeger Press, pp. 51–65.

Mitra, Anu M., Yen Hsieh and Ted Buswick (2010), "Learning how to look: developing leadership through intentional observation", *Journal of Business Strategy*, **31**(4), (July/August).

Serra, Richard (2008), "Commencement speech to Williams College graduates", *The New York Times*, 8 June.

Sturken, Marita and Lisa Cartwright (2001), *Practices of Looking: An Introduction to Visual Culture*, New York: Oxford University Press.

Suh, H.A. (ed.) (2005), *Leonardo's Notebooks*, New York: Black Dog and Leventhal Publishers.

PART III

Integration

16. Questioning leadership: an integrative model

Michael Harvey

> He said, "This is what the king who will reign over you will claim as his rights: He will take your sons and make them serve with his chariots and horses. . . . He will take your daughters to be perfumers and cooks and bakers. . . . you yourselves will become his slaves. When that day comes, you will cry out for relief from the king you have chosen. . . ." But the people refused to listen to Samuel. "No!" they said. "We want a king over us. Then we will be like all the other nations, with a king to lead us and to go out before us and fight our battles."
>
> (1 Samuel 8:10–20, New International Version)

> We search eagerly for leadership yet seek to tame and cage it. We recoil from power yet we are bewitched or titillated by it.
>
> (James MacGregor Burns, *Leadership* (1978: 9)

> Well, you've gotta question everything.
>
> (Football coach Rex Ryan after a 45–3 loss)

Leadership – by which I mean an interaction between leaders and followers rather than the traits or actions of leaders alone – is the most complex of human relationships. I think there are three main reasons. First, the overarching nature of leadership. It can concern itself with everything from the group's identity and aspirations to any detail which might affect the group's well-being. Second, the sheer number of people involved. All the members of a group, with their multitudinous interests, perceptions and judgments, contribute to the group's experience of leadership. Third, our profound ambivalence about it. Both the Bible and Jim Burns speak to the commingling of hope and skepticism in how we view leadership.

If there is an ancient tradition of hope and skepticism about leadership, there is a more recent tradition of hope and skepticism about *thinking* about leadership. A new and uncertain field of leadership studies has arisen on the hope that we can discover important truths, but many are skeptical that there is really a discipline here, or that it can contribute much of value. Against skepticism, my colleague Ron Riggio argues at the beginning of this volume that leadership studies is indeed an emerging discipline. Beneath the extravagant diversity of methods, perspectives and purposes evidenced by leadership scholars, he suggests, there is an underlying unity of focus. In this chapter I suppose that Riggio is right, and take his modest suggestion about the disciplinary coherence of leadership studies as a challenge. What might a general model of leadership that draws on fields as diverse as classics, philosophy, psychology, sociology and management look like?

I begin with the premise that leadership happens in groups, and exists or evolved to serve fundamental group needs. As the sociologist, Philip Selznick, argued in his influential 1957 study of leadership, "certain very general activities of leaders … reflect equally general characteristics of all human groups" (p. 23). In the model presented here, group needs are understood as a set of questions which leaders must ask and answer. In other words, to lead is to ask. The central questions – about identity, purpose and survival – are presumed to be common to all groups. But the questions are quite different one from another, so leadership is a difficult yoking-together of different kinds of inquiry. Leaders enjoy privileged but not exclusive power to ask, and to assert certain answers as authoritative. In different groups, followers have more or less capacity themselves to ask questions, to contribute to decisions about appropriate answers, and to voice doubts – but they are always quick to harbor at least incipient doubts. As for answers, they are never final because the nature of the group and the world around it are constantly changing. Leadership is thus a disorderly and unending dialectic, question following question and yielding provisional and often-contested answers. Finally, the kind of inquiry proposed here as the work of leadership is not an end in itself, but an engaged inquiry whose success is measured, not by its truth or consistency, but by its ability to spark effective action on behalf of the group by its members.

The suggestion that leadership is a kind of inquiry is not new. It is implicit, I believe, in most serious thinking about leadership, ranging for instance from Plato, who claimed that the dialectic was the critical training tool for leaders (*Republic*, Book VII, especially 532b–541b (1991: 211–20)) to Peter Drucker (see, for instance, Drucker et al. 2008, with its "five most important questions"). But the argument presented here, inspired by the interdisciplinary vision of this volume, is a new effort to present an integrated model of leadership.

Proposing an integrated model is not necessary, to be sure, in order to establish leadership studies as a discipline. Disciplines can and do contain disparate models and methods, contrasting theories, divergent levels of analysis, and violent disagreements among scholars of all stripes about issues of all kinds. Political science, for instance, contains four quite different subfields: international relations; comparative politics; American politics; and political theory. Political scientists in these four subfields largely talk past each other, explore different questions with different methods, publish in different journals, and share little but departmental affiliation and an annual conference. But it is nevertheless instructive to see how much, if at all, we can get the different disciplines within leadership studies to talk with each other – and whether, out of this dialogue of disciplines, we can draw forth a vision of leadership and its study that is thematically coherent and productive of further research.

"[R]esearch", the scholar Robert Birnbaum drily observed in a study of college presidents, "cannot provide answers to the puzzles of leadership" (1992: xix). Birnbaum did not mean that research is useless, or provides no insights at all – but that research in any particular field is always too narrow to get at the biggest puzzles. So instead of more research, let's ask some reflective questions, beginning with the natural first question: what is leadership? It is a stock device among those who write about leadership to note the dozens, or scores, or hundreds of different definitions of leadership that one thinker or another has devised (Rost, 1991 provides the classic compilation). And yet, if we consider actual working conceptions of leadership, discipline by discipline, as evidenced in this collection of field reports, we might conclude that we are not too far from a general answer: *Leaders confront and solve problems associated with group survival and well-being.* Across all the chapters in this volume we find a recognition that leaders work for and within the context of a particular group. The prophet Samuel's caution to Israel, which serves as an epigram to this chapter, reminds us that this bargain between leader and followers is as much faith and hope as informed consent, and can transform into behaviors and outcomes few imagined or desired.

Defining leadership within the context of the group is the central thrust of modern scholarship in this emerging discipline, as a glance at several prominent scholars shows:

> Leadership may be considered as the process (act) of influencing the activities of an organized group in its efforts toward goal setting and goal achievement. (Stogdill, 1950: 3)

> Leaders are individuals who establish direction for a working group of individuals, who gain commitment from these group members to this direction, and who then motivate these members to achieve the direction's outcomes. (Conger, 1992: 18)

> A process whereby an individual influences a group to achieve a common goal. (Northouse, 2009: 3)

The renowned leadership scholar Fred Fiedler made the point as concisely and emphatically as it can be made: "Without a group there can be no leader" (1967: 16). In the present volume, the group peeps out from every chapter: the Greek *polis* discussed by Genovese and Tritle; Wren's "institutional and cultural elements that form the essence of the historical context"; the setting for Weber's understanding of charisma, as explored by Turner; the business enterprise setting for our two chapters on management; Provizer's political science emphasis on the state as the central site of leadership; and even the depiction of leadership lodged in particular communities in literary works like the *Iliad* and *O Pioneers!*, as elaborated by Warner. But the most detailed explorations of the group setting of leadership unfold in the chapters on sociology, by Ospina and Hittleman, and on psychology, by Goethals and Hoyt.

From their standpoint as sociologists, Ospina and Hittleman provide a group-centered understanding of leadership: "Leadership", they argue, is a set of group-based processes "that emerge to address organizing and action". These processes are "social and relational", so that they can only really be studied and understood in the context of a group or the community. Citing Selznick (1957), they emphasize leadership's special role in addressing the group's "recurrent problems", focusing on meaning-making, organization and action.

In their psychology chapter, Goethals and Hoyt provide a remarkably parallel perspective about what groups need, and what leaders provide. They say that leadership is best understood as an evolutionary response to "coordination problems associated with group life: problems like movement; intragroup conflict, competition and cooperation; and intergroup conflict, competition and cooperation". Leadership, they argue, facilitates decision-making and coordination. Beyond this, they suggest that leadership fulfills basic human psychological needs – people seek leaders "who confirm their worldview and make them feel they are a part of something larger than themselves". And leaders help followers make sense of the world, providing "a vision or narrative that frames past experience and points the way toward future behavior". Harvey (2006) distills this to three fundamental group needs that leadership can satisfy: survival, sense-making and managing power. Survival, in all ordinary human circumstances, comes first, as evidenced by the Israelites' insistence on acquiring a war leader, by Goethals and Hoyt's opening case of Ernest Shackleton and the *Endurance*, and by the business primacy of the bottom line – or, in a different arena, by Americans' arm's-length but easy acceptance in a post-9/11 world of waterboarding and other forms of torture, or "enhanced interrogation techniques" (Ross and Esposito, 2005).

As the example of torture shows, putting the group first does not ensure an ethical leadership, nor does it allow students of leadership to avoid the centrality of ethics. Instead, it places a particular ethical tension at the heart of leadership studies: on one side stands the group, understood ethically either in an ancient, tribalistic "us against them" perspective or a modern, relativistic "no-one outside the group can judge that group's ethical understanding". On the other side stands the individual, raised up by a universalist perspective predicated on Christ, Kant or another absolute morality. One can choose either perspective, and judge a group's morality from within the group or from a universalist perspective. For actual leaders, though, there isn't much of a choice: the group comes first. Max Weber, a seminal figure in the modern study of leadership, makes this point in "Politics as a vocation", one of the greatest meditations on the "ethical paradoxes" embedded in leadership (1946: 125). Contrasting the pure ethic of absolute ends and what he calls "an ethic of responsibility" – meaning responsibility for the survival and welfare of the group – Weber admits that the leader, or anyone who chooses to accept responsibility for others, "lets himself in for the diabolic forces lurking in all violence" (1946: 125–6). It is a reflection that President George W. Bush certainly confronted after 9/11 – though more likely by watching Jack Bauer in *24* than by reading Weber (see Lithwick, 2008).

With ethics in play, then, let us pursue the reflective question of what groups need. An immediate difficulty is that modern society is awash with groups, and we are all members of many of them. Can one generalize about one's membership in a state, a church, a company, a service organization, or a social club? Such groups make very different claims on one's loyalty, time, resources, labor and psyche, don't they? The bewildering array of modern groups can seem to kill in its first bloom any attempt to propose a general leadership model based on what groups need. In that light, one understands why our psychologists, Goethals and Hoyt, turn to what we might consider two ideal types, the stranded group in duress and the hypothesized early group in evolutionary perspective. A striking thing about these is that they are examples of what one might term a "total group", one that commands all of its members' allegiances, labor and aspirations. There is no viable escape in early human experience from the needs and demands of the hunter-gatherer group, just as Sir Ernest Shackleton's stranded men had no alternative to embracing his leadership except death.

Today people are members of more groups and have more discretion about joining and exiting them than in earlier eras of human existence. But that does not change the basic equation of what groups need. Groups complex or long-lived enough to need leadership (which would exclude incidental occurrences like carpools orgies, or a Disneyworld line, at least under normal circumstances) share a family resemblance. They exist for a purpose, to achieve some collective labor that requires coordination and collaboration. They seek to survive. They need members and ways of organizing them, resources and ways of allocating them, and the capacity to capture inputs and transform them into outputs. They have a setting, a culture, a history, and a claim of some kind on their members' participation and commitment. Even disputes about these things – things like how to divide and coordinate labor, what to aim at, who counts as a member and who does not, what the proper remembrance of history is and what lessons it teaches – are part of the fabric of leadership within the framework of the group. All of this contributes, as our sociologists teach us, to the group's distinctive social reality.

But to meet its needs, must a group turn to leadership? Are there "substitutes for leadership" (Kerr and Jermier, 1978) that might also serve? Some possible substitutes might be culture, spontaneity, heroism, bureaucracy, or pure democracy. But the evidence of history suggests that among these different mechanisms, leadership provides the best balance of creativity and authority. Culture is fundamental to the life of the group, and thus to leadership ("Cultural understanding", the scholar Edgar Schein observes [2010: 22], "is essential to leaders if they are to lead"). But culture alone, divorced from effective leadership, cannot respond to crisis. Chinua Achebe's classic 1958 novel *Things Fall Apart* explores this theme in colonial Africa.

As for spontaneity, in many ways the opposite of culture, it has its charms, especially for those who dream of reshaping human nature. Karl Marx mused that Communist society "makes it possible for me to do one thing today and another tomorrow, to hunt in the morning, fish in the afternoon, rear cattle in the evening, criticise after dinner, just as I have a mind..." (in Tucker, 1978: 160). But it is hard to find an actual group in the world that relies on spontaneity as its chief idea.

Heroism can only be a substitute for leadership in exceptional circumstances. It's endlessly popular in stories, however, reflecting some primal desire in us for the simple assuredness of the protector figure (see Campbell, 1953 for the classic study). The essence of the hero's story is self-reliance and separation from the group; but a reliance on others, while it may be the end of heroism, can be the beginning of the leader. Indeed the transformation of a man from hero to leader is, I have argued, the theme of the world's oldest extant leadership story, *Gilgamesh* (see Harvey, 2008).

Bureaucracy is another possible substitute for leadership. It has the advantage of applying rational analysis to the problems of the group. But the bureaucrat operates narrowly within a regime of rules, and has nothing, as a bureaucrat, to contribute to the group's deepest existential questions. The narrowness of the bureaucrat's work is brilliantly explored by Akira Kurosawa in his 1952 film *Ikiru*, which dramatizes the transformation of a man dying of stomach cancer from bureaucrat to leader. Finally, pure democracy alone cannot sustain collective purpose in the face of resistance, diffidence, or anxiety: the Athenians, as Genovese and Tritle remind us, often turned to demagogues during difficult times.

Compared to these substitutes, leadership excels at making authoritative choices while preserving space for innovation and new thinking in how to meet the needs of the group. Choices imply questions, so it seems useful to reframe the problem of what groups need into this: *What questions must groups and their leaders confront?* This is an important reframing, for it shifts the fundamental leadership function from action to inquiry that sparks action. Pondering the field reports in this volume, I suggest, yields seven fundamental questions that groups, and their leaders, must confront and answer:

Who are we?

Where are we?

How are we doing?

Where are we going?

How will we get there?

Why should we care?

Do we understand?

The first three questions each represent a kind of learning. The fourth envisions a desired future. The fifth, resolutely practical, is about how to align the group's people, resources and work with the vision. The sixth question concerns the group's members as human beings, and how they may be driven, through inspiration or something else, to support the group and its purposes. The final question concerns communication between the leader and followers. Let's consider the questions one by one, to see whether they add up to something suggestive about leadership.

Learning
Who are we?

The first leadership question concerns the identity of the group. Sometimes this occurs in the most literal fashion imaginable: the Old Testament Book of Numbers, for instance, is framed around two censuses that Moses conducts of the Israelites in the wilderness, so that he will be able to gauge his people's fighting strength. Leaders and others ascertain who are the group's members, who not, and how to distinguish between them. Within groups, leadership researchers have explored the important distinction between "in-group" and "out-group" members (Danserau et al., 1975). Leaders may not be the only ones to inquire about or assert the identity of a group, but they hold a privileged place in the work of asking and asserting (see Lührmann and Eberl, 2007). Genovese and Tritle, our classicists, note that Pericles, in his funeral oration, "outlined the ideals of a democratic society and how such a society stands apart from other polities or political forms". In other words, he gave the Athenians an enduring lesson in their identity. Mitra, in her chapter on the study of art, says that the first lesson of "learning to look" is gaining a better recognition of ourselves and our identities. Ospina and Hittleman, the sociologists, cite "naming and shaping identity" as a key leadership act.

Collins and Porras, in their influential 1996 study of long-term business success, argue that at the heart of such organizational success is an enduring identity or "core ideology". The most successful business leaders, they say, "understood that it is more important to know who you are than where you are going, for where you are going will change as the world around you changes" (1996: 66).

Asking and answering the question of "who we are", by raising the corollary question of "who we are not", can serve to exclude. Adolf Hitler cast Jews out of the German nation. The French scholar René Girard (1986) has explored how, throughout history, groups have made use of the scapegoat mechanism, sacrificing some to (ostensibly) preserve the group. More broadly, the scholars Lawrence and Nohria say that the division into "us" and "them" is basic to groups; they term it the "dyadic instinct" (2002: 102).

The great African-American leader Frederick Douglass wrestled with the question of identity throughout his life, embracing the aspirations of American democracy but rejecting the bitter history and hypocrisy of American slavery and racism. "What country have I?" he powerfully asked in an 1847 speech (in Blassingame et al., 1979, vol. 2: 57). Douglass was an unrelenting asker of hard questions. When the citizens of Rochester, New York invited the well-known abolitionist leader to speak at their Fourth of July celebration in 1852 he accepted, but used the occasion to challenge their complacency. The speech he gave – on 5 July, perhaps to mark his critical distance from the customary celebration – is one of the most astonishing and arresting in American history (for a thoughtful study see Colaiaco, 2006):

> What have I, or those I represent, to do with your national independence? Fellow-citizens, pardon me, allow me to ask, why am I called upon to speak here to-day? What have I, or those I represent, to do with your national independence? Are the

great principles of political freedom and of natural justice, embodied in that Declaration of Independence, extended to us? and am I, therefore, called upon to bring our humble offering to the national altar, and to confess the benefits and express devout gratitude for the blessings resulting from your independence to us? (in Blassingame et al., 1979, vol. 2: 359–87)

Tension between inclusion and separatism helped shape the leadership clash within the African-American political awakening of the mid-twentieth century, between a reform and civil-rights movement led by Martin Luther King, Jr, and a separatist movement led by Malcolm X. In November 1963 Malcolm X famously asserted a separatist identity:

> So we're all black people, so-called Negroes, second-class citizens, ex-slaves. You're nothing but an ex-slave. You don't like to be told that. But what else are you? You are ex-slaves. You didn't come here on the "Mayflower". You came here on a slave ship. In chains, like a horse, or a cow, or a chicken. And you were brought here by the people who came here on the *Mayflower*, you were brought here by the so-called Pilgrims, or Founding Fathers. They were the ones who brought you here.
>
> We have a common enemy. We have this in common: We have a common oppressor, a common exploiter, and a common discriminator. But once we all realize that we have this common enemy, then we unite – on the basis of what we have in common. And what we have foremost in common is that enemy – the white man. He's an enemy to all of us. I know some of you all think that some of them aren't enemies. Time will tell. (Malcolm X, 1965: 4–5)

For his part, Martin Luther King defined African-American identity within the staunchly patriotic context of American democratic idealism. He gave his most celebrated speech also in 1963, a few months before Malcolm's "message to the grassroots". He spoke at the heart of the nation, at the Lincoln Memorial, under the gaze, as it were, of the President who freed the slaves. He began his speech by citing Lincoln's example, alluding to the Emancipation Proclamation issued precisely a century earlier and echoing Lincoln's language ("Five score years ago"). Further cementing the identity of African-Americans within the mainstream of the American tradition, he quoted the Declaration of Independence and biblical verse, and built his peroration around the image of the Liberty Bell ringing from mountain to American mountain. His speech overwhelmed any superficial distinctions between black and white identity (King, 1986: 217–20).

Martin Luther King, Jr largely won the struggle with Malcolm X over the question of the identity of African-Americans. Separatism is quiescent as a political movement, and the Civil Rights movement has become enshrined as part of the grand patriotic fabric of America. But black identity as an unresolved question – a "problem", as Malcolm X put it (1965: 4) – endures in the psychology, if not the overt politics of African-American culture, especially among many young people. The most dramatic marker is the word "nigger", considered by most Americans an unspeakable insult, the "n-word". But in broad swathes of African-American youth culture the word has quite a contrary sense, as an assertion of separate identity so potent that whites may not even utter it (see Kennedy, 2002). Today the forbidden word is a staple of some categories of popular music. Some of its uses, at least, merit attention (see Ogbar, 2007 for a sharp examination of ideas in hip-hop music). The popular rap singer Nas (Nasir bin Olu Dara Jones), for instance, offers a surprisingly complex critical interrogation of the word in "Be a nigger too" (2008). Alongside Nas's staccato repetition of the term, his questions hang in the air:

> Why we fight each other in public
> in front of these arrogant fascists?
> They love it
> Putting old niggers versus the youngest
> Most of our elders failed us
> How can they judge us
> niggers?
> There's verbal books published by niggers
> Produced by niggers
> genuine niggers
> so I salute my
> niggers
>
> . . . .
> I'm a nigger
> he's a nigger
> she's a nigger
> we some niggers
> wouldn't you like to be a nigger too?
> They like to strangle niggers
> blaming niggers
> shooting niggers
> hanging niggers
> still you wanna be a nigger too?

Nas, it is fair to say, intends to shock the listener into a new sense of identity and allegiance, or at least a new willingness to question. Ralph Ellison made the same move, though on a far loftier scale, in his great novel *Invisible Man*:

> In my mind's eye I see the bronze statue of the college Founder, the cold Father symbol, his hands outstretched in the breathtaking gesture of lifting a veil that flutters in hard, metallic folds above the face of a kneeling slave; and I am standing puzzled, unable to decide whether the veil is really being lifted, or lowered more firmly in place; whether I am witnessing a revelation or a more efficient binding. (1952: 28)

The South African leader Nelson Mandela tells a striking story of his youth in his autobiography, of how a challenging question jolted him into a new awareness of identity and his responsibility as an aspiring leader. Meeting the queen regent of Basutoland (now Lesotho), he was unable to speak to her in Sesotho, her native tongue. "What kind of lawyer and leader will you be," she asked him, "who cannot speak the language of your own people?" "I had no response", Mandela relates:

> The question embarrassed and sobered me; it made me realize my parochialism and just how unprepared I was for the task of serving my people. I had unconsciously succumbed to the ethnic divisions fostered by the white government and I did not know how to speak to my own kith and kin. Without language, one cannot talk to people and understand them; one cannot share their hopes and aspirations, grasp their history, appreciate their poetry, or savor their songs. I again realized that we were not different people with separate languages; we were one people, with different tongues. (1994: 84)

We may close this discussion of the first leadership question, "Who are we?", by considering a concise and powerful answer: "We the people." These are the three words, written much larger than the rest in the original handwritten document in the National Archives, that begin the United States Constitution. Alexis de Tocqueville, the most perceptive observer of America as a civilization, was struck by the sheer visibility of this assertion of identity as a source of political power:

> The principle of the sovereignty of the people, which is always to be found, more or less, at the bottom of almost all human institutions, generally remains there concealed from view. It is obeyed without being recognized, or if for a moment it is brought to light, it is hastily cast back into the gloom of the sanctuary. . . . In America the principle of the sovereignty of the people is neither barren nor concealed, as it is with some other nations; it is recognized by the customs and proclaimed by the laws. . . . (Tocqueville, 1966: 51)

A great deal, as Tocqueville perceived, is contained in the assertion of a group's identity.

Learning
Where are we?

"Where are we?", the second leadership question in our model, can be a question of irritation, bewilderment, anxiety or wonder. To be lost – and this is perhaps especially true in our modern technological age, when the gadgets fail us – is to be plunged into a remarkably powerful primal state of fear and lack of control. In all its forms, from the trivial to the profound, "Where are we?"

is one of the first questions leaders and others in the group ask. Sometimes it is asked figuratively, when complexity and confusion reign. The "where" or context in which a group exists draws the attention of every discipline that contributes to leadership studies. Wren, the historian, speaks of the study of where, or context, as key to why history matters to leadership studies.

Leaders know where we are. This is something so basic to our expectation of leadership that we may take it for granted and miss the work that goes into the gaining of knowledge. In Akira Kurosawa's famed 1954 movie *The Seven Samurai*, Kambei, the samurai leader, upon arriving at the village he has chosen to defend, walks the fields and hills surrounding it, drawing up a map and planning his campaign. The context-setting question "where are we?" often plays out quite literally in leadership, especially military leadership (both Sun Tzu and Machiavelli, in their advice on how leaders should wage war, stress the vital importance of knowing the terrain). In the metaphoric warfare of business competition, scholars in the subfield of strategy stress the fundamental importance of "external analysis", the study of a business's industry and competitive environment, including competitors, customers, suppliers, potential new entrants, and other external factors, often presented shorthand as PESTEL analysis or a similar acronym (for political, economic, sociocultural, technological, environmental and legal factors; see Aguilar, 1967).

For territory-based groups, the question of "where are we" takes on deep emotional and psychic resonance (Herb and Kaplan, 2000). In Willa Cather's novel *O Pioneers!*, explored by Warner in his chapter on literature and leadership, the setting is the American frontier, the living land so dynamic and personified in Cather's telling that it is virtually a character itself. Part of what marks Alexandra as the story's central figure and leader is her deep sympathy and even reverence for the land: "For the first time, perhaps, since that land emerged from the waters of geologic ages, a human face was set toward it with love and yearning" (1992: 33). A striking echo of this occurs in the 2003 New Zealand film *Whale Rider* (based on the novel by Witi Ihimaera), also about a visionary female leader: "In the old days, the land felt a great emptiness. It was waiting. Waiting to be filled up. Waiting for someone to love it. Waiting for a leader" (Gavin et al., 2003).

The question of "where are we" is usually answered over time, in an ongoing exploration of the literal or symbolic terrain around the group. Sometimes, however, the question can explode into sudden, urgent recognition and action. An unexpected but powerful instance occurred with United Airlines Flight 93 on 11 September 2001. Because this flight from Newark to San Francisco had been delayed, and because some passengers and crew members used phones to communicate with those on the ground, they learned that they were not in an ordinary hijacking, but on board a missile aimed at Washington, DC. They were in a strange new reality, where the old rules and logic no longer applied. The normal mode of action in a hijacking – "Don't worry," as a friend on the ground tried to reassure passenger Marion Britton, "they hijacked the plane, they're gonna take you for a ride, you go to their country, and you come back" – was rendered beside the point (Pauley, 2006). Once the shock had been digested, some or all understood the implications. The recognition crystallized into a swift plan of action, and a group stormed the cabin. That they died does not mean that they failed; their on-the-fly adaptation, hasty coordination, and sacrifice stand as tributes to the courage of acknowledging where you are.

Learning
How are we doing?

I begin this section with a personal perspective. I serve on my local school board, and so I encounter a good deal of information on test scores, graduation rates, teacher hiring, and so on. Reading through the school system's "master plan update", a turgid doorstop of a document required by the state, I came across a table showing that the school system, on its three-tier scale ("satisfactory", "needs improvement" and "unsatisfactory"), rates 98 per cent of its teachers as satisfactory. The other 2 per cent need improvement. Not a single teacher is unsatisfactory! Either my family is part of the best school district in America, or our evaluation system is broken. If the latter, what does that mean about our ability or will to identify, hire and train good teachers? If we can't distinguish between good and bad teaching, can we succeed in our core mission of helping children learn?

Honestly asking "how are we doing?" is a critical but contentious task for groups. In contemporary American education it has largely been forced on wary bureaucracies by external reformers. The result has been a messy hodgepodge of change, churn, and the rise of a testing culture that, ironically, can interfere with the core mission of good schools (see Ravitch, 2010). It is with this question that business contributes the most to the interdisciplinary field of leadership studies. Business leaders and their organizations have the most immediately powerful incentive – profit or die – to make an accurate reckoning. Indeed the history of modern business management is in a sense an elaboration on the question, from Frederick Taylor's scientific management to Peter Drucker's mid-twentieth-century managerial revolution to the recently ascendant quality movements like Total Quality Management (TQM), "Six Sigma" and the "Toyota way" (see Taylor, 1911; Drucker, 1974; Deming, 1986; Pande et al., 2000; Liker, 2004; and Liker and Hoseus, 2008). Even earlier, the development of double-entry bookkeeping in the Islamic world and in early modern Italy can be understood as developing a new tool to help answer this old question. On the other hand, one of the deepest critiques of business is that it frames and answers the question of "how are we doing" narrowly, avoiding "externalities"; any costs or impacts, like pollution, that can be shifted to others (though for a hopeful alternative, see Meyer and Kirby, 2010).

One of the most consequential efforts to address the question of "how we are doing" was made by W. Edwards Deming, the American statistical scientist and management thinker whose ideas were popularized as Total Quality Management. Deming believed that the systematic use of data – in particular, careful statistical analysis of variance – could help organizations identify weaknesses and systematically improve (see also Shewhart, 1931). Deming saw his approach as more than a measurement system. He came to view it as a new philosophy of leadership, a "system of profound knowledge", as he called it, that could fundamentally transform the nature of enterprise (see Deming, 1993). Chapter 5 of his famous book *Out of the Crisis* (1986), entitled "Questions to help managers", consists of nothing but questions, more than a hundred in all, meant to stimulate the kind of reflection and learning he felt were vital to effective leadership. The heyday of TQM as an organizational fad has passed, but Deming's commitment to learning endures in many organizations, notably in Japan, where he spent most of his working life. Toyota, for instance, one of the most successful companies in the world, traces its famous "Toyota way" to Deming's influence: "Every day I think about what he meant to us", the president of Toyota said in 1991. "Deming is the core of our management" (quoted in Magee, 2007: 43). That management "core" is less about complex measurement systems than a basic commitment to ask questions, as one scholar learned:

> I recall interviewing Yuichi Okamoto, a former Toyota Technical Center vice president, about the secret to the success of Toyota's product development system. I was expecting a description of a sophisticated process. … Instead, he answered with an underlying tone of sarcasm, "We have a very sophisticated technique for developing new products. It is called five-why. We ask why five times." (Liker, 2004: 252)

This is Toyota's well-known five-why analysis, an attempt to get at the hidden root causes of superficially evident problems. "Asking 'Why?' five times", Liker observes, "requires taking the answer to the first why and then asking why that occurs" (2004: 253). At Toyota, five-why analysis is part of a culture that embeds the question "how are we doing?" in the everyday work of the whole group (see Ohno, 1988).

"How are we doing?" is a question that has been most systematically confronted by businesses like Toyota, facing the everyday pressures of market competition. Groups insulated from market forces, like public schools and government agencies, can often count on survival regardless of how or even whether they answer this question. But only in the short term. Eventually, all groups face a reckoning. This is as true for my small local school system as the largest global business firm. In the end, it is a question all groups and their leaders must confront.

The kinds of inquiry implied by the first three questions in this questioning model of leadership – "who are we?", "where are we?" and "how are we doing" – are all answered by the same basic task: learning. Leadership must learn about the group's history and culture, the environment it operates in, and its condition and effectiveness. To learn to the depth demanded by leadership requires the curiosity of a philosopher or historian, the patience of a scientist, and the courage to accept the truth as one finds it.

Envisioning
Where are we going?

Our next question shifts the focus to the future, and to the group's goal. This is the most familiar and immediately appealing image of what leaders do, envisioning a stirring imagined destination: Martin Luther King's dream; John Winthrop's (and John F. Kennedy's and Ronald Reagan's) "city on a hill"; Henry V's Agincourt speech (as written by Shakespeare) with its glorious imagined future of precious memories of the battle; or, at the root of countless proffered visions in Western culture, Moses' evocation of a promised land to the ever-doubting Israelites in the Pentateuch (a vision brutally satirized in George Orwell's *Animal Farm* as "Sugarcandy Mountain", a fable told to the animals by the tame raven Moses).

Collins and Porras argue that the most successful business leaders articulate a vivid "envisioned future" in a way that resonates with followers (1996: 73). They note the famous instance of Henry Ford, who was able to imagine such a future in 1907, a year *before* he introduced the epochal Model T:

> I will build a motor car for the great multitude. … It will be so low in price that no man making a good salary will be unable to own one and enjoy with his family the blessing of hours of pleasure in God's great open spaces. … When I'm through, everybody will be able to afford one, and everyone will have one. The horse will have disappeared from our highways, the automobile will be taken for granted … [and we will] give a large number of men employment at good wages. (Quoted in Collins and Porras 1996: 74)

To answer the question "where are we going?" some stirring sense of purpose or destination beyond the immediate task is needed. Leadership supplies this, "to help people", as Ospina and Hittleman put it, "make sense of events or give legitimacy to organizational realities and decisions." The answer to "where are we going" is perhaps rightly understood as a simplification of a more complex reality. A group always has, in reality, a thousand purposes and desires – as many as there might be followers. Leadership, especially at times of crisis, but in ordinary times as well, directs attention to an overriding goal. In a sense, leaders capture and gather a thousand gleams and glints, and condense them into brilliant stabs of brightness that all can see, and follow. William Manchester, summarizing his portrait of Winston Churchill, characterized the great wartime leader in just this fashion: "an artist who knew how to gather the blazing light of history into his prism and then distort it to his ends, an embodiment of inflexible resolution who could impose his will and his imagination on his people" (Manchester, 1983: 4).

Aligning
How will we get there?

There is something poetic or prophetic about stepping forth to answer the question "where are we going?" The tone is very different with the next question: "how will we get there?" This is the clearheaded mood of the day after, the mindset of the one who must pay the bills, pack the luggage, or look up at the mountain and start thinking exactly what route to take, what equipment will be needed, and what the weather will be like. Jon Krakauer's *Into Thin Air* (1999) brings home the life-and-death seriousness of leaders' attention to these mundane details.

During the 2008 Presidential campaign, frustrated by the success of Barack Obama's soaring rhetoric ("You and I together, we will remake this country and we will remake the world" (Clark and Nista, 2008)), Hillary Clinton spoke at a rally in Rhode Island from the stolid, anti-rhetorical perspective of "how":

> Now, I could stand up here and say, "Let's just get everybody together. Let's get unified." The skies will open, the light will come down, celestial choirs will be singing and everyone will know we should do the right thing and the world will be perfect. Maybe I've just lived a little long, but I have no illusions about how hard this is going to be. You are not going to wave a magic wand to make special interests disappear. (Quoted in Zorn 2008)

Our sociologists Ospina and Hittleman suggest that answering the "how" question gets at the real work of leadership. They quote Selznick to make the point: "A theory of leadership is dependent on a theory of social organization" (1957: 23). Genovese and Tritle, exploring leadership in the classics, make a similar point, citing the Herodotean tripartite scheme of regimes – kingship, aristocracy and democracy – as a key step in the development of the ancient Greek understanding of leadership and groups.

Some leaders are reluctant to distinguish the "where" and the "how", and blur the line between aspiration and attainment. This is the nature of charismatic leadership as studied by Weber (see Turner, Chapter 7 in this volume). For Weber, charisma was not merely attractiveness or appeal, but a powerful claim of magical power; "the leader as path", Turner summarizes Weber's treatment of charismatic power. Turner notes Weber's repeated citations of Christ, his ideal-type of charismatic leadership: "I am the way and the truth and the life. No one comes to the Father except through me" (John, 14:6, New International Version). In terms of our questions, the charismatic leader presents himself or herself as a living answer to the "how?" question. Naturally this is a fragile arrangement, and Weber, in addition to a host of recent scholars, explored the sudden collapse of charismatic leadership – and sometimes the group as a whole – when the leader's magical power ebbed, or the curtain was pulled back. One classic study is Charles Lindholm's (1990) account of Jim Jones and the Peoples Temple.

But most leaders confront the question of "how" with less magic and more method. The great American business example is surely Alfred Sloan, who took over a nearly bankrupt General Motors in 1923 and carefully reorganized it back to profitability and then dominance, along the way largely inventing the modern concept of the divisionalized corporation. Henry Ford, on the other hand, almost ruined his company during these years by proving slow to adapt to the challenges of growth and competition. Ford tried to lead his company the way he began it, with strict personal control, and only changed under duress. The contrast between Ford, the visionary and Sloan, the organizer is striking, and suggests some of the complexities involved in judging the most effective kind of leadership (for Ford see Tedlow, 2001; for Sloan the classic account – though lacking critical perspective, of course – is his own memoir (Sloan, 1990)).

In American political history, one of the most striking instances of the "how do we get there?" question comes from the interplay between Martin Luther King, Jr and President Lyndon B. Johnson. Johnson had suddenly become President after the assassination of John Kennedy in November 1963, a few months after King's "I have a dream" speech. Johnson devoted much of his early presidency to translating King's vision into reality, with the Civil Rights Act of 1964 and the Voting Rights Act of 1965. King and Johnson worked warily together – Johnson laboring as much to gain King's trust as to navigate the difficulties of passing historic legislation. In a 1965 telephone conversation, Johnson, the former Congressional leader and master of the legislative process, analyzed the "practical political problem" both men faced:

> **President Johnson:** I think that we are confronted with the realistic problem that we have faced all through the years, a combination of the South and the Republicans. . . . We've lost a good deal of the gain we made last November. I don't know. I have the problem . . . You know my practical political problem in the Senate. ...

> **King:** Yes.
>
> …
>
> **President Johnson:** So I would say there are about two things that ought to be done. You ought to have the strongest man that can speak for you – and the most knowledgeable legislative-wise – authorized to speak and authorized to tell people like the Speaker what you want. And you don't want this fight going on, and you ought to find out who you believe you can trust, if you can trust me, if you can trust the Attorney General. If you can't trust us, why, trust Teddy Kennedy or whoever you want to trust and then get behind them and see that they take the thing because I'll give every bit, ounce of energy and ability of any that I have to passing the most effective bill that can be written.
>
> …
>
> Well, you helped, I think, dramatize and bring it to a point where I could go before the Congress in that night session, and I think that was one of the most effective things that had ever happened, but you had worked for months to help create the sentiment that supported it.
>
> **King:** Yes.
>
> **President Johnson:** Now the trouble is that fire has gone out.
>
> **King:** That's right.
> (Miller Center of Public Affairs, n.d.)

We all recognize that leadership is more than planning, and that there is something unreal about a plan by itself. "They all have a plan", the champion boxer Mike Tyson famously observed, "until they get hit" (quoted in Jackman, 1989). But the question "how will we get there?", in its cool insistence on identifying what is practical and possible, clarifies another aspect of leadership: the leader as aligner, ensuring that people, resources, capacities and tasks match the purposes and goals of the group.

Driving
Why should we care?

The modern era of leadership research began in the 1940s. Until then, the leading approach had been to identify the personal characteristics of effective leaders. Dissatisfied with the narrowness of this focus on individual traits, a team of scholars at Ohio State University led by Ralph Stogdill broadened their inquiry to include the working group, the context in which leadership occurs.

Stogdill and his colleagues drew up close to 2000 questionnaire items on leadership behaviors in groups. Further work distilled these to nine dimensions of leadership activity, and eventually to just two dimensions, one focused on the work of the group, and the other on its members. Stogdill and his colleagues called the first dimension "initiating structure". The term refers to how a leader attends to organizing the group, managing work and achieving goals. They called the second dimension "consideration". It refers to how a leader treats group members as individuals, and includes things like respect, encouragement and concern (Halpin and Winer, 1957). This recognition of the double nature of the leader's work is in my opinion the most significant achievement of modern leadership research. Since the Ohio State studies, remarkably, most major leadership models have identified the same basic distinction in the work of leadership, between attention to the task and attention to the group. Table 16.1, for instance, summarizes the historical overview of Peter Northouse (2009) in his influential leadership textbook. "Consideration and Initiating Structure", one scholar says, "have proven to be among the most robust of leadership concepts." (Fleishman, 1995: 51; see also Judge et al., 2004).

One might wonder why this double nature of the leader's work should exist, since from one perspective accomplishing the task serves the interest of the group's members. "What is the city," the tribunes ask in Shakespeare's *Coriolanus*, "but the people?" (3.1.198, in Shakespeare, 1997). But the answer is not so surprising. How things look from the perspective of leadership, which occupies a strategic perch and has overall responsibility for the survival and well-being of the group, is often not how they look from the perspective of followers, who of necessity have a narrower focus. In the group's division of labor, leaders think more readily of the whole and the future, and followers think more readily of the particular and the now. Since antiquity, thoughtful

Table 16.1 The two dimensions of leadership research

Model	**Task focus**	**People focus**
Ohio State	Initiating structure	Consideration
University of Michigan	Production orientation	Employee orientation
Style approach	Task behaviors	Relationship behaviors
Managerial Grid	Concern for production	Concern for people
Hersey and Blanchard's situational approach	Directive behaviors	Supportive behaviors
Fiedler's contingency theory	Task-related style	Relationship-related style
Path–goal theory	Directive leadership	Supportive leadership

students of leadership have recognized this distinction, often concluding that it is due to an innate selfishness or untrustworthiness on the part of followers. In the *Republic*, for instance, Plato makes the audacious proposal that his ideal community must be founded on a vast "Noble Lie", as the only way to get the city's followers – ordinary human beings – to overcome their natural propensity for self-interested behavior (*Republic*, 414b–417b (Plato, 1991: 95–6)). The irony that Plato's ideal rulers are lying philosophers has fascinated and troubled countless readers over the centuries, but the idea has remarkable staying power. The sociologist Philip Selznick, for instance, concludes his study of leadership by asserting "the necessity of the myth" that leaders must create and institutionalize (1957: 151). Machiavelli took a similar tack in *The Prince*, blaming human fickleness and selfishness for the inconstancy in followers' support for leaders. He concluded that leaders must be willing to lie, commit violence, or use any other necessary means to win ongoing allegiance. Because of followers' all-too-human fickleness, he bleakly warned in Chapter 6 of *The Prince*, all unarmed prophets fail.

But from a modern, more democratic perspective, we might simply say that the work of following is different from the work of leadership. Each has its burdens and concerns. Leaders, relentlessly optimistic (or at least representing themselves as such), inhabit an airy world of promises made and dreams always about to become real. Or perhaps it is kinder to leadership to suggest that it tends to take a Burkean view of the group; the great English conservative thinker Edmund Burke saw society as "a partnership not only between those who are living, but between those who are living, those who are dead, and those who are to be born" (in Clark, 2001: 261). In other words, to leaders the city isn't just the people, but what the city has been and especially what it might be in the future. This perspective, organized into three simple paragraphs on past, present and future, shapes what is widely considered the greatest and most consequential speech in American history, Lincoln's Gettysburg Address (see Wills, 1992). But followers don't have nearly as much incentive to take the long view. Relentlessly sober, they inhabit a more concrete world of promises unmet and dreams ever receding – and their own less glorious work that, regardless, always needs attending to. The Israelites who followed or were driven by Moses into the desert ask repeatedly, "How will we eat today?" (Nor, unlike Moses, Joshua and a few others, is memory of the people preserved – except dismissively – in the journey's authorized history.)

What does this distinction between task and people mean for any sensible effort to put forth a model of leadership? For one thing, it means that a strategic perspective – attention to the goal, the task, coordination, organization of resources, and effectiveness – is not enough. Leaders must also perceive members of the group as human beings engaged in day-to-day work that requires ongoing, constantly reaffirmed commitment and dedication. Beyond appealing to the beauty of the dream or the greatness of the task, leaders must be able to help followers find a meaningful answer to the everyday question, "why should I care?" Most modern leadership literature, both scholarly and popular, casts this as finding the right way to inspire or win people's hearts, whether through authenticity, transformation, empowerment, collaboration, team-building or other means. One prominent example is Kouzes and Posner's (2007) best-selling book, *The Leadership Challenge*. A darker tradition, expressed most famously by Machiavelli in Chapter 17 of *The Prince*, argues that it is wiser to rely on fear (though not hate) to hold followers' support. The largely unstated reality of most modern groups is that fear is widely relied on, either in overt ways or indirectly by ensuring that workers perceive the precarious nature of organizational survival and their employment.

However leaders choose to address the followers' question, "why should we care?", useful answers require a measure of empathy or emotional intelligence (see Goleman, 1996 and Goleman et al., 2004), and an understanding of motivation (well explored by Goethals and Hoyt in Chapter 9 of this volume). The most enduringly effective leadership, a long tradition of research suggests, requires a view of followers not simply as factors of production or fodder for the work of the group, but as individuals in their own right (see McGregor, 1960). It is in this sense, I think, that the philosopher Joanne Ciulla (1998) calls ethics "the heart of leadership".

Communicating
Do we understand?

"Do we understand?" is the question followers ask as they interact (mainly by listening) with leaders. Leaders face an immense communicative challenge. Followers generally have less at stake, pay less attention, and are mostly preoccupied with daily concerns rather than far-off challenges or visions. They are, for the most part, rooted in the present, while leaders in a sense live in or for the future. (One suspects that 2014, the year that most of the Affordable Care Act takes effect, seems much sooner to President Obama than ordinary Americans.) The dreams and changes that leaders imagine become in a sense real to them, if they are sincere, while to the rest of us they are likely to be just words, words, words, especially because in every group there is far more promise of change and progress than actual change and progress. Nor are most followers likely to be as interested as leaders in the complexities of information-gathering, decision-making and plan formulation. They expect clarity, direction and action. Leaders must bridge this gap between the complexities they face and the clarity followers demand. To do so, the best leaders simplify without condescending. Many of the chapters in this volume speak of the importance of storytelling to leadership – not because stories are more true than other forms of communication, but because, well chosen and well told, they convey a kind of condensed truth, like Christ's parables ("true" to believers, at least).

The best communicators among American presidents – figures like Abraham Lincoln, Franklin Delano Roosevelt and Ronald Reagan – are not coincidentally judged among the greatest presidents by historians and popular memory. Roosevelt was the first president to perceive and exploit the potential of radio to reach millions of citizens. Over the dozen years of his presidency, he made 30 "fireside chats" over the radio, using these informal addresses to inform, to persuade, and to forge a sense of personal connection with Americans. His first chat, meant to soothe the bank panic of March 1933, and delivered when he had been in office just a week, is striking in its uncondescending simplicity and familiarity:

> My friends, I want to talk for a few minutes with the people of the United States about banking – to talk with the comparatively few who understand the mechanics of banking, but more particularly with the overwhelming majority of you who use banks for the making of deposits and the drawing of checks. I want to tell you what has been done in the last few days, and why it was done, and what the next steps are going to be.
>
> I recognize that the many proclamations from state capitals and from Washington, the legislation, the Treasury regulations, and so forth, couched for the most part in banking and legal terms, ought to be explained for the benefit of the average citizen. … And I know that when you understand what we in Washington have been about, I shall continue to have your cooperation as fully as I have had your sympathy and help during the past week. (In Kiewe, 2007: 1)

The humorist Will Rogers summarized the impact: "Our president took such a dry subject as banking and made everyone understand it, even bankers" (quoted in Levin and Levine, 2002: ix).

FDR's first fireside chat (or Malcolm X's message to the grassroots, for that matter) suggests the essentials of how effective leaders communicate: absorb a vast amount of information; distill and simplify the complex; take apparently discrete and disconnected phenomena and show their connection; use personal example, tone and emotion as well as words; communicate swiftly, while followers feel a sense of urgency; and rouse followers to action and commitment. After Roosevelt's death, the writer Carl Carmer wrote a poem trying to convey the impact of his voice:

> I never saw him –
> But I *knew* him. Can you have forgotten
> How, with his voice, he came into our house,
> The President of these United States,
> Calling us friends. . . . (in Levine and Levine, 2002: ix)

QUESTIONING THE QUESTIONS

Presenting these seven questions and their related tasks as a model of leadership raises a host of attendant questions. First of all, why these questions in this sequence? The answer emerges from the widespread recognition by leadership scholars that the group is the natural setting for leadership. The seven questions attempt to capture the needs of a group, as recognized in fields like sociology, history and psychology: from the forging of the group's social identity, a natural analytic starting-point; to its setting and condition; to its purpose and aspirations; to its way of accomplishing that purpose. And since the most durable research finding of modern leadership studies is the importance of two kinds of leadership work, that directed toward the task and that directed toward the individual members of the group, the sixth question ("why should we care?") creates space for this distinction. The final question suggests that communication is implicit in all of the previous questions, and that leaders must ceaselessly toil to help followers understand. In some ways the sequence is similar to the classic managerial model of Henri Fayol, the late-nineteenth- and early-twentieth-century French engineer and pioneering management thinker. "To manage", Fayol said, "is to plan, organize, coordinate, command, and control" (1987: 13). Like Fayol's model, this one is essentially strategic, seeing leadership as a comprehensive responsibility for the survival and well-being of the group. (For an interesting reading of Fayol that stresses his relevance to contemporary approaches to leadership, see Parker and Ritson, 2005.) A second question or challenge to the model is who exactly asks and answers the questions. The simplest answer is leaders, but in many situations leaders will share or delegate some of the responsibilities attached to the questions. Or groups may employ distributed leadership, so that different questions and answers are the responsibility of different leaders within a group, or different parts of an organization. Large organizations divide the tasks of answering the questions into different formal areas. But any such division creates a new complexity for leadership, which must still synthesize the pieces into a coherent understanding. The questions can also serve to challenge leaders. This is the heart of modern democratic politics. But over human history, even without formal mechanisms for debate and decision, challenges to leadership arise as struggles over whether the answers to the seven questions, as currently understood and articulated by leaders, are appropriate for the group. One of the most poignant moments in the Bible occurs with such a challenge to Moses, a kind of proto-democratic and proto-Protestant objection to his rule:

> Korah . . . and certain Reubenites – Dathan and Abiram, sons of Eliab, and On son of Peleth – became insolent and rose up against Moses. With them were 250 Israelite men, well-known community leaders who had been appointed members of

> the council. They came as a group to oppose Moses and Aaron and said to them, "You have gone too far! The whole community is holy, every one of them, and the LORD is with them. Why then do you set yourselves above the LORD's assembly?" (Numbers, 16:1–3, New International Version)

Korah challenges Moses on the fourth question, "how will we get there?" But his challenge implicates the whole of Moses' project, because it calls into question his answers about the identity, condition and aspirations of the Israelites. (The Bible has a stark answer to Korah's challenge: the earth opens up and swallows him and his fellow rebels.)

All leaders' answers are contested. A large part of the work of leadership consists of pushing back against the reopening of "settled" questions. Even the most iconic leadership myths, from that of Moses in the wilderness to George Washington during the Revolutionary War, reveal themselves upon closer inquiry as stories of dispute and discord (on Moses see Buber, 1946; on Washington see Flexner, 1994). Rivals jockey for power. Those close to the leader resent the leader's advancement and suppose that they could do better. Followers watch from a discreet distance and speculate and gossip about every scrap of information. Most leadership advice literature, from ancient texts to modern best-sellers, proposes to help leaders overcome opposition by means ranging from kindness and love to violence and fear.

A fourth question about the questioning model is, can the questions be asked in the first-person singular? Yes. Indeed "why should we care?" and "do we understand?" are perhaps just as easily interpreted as questions that individuals may ask, for the answers may be made by individuals gauging their level of commitment and understanding. All of the questions may be asked by leaders as individuals, generally as a private matter. But sharing this with followers is the exception, not the rule. A striking example of private questions comes from the life of Mother Teresa, the Catholic nun who founded the Missionaries of Charity and spent her life working to aid the poor in Calcutta. Despite her lifelong devotion to the Church and her carefully constructed persona of tranquil reverence, for most of her life she suffered intense spiritual doubts, as attested by an undated letter to one of her seniors in the Church:

> The place of God in my soul is blank – There is no God in me – when the pain of longing is so great – I just long & long for God – and then it is that I feel – He does not want me – He is not there – . . . God does not want me – Sometimes – I just hear my own heart cry out – "My God" and nothing else comes – The torture and pain I can't explain. (Teresa and Kolodiejchuk, 2007: 2)

The shocking thing about the inner leadership story of Mother Teresa is not that she felt such doubts, but that she felt them for most of her life, even as she went about her leadership work. In public she showed no trace of doubt, and she asked that her letters be burnt after her death. Most leaders, most of the time, make the choice she did: to present a simplified, more positive version of themselves and their answers, in order to avoid unsettling followers. The choices leaders make about whether and how to simplify their questions and answers, and their overall presentation of self, is one of the most fascinating and melancholy aspects of leadership. As a colleague of Abraham Lincoln observed, "He made simplicity and candor a mask of deep feelings carefully concealed" (quoted in Oates, 1977: 99). I suspect that this very flattening that leaders perforce engage in – demanded by the dynamics of decision-making, action, and authority in the group – has obscured the fundamental role that questions play in the work of leadership.

Finally, what counts as a good answer? From within our framework, a good answer is one that contributes to the survival or well-being of the group. This largely resolves Joanne Ciulla's "Hitler problem", at least for Hitler himself. In her chapter on philosophy, Ciulla considers whether Hitler was a good leader, and concludes that it is a thorny question because he was "effective", but evil. From our perspective we would ask whether Hitler contributed to the survival or well-being of his group. The answer is an emphatic no. For a time Hitler made his nation powerful, but he fell far short of his dream of a "Thousand-Year Reich", and provoked opposition that soon devastated Germany. Far from strengthening his nation, he nearly destroyed it, and made restraining Germany one of the centerpieces of post-war international relations. (The famous joke about NATO is that it was established "to keep the Russians out, the Americans in, and the Germans down".) As a legacy, Hitler left a black mark of guilt that still stains German identity. To call Hitler effective would be like saying that someone who had maxed out his credit cards was wealthy.

THE LEADERSHIP CYCLE

The work of leadership is never done. There is no final answer to "who are we?" or any of the questions – only an endless iterative process as the problems and circumstances facing the group, and the group itself, change. The questions only end when the group does. To convey this ongoing nature, it is best to arrange the questions in a circle. Learning, envisioning, aligning and driving follow a roughly logical sequence and are placed around the circle. One task and question are placed at the center: communicating and the question "do we understand?" Because leadership involves working not just with but *through* others, leaders must labor to constantly communicate with, and be understood by, followers: "You communicate, you communicate, and then you communicate some more. Consistency, simplicity, and repetition is what it's all about..." (former GE leader Jack Welch, quoted in Slater, 1999: 55). The

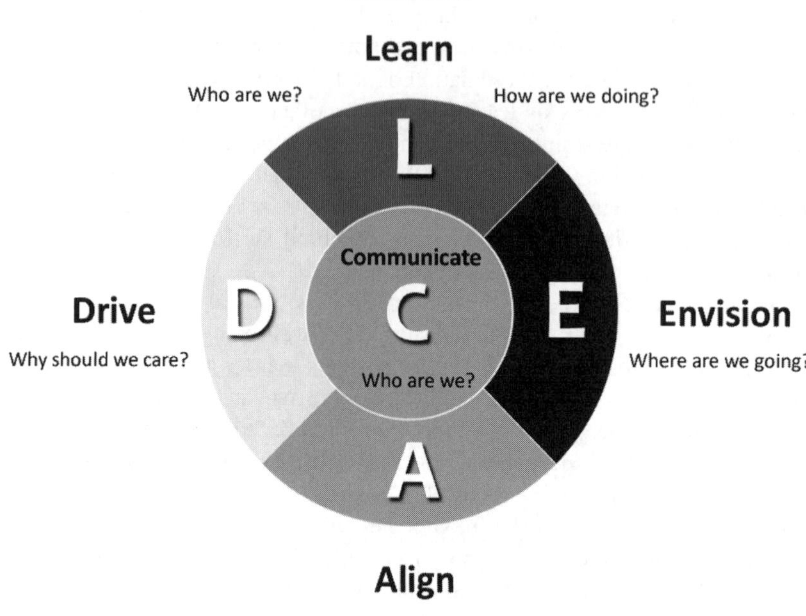

Figure 16.1 The leadership cycle

leadership model we emerge with calls attention both to the different faces of leadership, and to its underlying unity (see Figure 16.1).

This inquiry-based model helps us see that it is not enough for a leader to do or be one thing: honest, or charismatic, or "genuine", or hard-working, or prophetic, or empathetic, or organized. Leadership is the executive function of the group, and as such it is comprised of distinct tasks concerned with gathering information about the group and its environment, envisioning a goal, translating that choice into results, and ensuring that followers understand and remain committed to the task, and the group. "Leadership reconciles internal strivings and environmental pressures", Philip Selznick observed a half-century ago. "It entails a self-assessment to discover the true commitments of the organization" (1957: 62). It is this complex dynamic of endless, ongoing inquiry that the questioning leadership model attempts to capture.

Modernity has vastly complicated the nature of groups. Companies may have hundreds of thousands of employees, armies millions of soldiers, and countries hundreds of millions of citizens. This division of labor and extreme scaling-up is part of what makes leadership so confusing to contemplate. Organizationally, it is not surprising that the leadership of large groups is broken into manageable pieces like R&D, public relations, human resources or logistics. Quite the contrary, actually: the real surprise comes from surveying a complex, rapidly changing environment filled with organizations that are faster, bigger and more dynamic than anything our ancestors experienced – and still finding leadership patterns they would surely have recognized and responded to. Leaders still, as they have always done, must learn, envision, align, drive and communicate. It is in the nature of us as individuals and as social beings who work together in groups.

The model presented here puts questions at the heart of leadership. "Ask questions about everything", wrote the great Qing Dynasty emperor Kangxi, "and investigate everything" (in Spence, 1988: 68). Summing up the nature of the CEO's work, Jack Welch observed that "a series of questions" inspired by a nineteenth-century Prussian general "were much more useful to me over the years than all the data crunching in strategic plans" (Welch and Byrne, 2001: 390). One may object that leadership is about answers, not questions. But questions must precede answers. If leaders do not ask, who will? Perhaps it is even right to say that questions are the sparks that create the possibility of leadership.

The ancient world was dominated by a style of leadership that stressed the certainty of the leader's answers rather than the questions that precede them. Even so, one finds in an ancient text like *Gilgamesh* a dramatization of the leader's journey as a questioning exploration into the heart of the human condition. We might say that Gilgamesh begins his journey with one question: "who am I?", the individual's question. He ends his journey, back where he started, with another: "who are we?", the leader's question. The answers that Gilgamesh finds through suffering and discovery are powerful affirmations of the importance of the group in our lives. So is the symbolic circle of his journey, which begins and ends in his city of Uruk. The structure of the story betrays the same circularity, opening and closing with the same words about the same place, the city built and sustained by leadership and collective labor:

> Study the brickwork, study the fortification;
> climb the great ancient staircase to the terrace;
>
> study how it is made; from the terrace see
> the planted and fallow fields, the ponds and orchards.
>
> This is Uruk, the city of Gilgamesh. . . . (Ferry, 1992: 3; cf. 81)

The real hero of the ancient story is the city itself. It is where Gilgamesh finds the only kind of immortality available to leaders, through their service to the group.

In the end, the answers that elude Gilgamesh in his journey, and that he recognizes upon his return to the city, are only as important as the questions that drive him. His questions spark his sense of mortality and empathy. They impel him to seek, make him willing to learn, and teach him how to lead. As for us, it is our urge to question, our capacity for wonder and imagination, that ensures that as long as we live, and as long as we depend on each other for the collective labor that makes our lives possible and meaningful, we will ask for leadership.

REFERENCES

Achebe, C. (1958 [1994]), *Things Fall Apart,* New York: Anchor Books.

Aguilar, F.J. (1967), *Scanning the Business Environment*, New York: Macmillan.

Birnbaum, R. (1992), *How Academic Leadership Works: Understanding Success and Failure in the College Presidency*, San Francisco, CA: Jossey-Bass.

Blassingame, J. et al. (eds) (1979), *The Frederick Douglass Papers: Series One – Speeches, Debates, and Interviews*, New Haven, CT: Yale University Press.

Buber, M. (1946), *Moses: The Revelation and the Covenant*, New York: Harper and Brothers.

Burns, J.M. (1978), *Leadership*, New York: Harper and Row.

Campbell, J. (1953), *The Hero with a Thousand Faces*, New York: Pantheon Press.

Cather, W. (1992), *O Pioneers!*, New York: Vintage Classics.

Ciulla, J. (1998), *Ethics, the Heart of Leadership*, Westport, CT: Praeger.

Clark, J.C.D. (ed.) (2001), *Reflections on the Revolution in France. A Critical Edition*, Stanford, CA: Stanford University Press.

Clark, P. and L. Nista (2008), "Anatomy of a stump speech", *Washington Post*, 26 February, accessed at www.washingtonpost.com/wpdyn/content/graphic/2008/02/26/GR2008022600417.html.

Colaiaco, J.A. (2006), *Frederick Douglass and the Fourth of July Oration*, New York: Palgrave Macmillan.

Collins, J.C. and J.I. Porras (1996), "Building your company's vision", *Harvard Business Review*, September–October, pp. 65–77.

Conger, J.A. (1992), *Learning to Lead*, San Francisco, CA: Jossey-Bass.

Danserau, F., G. Graen and B.A. Haga (1975), "A vertical-dyad linkage approach to leadership within formal organizations: A longitudinal investigation of the role making process", *Organizational Behavior and Human Performance*, **13**, 46–78.

Deming, W.E. (1986), *Out of the Crisis*, Cambridge, MA: MIT Press.

Deming, W.E. (1993), *The New Economics for Industry, Government, Education*, Cambridge, MA: MIT CAES.

Drucker, P.F. (1974). *Management: Tasks, Responsibilities, Practices*, New York: Harper & Row.

Drucker, P., J. Collins, P. Kotler, J. Kouzes, J. Rodin, K. Rangan and F. Hesselbein (2008), *The Five Most Important Questions You Will Ever Ask About Your Organization*, Leader to Leader Institute, San Francisco, CA: Jossey-Bass.

Ellison, R. (1952), *Invisible Man*, New York: Random House.

Fayol, H. (1916 [1987]), *General and Industrial Management*, revised by Irwin Gray, New York: Pittman.

Ferry, D. (1992), *Gilgamesh: A New Rendering in English Verse*, New York: Farrar, Straus, and Giroux.

Fiedler, F.E. (1967), *A Theory of Leadership Effectiveness*, New York: McGraw-Hill.

Fleishman, E.A. (1995), "Consideration and structure: another look at their role in leadership research", in F. Dansereau and F.J. Yammarino (eds), *Leadership: The Multiple-level Approaches*, Stamford, CT: JAI Press, pp. 51–60.

Flexner, J.T. (1994), *Washington: The Indispensable Man*, Boston, MA: Back Bay Books.

Gavin, B. et al. (Producers) and N. Caro (Director) (2003), *Whale Rider* [motion picture], New Zealand: Sony Studios.

Girard, R. (1986), *The Scapegoat*, Baltimore, MD: The Johns Hopkins University Press.

Goleman, D. (1996), *Emotional Intelligence: Why it Can Matter More Than IQ*, 10th anniversary edn, New York: Bantam.

Goleman, D., R. Boyatzis and A. McKee (2004), *Primal Leadership: Realizing the Power of Emotional Intelligence*, Boston, MA: Harvard Business Press.

Halpin, A.W. and B.J. Winer (1957), "A factorial study of the leader behavior descriptions", in R.M. Stogdill and A.E. Coons (eds), *Leader Behavior: Its Description and Measurement*, Columbus, OH: Bureau of Business Research, Ohio State University, pp. 39–51.

Harvey, M. (2006), "Leadership and the human condition", Chapter 2 of George R. Goethals and Georgia L.J. Sorenson (eds), *The Quest for a General Theory of Leadership* Cheltenham, UK and Northampton, MA, USA: Edward Elgar.

Harvey, M. (2008), "Against the heroic: Gilgamesh and his city", in Joanne B. Ciulla (ed.), *Leadership and the Humanities*, vol. 3 of *Leadership at the Crossroads*, Westport, CT: Praeger Press, pp. 51–65.

Herb, G.H.and D.H. Kaplan (eds), (2000), *Nested Identities: Nationalism, Territory, and Scale*, Lanham, MD: Rowman and Littlefield.

Jackman, P. (1989), "Tyson biographer says nothing can distract champ; Torres says once he's in the ring, fighting supersedes everything else", *Los Angeles Times*, 21 July, Section 3, p. 1.

Judge, T.A., R.F. Piccolo and R. Ilies (2004), "The forgotten ones? The validity of consideration and initiating structure in leadership research", *Journal of Applied Psychology*, **89**(1), 36–51.

Kennedy, R. (2002), *Nigger: The Strange Career of a Troublesome Word*, New York: Pantheon Books.

Kerr, S. and J.M. Jermier (1978), "Substitutes for leadership: their meaning and measurement", *Organizational Behavior and Human Performance*, **22**, 374–403.

Kiewe, A. (2007), *FDR's First Fireside Chat: Public Confidence and the Banking Crisis*, College Station, TX: TAMU Press.

King, M.L. (1986), *A Testament of Hope: The Essential Writings and Speeches of Martin Luther King, Jr*, edited by J.M. Washington, New York: HarperCollins.

Kouzes, J.M. and B.Z. Posner (2007), *The Leadership Challenge*, 4th edn, San Francisco, CA: Jossey-Bass.

Krakauer, J. (1999), *Into Thin Air*, New York: Anchor.

Lawrence, P.R. and N. Nohria (2002), *Driven: How Human Nature Shapes our Choices*, San Francisco, CA: Jossey-Bass.

Levine, L.W. and C.R. Levine (2002), *The People and the President: America's Conversation with FDR*, Boston, MA: Beacon Press.

Liker, J.K. (2004), *The Toyota Way: 14 Management Principles from the World's Greatest Manufacturer*, New York: McGraw-Hill.

Liker, J.K. and M. Hoseus (2008), *Toyota Culture: The Heart and Soul of the Toyota Way*, New York: McGraw-Hill.

Lindholm, C. (1990), *Charisma*, London: Blackwell.

Lithwick, D. (2008), "The fiction behind torture policy", *Newsweek*, 26 July, accessed at www.newsweek.com/2008/07/25/the-fiction-behind-torture-policy.html.

Lührmann, T. and P. Eberl (2007), "Leadership and identity construction: reframing the leader-follower interaction from an identity theory perspective", *Leadership*, **3** (February), 115–27.

Machiavelli, Niccolò (1532 [1985]), *The Prince,* translated by Harvey C. Mansfield, Jr, Chicago, IL: University of Chicago Press.

Magee, D. (2007), *How Toyota Became Number One*, New York: Penguin.

Malcolm X. (1965), *Malcolm X Speaks: Selected Speeches and Statements*, edited by G. Breitman, New York: Merit.

Manchester, W. (1983), *The Last Lion: The Lion at Bay*, Boston, MA: Little, Brown.

Mandela, N. (1994), *Long Walk to Freedom*, Boston, MA: Little, Brown.

McGregor, D. (1960), *The Human Side of Enterprise*, New York: McGraw-Hill.

Meyer, C. and J. Kirby (2010), "Leadership in the age of transparency", *Harvard Business Review*, **88**(4), 39–46.

Miller Center of Public Affairs (n.d.), phone conversation between Lyndon Johnson and Dr Martin Luther King, Jr, Presidential Recordings Program: White House Tapes, University of Virginia, WH6507-02-8311-8312-8313, 7 July 1965, accessed at http://whitehousetapes.net/transcript/johnson/wh6507-02-8311-8312-8313.

Nas (2008), "Be a nigger too" [lyrics], accessed at www.hiphopmusic.com.

Northouse, P. (2009), *Leadership: Theory and Practice*, 5th edn, Thousand Oaks, CA: Sage.

Oates, S.B. (1977), *With Malice Toward None: The Life of Abraham Lincoln*, New York: Harper & Row.

Ogbar, J.O.G. (2007), *Hip-hop Revolution: The Culture and Politics of Rap*, Lawrence, KS: University Press of Kansas.

Ohno, T. (1988), *Toyota Production System: Beyond Large-scale Production*, Portland, OR: Productivity Press.

Pande, P.S., R.P. Neuman and R.R. Cavanagh (2000), *The Six Sigma Way: How GE, Motorola, and Other Top Companies are Honing their Performance*, New York: McGraw-Hill.

Parker, L.D. and P.A. Ritson (2005), "Re-visiting Fayol: anticipating contemporary management", *British Journal of Management*, **16**(3) (September), 175–94.

Pauley, J. (2006), "No greater love", *Dateline NBC*, accessed at www.msnbc.msn.com/id/14789502/.

Plato (1991), *The Republic*, 2nd edn, translated by Allan Bloom, New York: Basic Books.

Ravitch, D. (2010), *The Death and Life of the Great American School System: How Testing and Choice are Undermining Education*, New York: Basic Books.

Ross, B. and R. Esposito (2005), "CIA's harsh interrogation techniques described: sources say agency's tactics lead to questionable confessions, sometimes to death", ABC News. 18 November at http://abcnews.go.com/Blotter/Investigation/story?id=1322866.

Rost, J. (1991), *Leadership for the Twenty-first Century*, New York: Praeger.

Schein, E.H. (2010), *Organizational Culture and Leadership*, 4th edn, San Francisco, CA: Jossey-Bass.

Selznick, P. (1957), *Leadership in Administration: A Sociological Interpretation*, New York: Harper & Row.

Shakespeare, W. (1997), *The Norton Shakespeare*, edited by Stephen Greenblatt, New York: W.W. Norton.
Shewhart, W.A. (1931), *Economic Control of Quality of Manufactured Product*, New York: D. Van Nostrand.
Slater, R. (1999), *Jack Welch and the GE Way*, New York: McGraw-Hill.
Sloan, A. (1964 [1990]), *My Years with General Motors*, New York: Crown.
Spence, J.D. (1988), *Emperor of China: Self-portrait of K'ang-hsi*, New York: Vintage.
Stogdill, R.M. (1950), "Leadership, membership, and organization", *Psychological Bulletin*, **47**, 1–14.
Sun Tzu (1963), *The Art of War*, translated by Samuel B. Griffith, London: Oxford University Press.
Taylor, F. (1911), *Principles of Scientific Management*, New York: Harper and Brothers.
Tedlow, R.S. (2001), *Giants of Enterprise: Seven Business Innovators and the Empires They Built*, New York: Collins.
Teresa, Mother and B. Kolodiejchuk (2007), *Mother Teresa: Come be My Light*, New York: Doubleday.
Tocqueville, A. de (1835 [1966]). *Democracy in America*, translated by George Lawrence, J.P. Mayer and Max Lerner (eds), New York: Harper & Row.
Tucker, R.C. (ed.) (1978), *The Marx–Engels Reader*, 2nd edn, New York: W.W. Norton.
Weber, M. (1946), *From Max Weber: Essays in Sociology*, ed. and trans. H.H. Gerth and C. Wright Mills, New York: Oxford University Press.
Welch, J. and J.A. Byrne, (2001), *Jack: Straight from the Gut,* New York: Warner Business Books.
Wills, G. (1992), *Lincoln at Gettysburg: The Words that Remade America*, New York: Touchstone.
Zorn, E. (2008), "Clinton mocks . . . Obama? Change of subject blog", *Chicago Tribune*, 26 February, accessed at http://blogs.chicagotribune.com/news_columnists_ezorn/2008/02/the-mockery-gam.html.

Name index

Subject index